2 TIMOTHY

2 TIMOTHY

Fight the Good Fight, Finish the Race, Keep the Faith

Paul S. Jeon

PICKWICK *Publications* · Eugene, Oregon

2 TIMOTHY
Fight the Good Fight, Finish the Race, Keep the Faith

Pickwick Publications
An Imprint of Wipf and Stock Publishers
199 W. 8th Ave., Suite 3
Eugene, OR 97401

www.wipfandstock.com

PAPERBACK ISBN: 978-1-7252-6933-0
HARDCOVER ISBN: 978-1-7252-6932-3
EBOOK ISBN: 978-1-7252-6934-7

Cataloging-in-Publication data:

Names: Jeon, Paul S.

Title: 2 Timothy: fight the good fight, finish the race, keep the faith / by Paul S. Jeon.

Description: Eugene, OR: Pickwick Publications, 2020 | Includes bibliographical references.

Identifiers: ISBN 978-1-7252-6933-0 (paperback) | ISBN 978-1-7252-6932-3 (hardcover) | ISBN 978-1-7252-6934-7 (ebook)

Subjects: LCSH: Bible. Timothy, 2nd—Commentaries.| Bible. Timothy, 2nd—Criticism, interpretation, etc.

Classification: LCC BS2735.52 J46 2020 (print) | LCC BS2735.52 (ebook)

Manufactured in the U.S.A.   OCTOBER 1, 2020

To John Paul Heil,
Mentor and Inspiration,
And
To Cat and Ji,
Pillars in Every Sense

Contents

Preface

IT IS A DELIGHT to publish this final installment in my "trilogy" on the Pastoral Epistles. So much has happened between the time the idea for these commentaries was suggested by my dissertation advisor John Paul Heil and now. It is only by the grace of God—expressed tangibly through a patient and supportive wife, my diligent and gracious publisher, and the friendship of so many at NewCity Church—that this last commentary is done. As every sober author notes, any good in these commentaries is mainly a consequence of the love and labors of others; I take full responsibility for any (or the many?) deficiencies.

I first taught this short letter as a youth director in Philadelphia during my first year of seminary studies (2002). For whatever reason I thought it would be a brilliant idea to memorize the letter with five teenage fellows and meet weekly on Saturday to discuss our observations and reflections. Shockingly they all agreed to this outrageous plan, and each of us benefited very much, I in particular. Little did I know then how formative this letter would be in the way I experienced ministry over the next two decades.

In my meager assessment, 2 Timothy basically addresses the following question: "What do you do when you have tried to do the right thing and have lost?" Obviously, the letter should be read in light of 1 Timothy where Paul summons Timothy and the believers with him to do everything possible to preserve truth and promote godliness in the household of God. But in the end, as 2 Timothy suggests, the heretics have won and many are abandoning ship. What do you tell your apprentice, your beloved son? How do you encourage faithfulness when the temptation to give up is all too real? Such questions persist today among many women and men that have tried to do the right thing but feel like they are on the losing side. Thankfully, in God's providence, 2 Timothy has been given to address such questions. I encourage you to first and foremost read, memorize, and meditate on the letter. Then, and only then, consider reading this and many other commendable commentaries that might provide some insight. Most of all, know that every good endeavor pursued in faith is never in vain. Therefore, "fight the good fight, finish the race, keep the faith."

Acknowledgments

First, I thank my parents; you embody much of the faith in 2 Timothy and have enabled me to do what I am able to do today. Second, I thank God for my wife and three children; specifically, I thank God that they are never impressed by me. Third, I thank Brian Forman, Rebecca Gibson, and Zackary Martin whose efforts brought this book to fruition. Finally, I thank John Paul Heil who encouraged me to read my Bible deliberately.

Abbreviations

BDAG Bauer, Danker, Arndt, and Gingrich—
    Greek-English Lexicon of the New Testament

ESV English Standard Version

JSNT Journal for the Study of the New Testament

JSNTSup JSNT, Supplement Series

LTT Letters to Timothy and Titus

LXX Septuagint

NASB New American Standard Bible

NIV New International Version

NRSV New Revised Standard Version

NT New Testament

NLT New Living Translation

OT Old Testament

PE Pastoral Epistles

RSV Revised Standard Version

1

Introduction[1]

Explanation of the Message of the Letter
and Title of the Book

THE TITLE OF THIS book, 2 *Timothy: Fight the Good Fight, Finish the Race, Keep the Faith*, reflects what I believe was Paul's main burden in scripting this letter.[2] Despite fiery trials, Paul himself has endured in the faith because God remained faithful to him even when all had abandoned him (2 Tim 4:16–17). Now Paul prays and hopes for the same for his spiritual son Timothy, and all the believers with him.

This theme of struggling to finish the race and uphold the faith reminds me of Phil Knight's fascinating memoir *Shoe Dog*.[3] Many know Knight as the founder of Nike and one of the most generous billionaire philanthropists. Few know of the many battles he fought, including those with himself, to establish one of the most iconic and influential companies in the world. His story is very much about fighting, about running, and about staying the course until his dream was realized. While far less glorious, at least in this life, 2 Timothy reflects these themes of struggle, doggedness, and faith in implicit and explicit ways.

Later in this book we will examine more carefully what I dub as the chiastic arrangement of the letter. For now, a basic survey of the four chapters will show how pervasive this theme is. In the first chapter, Paul

---

1. The organization of this chapter follows in large part the works of Heil (see, e.g., *Ephesians*). See also my comments in the introduction of 1 *Timothy*.

2. I will briefly address the question of 2 Timothy's authorship in the next chapter.

3. Knight, *Shoe Dog*.

begins by identifying Timothy as his "beloved child" (1:2). This is certainly deliberate. By doing so, he reiterates the bond between them and hopes that Timothy will share not just in his father's sufferings for the gospel but also in his expectation of future redemption and glory. Paul then reminds Timothy of their respective spiritual lineages (1:3–6). Their faith is an inherited faith, the fruit of their predecessors who kept the faith in the face of opposition. Having reminded Timothy of his spiritual ancestry, Paul proceeds to exhort his son to remember his calling (1:6) and the Spirit of power and love that dwells in them, and to share "in suffering for the gospel by the power of God" (1:8). In typical Pauline fashion, the apostle presents himself as a model of endurance to the revealed gospel (1:9–12) and challenges his son to imitate him through the Holy Spirit (1:13–14). This challenge is made in the context of general apostasy: all except Onesiphorus have abandoned Paul (1:15–18). Paul hopes that Timothy will not follow in the steps of "all who are in Asia" (1:15) but will adopt Onesiphorus's example of fighting to keep the faith.

Following the command to entrust this same gospel to other faithful men (2:1–2), Paul gives a myriad of rich images that furthers the theme of fighting, finishing, and keeping. Perhaps most notable is the image of a soldier who does not get bogged down in civilian affairs but lives to please the one that enlisted him (2:3–4). But no less compelling are the analogies of a world-class athlete (2:5) and hard-working farmer (2:6). All three persons cannot succeed unless they display grit in the face of struggle. After presenting himself again as an example of endurance (2:8–13), Paul reminds Timothy of his task to shepherd those under his care (2:14–19). Central to Timothy's own endurance is being deliberate and careful around troublemakers whose talk had "spread like gangrene" (2:17). They represent the opposite of Onesiphorus and what Paul highlights as the theme of enduring in the faith. Such persons are likened to dishonorable vessels in God's house (2:20). In stark contrast, Timothy and all the believers with him are to continually purify themselves by fleeing passions and pursuing righteousness. Only in this way can they become vessels for honorable use (2:21–22). Nevertheless, in all his conduct, even toward the troublemakers, Timothy is to display perfect patience in hope that his character and instruction might lead even the rebels to repentance (2:23–26).

In the first half of the third chapter, Paul does not shy from underscoring the difficult arena in which Timothy must run the race of faith. "There will come times of difficulty. For people will be lovers of self, lovers of money . . . lovers of pleasure rather than lovers of God, having the appearance of godliness, but denying its power" (3:1–5). Such persons who constantly learn but never change because they never repent are the sons of "Jannes and Jambres" (3:6–8). But Paul also does not shy from highlighting their fate: "they will not get very far" (3:9). Paul then reminds Timothy of the apostle's own example and Timothy's relationship to him. In perhaps the most sobering declaration of the letter Paul plainly states: "Indeed, all who desire to live in-a-godly-manner in Christ Jesus will be persecuted" (3:12). Such is the normal existence of those who have been brought into the kingdom of God and confess Jesus as Lord. With this reiteration of both the fates of the sons of "Janes and Jambres" and the sons of Moses and Paul, the third chapter ends with another summons to fight to keep the faith in such a battlefield (3:14). This is done especially by rooting oneself more deeply in God's inspired Scripture, which is able to equip Timothy for the successful completion of every good task (3:15–17).

The final chapter begins with an explicit summons for Timothy to complete the work he has begun, especially in the face of opposition (4:1–4). Once again, Paul could not be clearer about the ensuing battle: "For the time is coming when people will not endure sound teaching, but having itching ears they will accumulate for themselves teachers to suit their own passion, and will turn away from listening to the truth and wander off into myths" (4:3–4). Timothy, however, is to swim against this current and "fulfill your ministry" (4:5) irrespective of what people demand. Paul then devotes the majority of the chapter to his own struggle and endurance. Acknowledging that he is entering a final or penultimate stage of ministry and life, he looks back and declares, "I have fought the good fight, I have finished the race, I have kept the faith" (4:7). But he doesn't end there. He goes on to highlight, "*Henceforth* there is laid up for me the crown of righteousness, which the Lord, the righteous judge, will award to me on that day, *and not only to me but also to all who have loved his appearing*" (4:8).

Herein lies perhaps the explicit purpose of this letter—to summon Timothy to follow in the legacy of his father in hope that he will share in the same crown of righteousness. As the letter has already made clear, such future hope does not blind one to the present realities of suffering and persecution. In fact, the letter ends by reiterating Paul's aloneness and suffering on account of the gospel (4:9–16). At the same time, while these fiery trials can burn up a person's faith, they can also refine and deepen it. For Paul, near-universal abandonment and unjust suffering afforded the unique opportunity to experience God's tangible deliverance (4:16); and it was this deliverance that buttressed his faith and enabled him to look forward with faith versus fear (4:17–18). Such power is available to all who share in the faith of the believers (4:19–22).

Reductionism is always a risky affair; and none can doubt that 2 Timothy has much to teach us in addition to endurance. But it cannot be overstated that the letter's primary motivation is to stir Timothy and believers, through the use of rhetoric and personal example, to engage in battle, complete the work set before them, and to uphold the faith even in the face of tremendous opposition. By nature, parents don't want to see their children suffer. But there are instances when they allow suffering. This happens when they know that a much greater glory awaits the end of the battle, the end of the race, the end of the journey. Being at the finish line, Paul is able to say, "Henceforth there is laid up for me the crown of righteousness." As a loving parent in the Lord, there is nothing he wants more for Timothy—and for us—than to share in this glory on that Day when Christ appears in full glory. Therefore, the letter is a summons to fight, finish, and fulfill.

We find a summary of everything stated above in the opening verse of the letter. Here Paul identifies both his vocation and hope: "Paul, an apostle of Christ Jesus by the will of God according to the promise of life that is in Christ Jesus" (1:1). This verse expresses with slight variation the same theme we have explored in more length; namely, that the promise of eternal life has enabled Paul to fulfill his apostolic calling despite much persecution. Paul writes this letter to encourage Timothy to follow in the footsteps of his spiritual father by fulfilling his ministry (4:5). Timothy and all the believers can accomplish this even in the face of great obstacles because the same God who delivered Paul continues to dwell in them through his Spirit. By this Spirit, Timothy and all believers can "guard the good deposit" until the Day of Christ. That is, they too can fight the good fight, finish the race, and keep the faith.

Authorship, Audience, and Historical Setting of the Letter

Many commentators have written comprehensive and detailed introductions that cover the basic topics of authorship and historical setting.[4] I

4. One of the best recent treatments of these topics can be found in Köstenberger,

rest on and refer to their work and opt to highlight only a few notes that are most pertinent to this commentary.

First, I remain unconvinced that Paul did not write 2 Timothy,[5] that is, I reject the idea that a later disciple scripted these letters and then attributed them to the apostle.[6] I do so for several reasons. First, there is no reason to reject the clear claims of Pauline authorship we find in all three letters (1 Tim 1:1; 2 Tim 1:1; Titus 1:1). Arguments for pseudonymity or allonymity appear far more speculative and forced than authentic Pauline authorship.[7] Also, contrary to the impression some have sought to establish, pseudonymity was neither pervasively nor readily accepted.[8] Second, much of the rhetorical force of the letter between Paul and his spiritual son depends on both Paul being the actual author and Timothy the actual, primary recipient. Paul's expectation of compliance and faithfulness assumes that Timothy will respond positively in no small part because of their personal relationship.

Third, arguments against Pauline authorship based on differences in style, vocabulary, and theology are fraught with difficulties. Every serious writer can attest to how his style and vocabulary continue to evolve and change over time. This is especially true in the case of ministry. As a person encounters people from diverse cultures and seeks to "incarnate" into their lives, both their style and vocabulary must adapt.[9] Similarly, as any pastor knows all too well, different ministry contexts require different theological emphases. A church caught up in legalism needs to hear that God's salvation comes as a result of mercy, not merit. In another setting,

---

1–2 Timothy and Titus, 1–54. See also my comments in Jeon, *1 Timothy*.

5. I hold this to be the case for all three letters, which are often classified together as the Pastoral Epistles.

6. The amount of literature on the topic of Pauline authorship (with respect to the Pastoral Epistles) is legion. Some representative and key articles include Van Nes, "On the Origin of the Pastorals' Authenticity Criticism," 315–20; James, *Genuineness and Authorship of the Pastoral Epistles*; "Authorship of the Pastoral Epistles," in Kierspel, *Charts on the Life, Letters, and Theology of Paul*, 136.

7. Some notable scholars do advocate these positions, including Hagner, *New Testament*, 614–26; Marshall, *Pastoral Epistles*, 83–84; Schnabel, "Paul, Timothy, and Titus," 383–403.

8. See Duff, "Reconsideration of Pseudepigraphy in Early Christianity"; Lea, "Early Christian View of Pseudepigraphic Writings," 65–75; Bauckham, "Pseudo-Apostolic Letters," 487.

9. See Pitts, "Style and Pseudonymity in Pauline Scholarship," esp. 113; Schnabel, "Paul, Timothy, and Titus," 386–91.

this same pastor might encounter a spirit of licentiousness and therefore underscore the necessity of good works as a sign of true faith. Moreover, any careful exploration of the theology of the Pastoral Epistles in comparison to the theology of Paul's undisputed letters shows little in the way of substantial difference. Köstenberger makes this helpful summary comment, "The theology of the LTT is not identical in form to that of Paul's other letters, but it can plausibly be viewed as complementary rather than contradictory and as no less Pauline than the earlier undisputed letters.[10]

Plenty more could be said on authorship. Perhaps what will most aid readers of this commentary will be for them to peruse the positions that reject authentic authorship and to consider whether these positions enhance their understand of the letters themselves. My own experience is that acceptance of Pauline authorship fits well with the style and objective of all three letters, but especially that of 2 Timothy.

The setting of the letter is similar to that of 1 Timothy, namely the presence and toxic influence of false teachers.[11] Assuming the traditional order of 1 Timothy and 2 Timothy, it appears that false teachers have come out on top despite Paul's efforts to check them in 1 Timothy. In contrast to the preceding letter, 2 Timothy reads more like a summons for Timothy to persevere even if it seems like Paul is losing. We can imagine a group of spectators that have begun to leave even before the game is over because they know that their home team has lost. Paul is urging Timothy not to abandon his call but to endure even if it seems like they are the few that have remained faithful to the gospel.

Because 2 Timothy focuses more on the theme of endurance and because neither 1 nor 2 Timothy are concerned with describing the false teaching but with refuting it, we can only speculate what these teachings entailed. The text offers some clues. For instance, we're told that the false teachers were argumentative (2:14) and heterodox (2:25). There is some insinuation that they were narcissistic and greedy (3:2). Finally, they aimed to please their audience with soothing words rather than the truth of the gospel (4:3). But beyond this we can only speculate what they were

---

10. Köstenberger, *1–2 Timothy and Titus*, 23.

11. See my comments in Jeon, *1 Timothy*; Köstenberger, *1–2 Timothy and Titus*, 45–54. It is safe to assume that the same troublemakers are in view in 1 and 2 Timothy; see Thornton, *Hostility in the House of God*. For further details on the historic context, see Köstenberger, *1–2 Timothy and Titus*, 33–44. Here Köstenberger gives a useful survey of the studies that have been proposed and how they have interacted with one another in the past few decades.

teaching. However, this should not lead us to despair in grasping the basic message of the letter. Reflecting on the various proposals that scholars have proposed about the social setting of all the Pastorals, Köstenberger notes:

> One must guard against reductionism (i.e., the tendency to explain biblical phenomena *solely* or *primarily* on the basis of social factors) and anachronism (i.e., one must ensure a given model of analysis is appropriate to the time frame studied) . . . Those who maintain Pauline authorship of the LTT, however, will discern a closer affinity with the other Pauline NT letters. They will stress continuity with OT paradigms, practices, and principles, and look at the salvation-historical trajectory represented in these letters at the transition from the apostolic to the post-apostolic period.[12]

In some circles, there is the belief that we cannot fully understand the meaning of a letter unless we have a full picture of the social setting. I do not mean to minimize the potential usefulness of background studies. Often, they provide useful insights (though even this is not always the case). However, even if I knew little about Shakespeare and the historical context in which he wrote his books, I am able to understand the basic story line of *Hamlet*. As I suggest below, what is most important is paying attention to the text, using some basic lexical tools, and applying some common sense.[13]

---

12. Köstenberger, *1–2 Timothy and Titus*, 44–45.

13. Within the debate concerning "corpus reading," that is, whether 1 and 2 Timothy and Titus should be read together, I lean toward reading the letters separately. I am not suggesting that these letters do not share important concepts and language; see esp. chart 71, "Similarities between the Pastoral Epistles," in Kierspel, *Charts on the Life, Letters, and Theology of Paul*, 133–35. Moreover, in some places of this commentary I do reflect on "echoes" and "differences" relative to 1 Timothy. Finally, given my belief that 2 Timothy is part of God's full revelation as that which is contained in the Old and New Testaments, I am very much a proponent of a "canonical reading." But as far as a first and careful reading is concerned, I maintain that 2 Timothy can and even perhaps should be read as a self-contained literary work; see Prior, *Paul the Letter-Writer*; Johnson, *First and Second Letters to Timothy*; O'Connor, "2 Timothy Contrasted with 1 Timothy and Titus," 403–18.

My own position is well articulated by Köstenberger, *1 and 2 Timothy and Titus*, 7: "An investigation of the relationship among the three letters calls for judiciousness and balance. Two extremes should be avoided: (1) treating the three letters as completely separate without acknowledging points of contact among them (e.g., same recipient in 1 and 2 Timothy); both Timothy and Titus are Paul's apostolic delegates; the false teachers share some common characteristics); and (2) collapsing the boundaries

Finally, I maintain that even the seemingly personal letters of Paul—
1 & 2 Timothy, Titus, and Philemon—were written with the understanding that they would be read in the congregation of believers. I sometimes
use the notation "primary" and "secondary" audience to recognize that
the persons named were likely the primary audience. Nevertheless, the
term "secondary" may suggest that Paul didn't really care whether the believers with Timothy were really paying attention. As I note, Paul writes
with such deliberation and even eloquence because he wishes to impact
the audience as the letter is being read.

Various commentators have observed how the letter ends with the
plural form of the personal pronoun: "Grace be with you *all*" (4:22).
This alone strengthens the case that the audience extends beyond just
Timothy. The belief that these letters were "personal" correspondences
between the apostle and his son also creates some confusion. If 2 Timothy, for instance, were just a personal letter, why does Paul assert his
apostleship (1:1)? Why does he reiterate his appointment as a preacher,
apostle, and teacher (1:11)? This would be akin to my starting a lecture
with the reminder to my students that I have been appointed to serve as
their professor. They know this already. In the same way, Paul's assertions of his apostolic calling, coupled with the various exhortations and
warnings, give weight to the perspective that the audience of these letters
comprised Paul's delegates and the believers with them. We will assume
this position in our analysis.

Approach to 2 Timothy: Text-Centered, Literary-Rhetorical, Audience-Oriented

The best way to approach 2 Timothy is to interpret it as a single and co-
herent letter that was written to be performed in a communal setting
(most likely a liturgical one) as a substitute for Paul's actual presence.[14] In

---

between 1 and 2 Timothy, and Titus as distinct letters to the extent that their individu-
ality is insufficiently recognized. In the end it seems best to engage the three letters not
as a corpus but as a 'cluster,' being sensitive to both the things that bind them together
and the things that make them distinct."

14. Ward, "Pauline Voice and Presence," 95–96: "Oral performance . . . is a way in
which the author-in-the-work becomes an audible presence by means of the speech
and movement of the presenter." See Holland, "Delivery, Delivery, Delivery," 136;
Strange, "'His Letters Are Weighty,'" 115.

other words, Paul wrote this letter much in the way an individual might make a recording today with a message to be played in his absence.

In my analysis, I use a text-centered, literary-rhetorical, and audience-oriented method.[15] "Text-centered" means paying attention to what is actually contained and expressed in the language of the text versus speculations concerning what the author intended to say or include. "Literary-rhetorical" means that 2 Timothy falls under the literary genre of a "letter" with the rhetorical purpose of persuading the implied audience to the perspective of Paul, who is the author indicated in the text. "Audience-oriented" indicates an interpretive approach that seeks to determine how the implied audience members are required to respond to Paul's instructions and exhortations as they are heard through the performance of the letter.[16]

The selection of this text-centered, literary-rhetorical, and audience-oriented method is not random. Recent scholarship has already demonstrated its basis and utility.[17] The performance-aspect of the text was essential for communicating the meaning of the text. Such scholars note that the letters of Paul were "composed mentally and orally and then dictated to a scribe" with the intended purpose of being heard by the audience.[18] Once written, the letter was given to a carrier who, likely

15. Similarly, Horsley, *Text and Tradition*, 20: "Of greatest importance for understanding texts in oral performance is giving careful attention to three key interrelated facets of a text-in-performance. In order to hear and interpret New Testament texts, it is necessary to discern the contours of the *text*, to determine the historical *context* of the community of the responsive/interactive hearers, and to know as much as possible the cultural *tradition* out of which the voiced texts resonate with the hearers."

16. For more on the audience-oriented method in recent biblical studies, see Heil, *Gospel of John*; *1–3 John*; *Book of Revelation*; *Worship in the Letter to the Hebrews*.

17. Porter and Adams, "Pauline Epistolography," 2: "One of the main approaches in recent scholarship to understanding the form and purpose of the Pauline letter—and one that vies for preeminence in analyzing his letters—is the utilization of ancient rhetorical practice and categories . . . It is the perspective of these scholars that Paul had access to and used rhetorical methodology to shape his letters in order to have the greatest impact on his recipients." Horsley, *Text and Tradition*, 18: "Increased recent attention to the dominance of oral communication in antiquity leads to the consideration of New Testament texts as *communication* in the course and context of their composition and cultivation." Thompson, *Preaching Like Paul*, 28: "[Paul,] *like other writers of antiquity, dictated his letters to an amanuensis* [scribe]. Therefore, the letters were the results of an oral event, and Paul's communication was meant for the ear, not the eye."

18. Rhoads, "Art of Translating for Oral Performance," 27. Rhoads and Dewey, "Performance Criticism," 16: "Oral dictation was the primary means to get something

being present during the dictation of the letter, was trained by the author to perform—verbatim—the author's original dictation to the intended audience.[19] The purpose of the written letter, then, was to aid the carrier as he performed a replica dictation of what the author himself had dictated to the scribe.[20] By this procedure, not only would the content of the letter be communicated, but also the author's gestures, facial expressions, demeanor, and tone of voice would be performed as the author intended.[21] The performative function of 2 Timothy was meant to be a total experience of the presence of the author.[22]

---

transcribed into writing." Dewey, *Oral Ethos*, 16: "Paul himself was literate . . . however, we may overestimate the degree of Paul's literacy and his reliance on writing. Like other literates, he often dictated rather than wrote himself."

19. Sampley, "Ruminations," ix–x: "We may readily suppose that this person, with insider cachet, would not only read the letter in its entirety to the assembly of believers in the appointed town but would also be there to lend authoritative interpretation."

Not just anyone could perform the letter to the audience. Nässelqvist, *Public Reading in Early Christianity*, 26: "Few people—even among trained lectors—were able to read a text aloud impromptu, without extensive preparation." Witherington with Hyatt, *Paul's Letter to the Romans*, 23: "It must be kept steadily in view that Paul's letter was meant to be read aloud, indeed meant to be orally delivered by a Pauline co-worker, not merely handed over to a congregation." Timothy would not have been the first to perform the letter for the audience; yet, perhaps due to his close relationship with Paul, he likely would have been capable of repeating the performance for the audience in a similar manner that Paul intended. See Kuruvilla, *Text to Praxis*, 23; Botha, "Verbal Art of the Pauline Letters," 417.

20. Rhoads, "Art of Translating for Oral Performance," 27: "The scrolls served mainly to assist a performer's memory." Rhoads and Dewey, "Performance Criticism," 15–16: "What was important was not that Paul *wrote* a letter but that the performer of the letter conveyed what Paul was *saying* in his letter . . . when writing occurred, it mostly served the needs of performance of prepared readings or oral performances from memory . . . For all intent and purpose, one needed to have studied the content and known it virtually by memory in order to enact a public reading with facility and in such a way as to make the content lively and meaningful."

21. Thompson, *Preaching Like Paul*, 30–31: "The role of the letter carrier or public reader was decisive for the communication of the Pauline letter . . . in order that the emissary might present his intentions and symbols verbally and bodily to others." Rhoads, "Art of Translating for Oral Performance," 27: "Everything we know about storytellers and orators in the ancient world suggests that storytelling and public reading alike would have been animated, emotional, and engaging . . . In fact, they likely visualized their whole embodied performance—gestures, movements, and facial expressions—as they composed ahead of actually performing."

22. Ward, "Pauline Voice and Presence," 105: "The performer of Paul's letter became an icon for the apostolic presence of Paul."

For this reason, a text-centered, literary-rhetorical, and audience-oriented approach to 2 Timothy enables a contemporary audience to get closer to the meaning, purpose, and even presence of the original author.[23] The remainder of this commentary will focus on Paul's rhetorical use of *chiasms* for both hearing his encouragements and warnings in 2 Timothy and experiencing Paul's authoritative, apostolic presence from nearly two thousand years ago.

23. Thompson, *Preaching Like Paul*, 28–29: "In the epistles of Paul, we come close to the actual voice of Paul as he addresses his communities . . . Paul clearly communicates his power through his letters, which function as the surrogates for his personal presence. The letter, therefore, partakes of his apostolic authority"; such authority "provided the occasion for *hearing*" (35). Rhoads, "Performance Events," 180: "In a sense, the letter bore the 'apostolic presence.' However, it is not the letter on a handwritten scroll that people experienced, but the embodied letter—the performer being Paul in the official act of presenting the letter. So it was the *letter-performer* who bore the apostolic presence."

2

The Chiastic Structures of 2 Timothy

Chiasm in 2 Timothy[1]

A CHIASM IS A linguistic parallel structure that moves an audience through introductory themes toward a central pivot and then back to a conclusion that recalls and develops aspects of the initial themes. In this way, the structure of a chiasm is organized by an introductory element, a pivot, and a concluding element. The following is a visual representation of a typical chiastic arrangement:

A. Introductory Theme
  B. Introductory Theme
    C. Pivot Point
    C'. Pivot Point
  B'. Concluding Theme
A'. Concluding Theme

Such chiastic structures provide linguistic organization to the language of a text and the performance thereof. They also—and perhaps more importantly—foster aural comprehension and convey rhetorical force. In the case of ancient letters, which were performed in front of an audience, the chiastic patterns facilitated the verbal recitation of the performer *and* comprehension by the audience. That is, chiasms functioned

1. The first section of this chapter follows in large part the work of Heil (e.g., *Philippians*, 10–13; *Colossians*, 13–37; *Letter of James*, 6–28). See also my introduction in *1 Timothy*.

as mnemonic devices to help both the performer communicate the letter *and* the audience to follow the performance and grasp the meaning and force of the letter.[2]

Because linguistic chiasms were fairly common in ancient oral-auricular and rhetorical cultures such as Paul's first-century Greco-Roman audience, the original audience may not have been as intentional about noting and pondering over chiasms in the 2 Timothy letter as we are in this study.[3] Due to such familiarity, the first-century audience of 2 Timothy would likely have experienced these chiastic patterns unconsciously.[4] For this reason, the identification, delineation, and articulation of such chiastic structures in ancient documents like the 2 Timothy letter are necessary aids for modern interpreters of the text who are unaccustomed to such literary and performative devices.[5] My analysis of 2 Timothy and the oral performance thereof as a deliberately structured chiasm seeks to

2. Rhoads and Dewey, "Performance Criticism," 15: "Compositions were structured and styled to facilitate the memory of the performer and the audience." Van Iersel, *Mark*, 71: "It is . . . probable that the concentric structures [chiasms] found in much ancient literature were originally a structuring and mnemonic device, which had the function of helping reciters structure the text for their listeners." Shively, *Apocalyptic Imagination*, 50: "This concentric structure [chiasm] is also a device of the implied author to aid the process of interpretation."

3. Chiasms in the Greco-Roman world were prevalent. Kuruvilla, *Mark*, 3n19: students learned the Greek alphabet "in chiastic pairs beginning with the first and last letters (A–W), the second and penultimate letters (B–Y), the third and prepenultimate letters (G–C), and so on." See Thomson, *Chiasmus in the Pauline Letters*, 22–24; Brouwer, *Literary Development of John 13–17*, 23–27; White, "Apostolic Mission and Apostolic Message," 157; Herrick, *History and Theory of Rhetoric*, 40; Vena, *Jesus, Disciple of the Kingdom*, 55.

Chiasms were not only a Greco-Roman rhetorical strategy. Paul's use of chiasms would also have been an application of OT Jewish literary patterns; see Bailey, *Paul Through Mediterranean Eyes*, 22. Paul's letters, then, would have appealed broadly to both Greco-Roman and Jewish audience members.

Against the view that chiasms were common in ancient letters, see Smit, *Paradigms*, 160.

4. See Dewey, "Mark as Aural Narrative," 50–52; Hearon, "Implications," 4–17; Gray, *Opening Paul's Letters*, 51–52.

5. Van Iersel, *Mark*, 71–72: "The efficiency of such a structuring device [chiasm] is proportionate to the recognizability of the concentric structures concerned . . . This is, of course, even more true of present-day readers who are not used to this phenomenon and whose ability to appropriate a text aurally has decreased and in some respects even disappeared."

help a modern audience "hear" and experience the rhetorical method in the way Paul intended.[6]

In order to be credible, a proposed chiastic structure must be based on a meticulous and clear methodology.[7] The methodology must demonstrate that the chiasm exists and operates objectively within the language of the text. My investigation of chiasms in 2 Timothy follows seven criteria:[8]

1. There must be problems in recognizing the structure of the text in consideration, which traditional outlines have not been able to resolve.

2. There must be indications of parallelism and pendulum movements in the text that commentaries and specialized studies have already observed.

3. Chiasms must exist in the received text and do not require unsupported and excessive textual emendations for substantiation.

4. Precise verbal parallelism—supported by conceptual and syntactical parallels—should link the corresponding chiastic pairs.

5. Such verbal parallelism should involve significant terminology versus peripheral language and should be unique to the parallel units.[9]

6. Rhoads, "Performance Events," 183: "Of course we cannot recover any of these myriad live performances among early Christians. Nevertheless, we have the 'scripts' to analyze. In this regard, the contents of the New Testament scrolls contain 'stage directions' for performers. There are . . . clues in the texts that help us to infer the . . . features of performances. One is *oral arts* of communication embedded in the texts that convey various storytelling patterns and memorable language and sound effects and rhetorical sequences, all of which give us some clues as to the style of the performance. Many of these same features served to facilitate memory on the part of the performer as well as the audience." Harvey, *Listening to the Text*, 56: "Oral composition was the rule, not the exception . . . an investigation of oral patterning must focus on 'acoustic resonances' *heard* by the original audience rather than on conceptual parallels found by silently rereading the texts." My analysis of 2 Timothy examines *chiasm* as both the main "script" of the letter and the "'acoustic resonances' *heard* by the original audience."

7. See Heil, "Chiastic Structure," 179, esp. n4.

8. See Deppe, *Theological Intentions*, 97–98; Blomberg, "Structure of 2 Corinthians 1–7," 4–8; Jeremias, "Chiasms in den Paulusbriefen," 145–56; Welch, "Chiasmus in the New Testament," 211–49; Welch, "Criteria for Identifying and Evaluating the Presence of Chiasmus," 157–74.

9. Although what constitutes "significant" is not as clear as we might like and will depend on the work itself. That is, what appear as "insignificant" in one text may be

6. The pivot, that is, the center of the chiasm, should function as the turning point in the literary structure.

7. Chiasms must always be "framed," that is, parallel units must gravitate around the pivot.

The key feature of this study on 2 Timothy is that all chiasms in the letter are based on precise linguistic parallels in the original Greek text. These include cognates, synonyms, antonyms, alliterative terms, and, on occasion, identical grammatical forms of a word. In cases where linguistic parallels involve seemingly ordinary words, we will see that such parallel words were significant to the rhetorical strategy of the author and the situation of the original audience.

Since the proposed chiasms are based on linguistic parallels, the overall length of the parallel units or elements may not be the same. For example, the introductory element of a chiasm (A) may be longer than its corresponding concluding element (A'). While this may seem unusual to a contemporary audience, Paul's first-century audience would have been attuned to the key linguistic parallels that organize sections of language rather than to a balance in the length of the parallel sections. The main presupposition of this study is that a chiasm is operative—irrespective of a balance in length—wherever linguistic parallels and a pivotal section between them are evident.

Throughout my analysis, I identify three types of chiasms: *macrochiasm*, *microchiasm*, and *minichiasm*. A single *macrochiasm* encompasses the entire 2 Timothy letter. It is composed of eight parallel *units*: A-B-C-D-D'-C'-B'-A'. I refer to each *unit* of the overall macrochiasm as a *microchiasm*. A *minichiasm* can occur within a microchiasm and derives its significance therein.

The following provides a visual representation of the eight macrochiastic units of the 2 Timothy letter:

A Unit: First Microchiasm

    B Unit: Second Microchiasm

        C Unit: Third Microchiasm

            D Unit: Fourth Microchiasm

            D' Unit: Fifth Microchiasm

        C' Unit: Sixth Microchiasm

"significant" in another; for example, the interchange of the "you" and "we" in Ephesians; see Heil, *Ephesians*.

B' Unit: Seventh Microchiasm

A' Unit: Eighth Microchiasm

Outline of the Chiastic Structures of 2 Timothy

A Unit. 1:1–12: Do Not Be Ashamed but Share in Suffering according
to the Power of God

  B Unit. 1:13—2:3: Guard the Commendable Entrustment
in Faith like a Good Soldier for That Day

    C Unit. 2:4–19: That They May Obtain Salvation in Christ Jesus
Who Remains Faithful

      D Unit. 2:20—3:6: Reject Those Who
Deny the Power of Godliness

      D' Unit. 3:7–17: Remain in Salvation
through Faith in Christ Jesus

    C' Unit. 4:1–8: I Have Fought the Good Fight and Kept the
Faith for That Day

  B' Unit. 4:9–21: The Lord Will Save Me from Every Evil Work

A' Unit. 4:22: The Lord Be with Your Spirit and Grace Be with You

The Eight Microchiastic Units of 2 Timothy

A Unit

1:1–12

DO NOT BE ASHAMED BUT SHARE IN SUFFERING ACCORDING
TO THE POWER OF GOD

The first of eight microchiasms within 2 Timothy is composed of four
elements (A-B-B'-A'). Linguistic parallels are indicated by the Greek text.

A. ¹ Paul, apostle of Christ Jesus through (διά ἀπόστολος Χριστοῦ
Ἰησοῦ) the will of God according to the promise of life (ζωῆς)
that is in Christ Jesus, ² To Timothy beloved child: Grace, mercy,
peace from God the Father and Christ Jesus (Χριστοῦ Ἰησοῦ) our
Lord. ³ Grace I have to God, to-the-one I (ᾧ) serve from [the way
of my] forefathers in a pure conscience, as I have without-ceasing

memory concerning you in my supplications night and day
(ἡμέρας), 4 longing to see you, having-been-reminded of your
tears, so-that I might become-full of joy, 5 taking remembrance
of the without-hypocrisy faith (πίστεως) in you that housed first
in your grandmother Lois and your mother Eunice, but I am convinced (πέπεισμαι) [is] also in you. 6 Through this reason (Δι᾽ ἥν
αἰτίαν) I remind you to rekindle the gift of God, which is (ἐστιν)
in you through (διά) the laying of my hands.

> B: 7 For to us God did not (οὐ) give (ἔδωκεν ἡμῖν) a Spirit of
> cowardice; rather of power (δυνάμεως) and love and self-
> control. 8a Therefore do not be ashamed of the witness of
> our Lord nor of me his prisoner;
>
> B'. 8b rather suffer-together for the gospel according to the
> power (δύναμιν) of God 9 who saved us and called to a
> holy calling not (οὐ) according to our works; rather ac-
> cording to his own purpose and grace, which was given
> to us (δοθεῖσαν ἡμῖν) in Christ Jesus before eternal times,

A'. 10 but now was manifested through (διά) the manifestation of
our Savior Christ Jesus (Χριστοῦ Ἰησοῦ) who on-the-one-hand
abolished death, on-the-other-hand brought-to-light life (ζωήν)
and without-mortality through (διά) the gospel 11 toward which
I-myself was appointed preacher and apostle (ἀπόστολος) and
teacher; 12 through this reason (δι᾽ ἥν αἰτίαν) indeed these
I suffer; rather, I am not ashamed, for I know to-the-one (ᾧ) I
have faith (πεπίστευκα) and I am convinced (πέπεισμαι) that
he is (ἐστιν) powerful to guard my entrustment toward *that* day
(ἡμέραν).[10]

B Unit

1:13—2:3

GUARD THE COMMENDABLE ENTRUSTMENT IN FAITH LIKE A
GOOD SOLDIER FOR THAT DAY

---

10. The demonstrative "that" (ἐκείνην) is italicized because it serves as a transitive
word to the next B unit. This unit begins with "I have" (ἔχε), a verb that shares an
obvious phonetic similarity with "that."

The second of eight microchiasms is composed of four elements (A-B-B'-A'). Linguistic parallels identifying chiastic arrangements are indicated by the Greek text.

A. 13 Have the pattern of sound words that you heard from me (παρ᾽ ἐμοῦ ἤκουσας) in the faith and love that are in Christ Jesus (τῇ ἐν Χριστῷ Ἰησοῦ). 14 The commendable entrustment (καλὴν παραθήκην) guard through the Holy Spirit who is housed in us. 15 You know this, that all that are in Asia turned-from me, among whom are Phygelus and Hermogenes.

> B: 16 May the Lord give mercy (δῴη ἔλεος ὁ κύριος) to the household of Onesiphorus, that often he refreshed me and was not ashamed of my chain; 17 rather, being in Rome, earnestly he sought me and found (εὗρεν) [me];
> B'. 18 may the Lord give (δῴη . . . ὁ κύριος) to him to find mercy (εὑρεῖν ἔλεος) from the Lord (κυρίου) on that day. And the-many-ways in Ephesus he served, you know well.

A'. 2:1 You, therefore, my child, be-strengthened in the grace that is in Christ Jesus (τῇ ἐν Χριστῷ Ἰησοῦ), 2 and what you heard from me (ἤκουσας παρ᾽ ἐμοῦ) through many witnesses, these entrust (παράθου) to faithful human beings, who also will be able to teach others. 3 Share-in-suffering as a commendable (καλός) *soldier* of Christ Jesus.[11]

C Unit

2:4–19

THAT THEY MAY OBTAIN SALVATION IN CHRIST JESUS WHO REMAINS FAITHFUL

The third of eight microchiasms is composed of four elements (A-B-B'-A'). Linguistic parallels identifying chiastic arrangements are indicated by the Greek text.

---

11. "Soldier" is italicized because it serves as a transitive word to the next C unit. This unit begins with "who is a soldier" (στρατευόμενος), a participle that shares an obvious phonetic similarity with "soldier." See also the participle "one-who-enlists-soldiers" (στρατολογήσαντι) in the same verse.

A. 4 None (οὐδείς) who-is-a-solider gets-entangled in the affairs of life, that he might please the one-who-enlists-soldiers. 5 But also if someone (τις) competes-as-an-athlete, he is not crowned unless (ἐὰν μή) lawfully he competes-as-an-athlete. 6 It-is-necessary for the laboring farmer to first partake of the fruits. 7 Understand what I am saying (λέγω); for to you the Lord (κύριος) will give insight in all-things.

B. 8 Remember (μνημόνευε) Jesus Christ raised from the dead, from the seed of David, according to the gospel of mine, 9 in which I am suffering-as-an-evildoer until bonds; rather the word of God has not been bound; 10 for this [reason] all-things I endure (ὑπομένω) for-the-sake of the elect, that they themselves might also obtain the salvation that [is] in Christ Jesus with eternal glory. 11 Faithful is the word; for if we-died-together, also we will-live-together.

B'. 12 If we endure (ὑπομένομεν), also we will-reign-together; if we will-deny [him], he also will-deny-us; 13 if we are-without-faith, he remains (μένει) faithful, for he is not able to deny himself. 14a These things remind (ὑπομίμνησκε), charging before God

A'. 14b not (μή) to word-fight, upon no (οὐδέν) usefulness, upon catastrophe of-those-who-hear. 15 Strive to present yourself approved to God, a worker without-shame, handling-orthodoxly the word of truth. 16 The profane empty-sounds avoid; for upon more irreverence they will progress, 17 and the word of theirs like gangrene will have increase. Among whom are Hymenaeus and Philetus, 18 the-someones-who (οἵτινες) regarding the truth have swerved, saying (λέγοντες) the resurrection already has happened, and they are overturning the faith of some (τινων). 19 However, the strong foundation of God has stood, having this seal: "The Lord (κύριος) knows the-ones-who-are of him," and, "From without-*righteousness* must withdraw all that-name the name of the Lord (κυρίου)."[12]

---

12. The noun "without-righteousness" (ἀδικίας) is italicized because it serves as a transitive word to the next D unit. This unit begins with "house" (οἰκία), a noun that shares an obvious phonetic similarity with "without-righteousness." Notice also how the reference to "the strong foundation of God" in the C unit prepares the audience for Paul's discussion of "the great house" of God in the D unit.

D Unit

2:20—3:6

REJECT THOSE WHO DENY THE POWER OF GODLINESS

The fourth of eight microchiasms within the 2 Timothy macrochiasm is composed carefully of four elements (A-B-B'-A'). Linguistic parallels identifying chiastic arrangements are indicated by the Greek text.

A. ²⁰ But in a great house (οἰκίᾳ) there are not only golden and silver vessels; rather [there are] also wooden and clay [vessels], and on-the-one-hand some toward honor, but on-the-other-hand some toward without-honor; ²¹ therefore, if someone purifies himself from these (τούτων), he will be a vessel toward honor, sanctified, useful for the master, toward all good work ready. ²² But youthful desires (ἐπιθυμίας) flee, but pursue righteousness, faith, love, peace with those who invoke the Lord from a pure heart.

B. ²³ But moronic and without-instruction (ἀπαιδεύτους) controversies disregard, knowing that (ὅτι) they birth fights (μάχας);

B'. ²⁴ But it is necessary for the slave of the Lord not to fight (μάχεσθαι); rather to be gentle to all, able-to-teach, forbearing, ²⁵ in respectfulness instructing (παιδεύοντα) those who oppose—perchance to them God may give repentance toward a knowledge of truth ²⁶ and they may become-sober-again from the snare of the devil (διαβόλου), having-been-captured by him toward that will.

3:1 But this perceive that (ὅτι) in the last days there will come difficult times; ² For human beings will be lovers-of-self, lovers-of-money, boasters, arrogant, blasphemous, without-obedient to their parents, without-gratitude, without-holiness, ³ without-feeling, without-reconciliation, devilish (διάβολοι), without-self-control, without-tameness, without-loving-good, ⁴ treacherous, reckless, puffed-up, lovers-of-pleasure rather-than lovers-of-God, ⁵ᵃ having the form of godliness but its power denying;

A'. ⁵ᵇ and these (τούτους) turn-from. ⁶ For from these (τούτων) are those *who-slip* into the households (οἰκίας) and captivate foolish-women who-are-weighed with sins, led by many desires (ἐπιθυμίαις),[13]

D' Unit

3:7-17

REMAIN IN SALVATION THROUGH FAITH IN CHRIST JESUS

The fifth of eight microchiasms within the 2 Timothy macrochiasm is composed carefully of five elements (A-B-C-B'-A'). Linguistic parallels identifying chiastic arrangements are indicated by the Greek text.

A. 7 always learning (μανθάνοντα) and never having-power (δυνάμενα) to come toward a knowledge of the truth. 8a But in-the-manner Jannes and Jambres opposed Moses, thus these also oppose the truth, human beings corrupted in mind,

   B. 8b without-qualification regarding the faith (τὴν πίστιν). 9 Rather they will not progress upon much (προκόψουσιν ἐπὶ πλεῖον); for the without-minded of theirs will be plain to all, as was (ἐγένετο) that also of those.

   B'. 10 But you yourself have followed the teaching of mine, the way, the purpose, the faith (τῇ πίστει), the long-suffering, the love, the endurance, 11 the persecutions, the sufferings which were (ἐγένετο) to me at Antioch, at Iconium, at Lystra—which persecutions I also bore-up—and from all the Lord rescued me. 12 But also all who-desire to live in-a-godly-manner in Christ Jesus will be persecuted. 13 But evil human beings and impostors will progress to worse (προκόψουσιν ἐπὶ τὸ χεῖρον), deceiving and being deceived.

---

13. The participle "who-slip" (ἐνδύνοντες) is italicized because it serves as a transitive word to the next D' unit. This unit begins with "being-able" (δυνάμενα), a participle that shares an obvious phonetic similarity with "who slip." Notice also the following arrangement, which seems to place the preposition εἰς "chiasticially" relative to these transition words.

3:6: γάρ εἰσιν οἱ ἐνδύνοντες εἰς τὰς οἰκίας
3:7: καὶ μηδέποτε εἰς ἐπίγνωσιν ἀληθείας ἐλθεῖν δυνάμενα

A'. ¹⁴ But you yourself endure in the things you learned (ἔμαθες) and were-persuaded-of, knowing from those you learned (ἔμαθες), ¹⁵ and that from childhood the sacred writings you have known that have-power (δυνάμενά) to wisen you for salvation through faith in Christ Jesus. ¹⁶ All Scripture is God-Spirited and useful toward teaching, toward reproof, toward correction, toward training in righteousness, ¹⁷ that complete may be the human *of God*, toward all good work equipped.¹⁴

C' Unit

4:1–8

I HAVE FOUGHT THE GOOD FIGHT AND KEPT THE FAITH FOR THAT DAY

The sixth of eight microchiasms within the 2 Timothy macrochiasm is composed carefully of four elements (A-B-B'-A'). Linguistic parallels identifying chiastic arrangements are indicated by the Greek text.

A. ⁴:¹ I charge you in-the-presence-of God and Christ Jesus who is about to judge (κρίνειν) the living and the dead, and [by] the manifestation of his (τὴν ἐπιφάνειαν αὐτοῦ) and the kingdom of his:

  B. ² preach the word, stand-ready (ἐπίστηθι) in-season (εὐκαίρως), out-of-season (ἀκαίρως), reprove, rebuke, ex-hort, in all long-suffering and doctrine. ³ For there will be a season (γὰρ καιρός) when sound teaching they will not tol-erate; rather according to their own desires for-themselves they—itching [regarding] the hearing (τὴν ἀκοήν)—will accumulate teachers,

  B'. ⁴ and on-the-one-hand the hearing (τὴν ἀκοήν) of the truth they will-turn-away, on-the-other-hand upon the myths they will-turn-aside. ⁵ But you yourself be sober in all [things], bear-hardship, the work of an evangelist do, the service of yours fulfill.

---

14. The genitive "of God" (τοῦ θεοῦ) is italicized because it serves as a transitive word to the next C' unit. This unit also begins with the genitive "of God" (τοῦ θεοῦ).

Β'. ⁶ For (γάρ) I myself am already being-poured-out-as-a-drink-offering, and the time (καιρός) of my departure has stood-near (ἐφέστηκεν). ⁷ The commendable agony I have agonized, the race I have-finished, the faith I have kept. ⁸ᵃ Henceforth is-laid-up for me the crown of righteousness,

Α'. ⁸ᵇ which the Lord will recompense to me on that day, the just judge (κριτής), but not only to me; rather and to all who have *loved* the manifestation of his (τὴν ἐπιφάνειαν αὐτοῦ).¹⁵

B' Unit

4:9–21

THE LORD WILL SAVE ME FROM EVERY EVIL WORK

The seventh microchiasm within the 2 Timothy macrochiasm is composed carefully of four elements (A-B-B'-A'). Linguistic parallels identifying chiastic arrangements are indicated by the Greek text.

A. ⁹ Do-your-best to come (Σπούδασον ἐλθεῖν) to me quickly. ¹⁰ For Demas deserted me, loving the present age, and journeyed toward Thessalonica, Crescens toward Galatia, Titus toward Dalmatia. ¹¹ Luke alone is with me. Taking-up Mark, bring [him] with you, for to me he is useful toward service. ¹² But Tychicus I sent toward Ephesus. ¹³ The cloak that I left (ἀπέλιπον) in Troas with Carpus—when you come bring, and the books, especially the parchments. ¹⁴ᵃ Alexander the coppersmith displayed many evils to me;

B. ¹⁴ᵇ to him the Lord (κύριος) will recompense according to his works (ἔργα); ¹⁵ him you yourself guard [against], for strongly he opposed our words. ¹⁶ In my first defense none was present with me; rather all left me; may it not be charged to them! ¹⁷ But the Lord (κύριός) stood-by with me and strengthened me, so that through me the proclamation might be fulfilled and all the Gentiles might hear it, and I was rescued (ἐρρύσθην) from the lion's mouth.

B'. ¹⁸ Rescue (ῥύσεταί) me the Lord (κύριος) will from all evil work (ἔργου) and will save [me] into his heavenly kingdom; to him be the glory for the eternities of eternities, amen. ¹⁹ Greet Prisca and

---

15. The verb "loved" (ἠγαπηκόσιν) is italicized because it serves as a transitive word to the next B' unit. This unit also begins with the verb "loving" (ἀγαπήσας).

Aquila and the household of Onesiphorus. [20a] Erastus remained at Corinth,

A'. [20b] but Trophimus being ill, I left (ἀπέλιπον) at Miletus. [21] Do-your-best to come (Σπούδασον . . . ἐλθεῖν) before winter. Eubulus and Pudens and Linus and Claudia and all the brothers greets *you*.[16]

A' Unit

4:22

THE LORD BE WITH YOUR SPIRIT AND GRACE BE WITH YOU

The eighth and final microchiasm of the 2 Timothy macrochiasm is composed carefully of three elements (A-B-A'). Linguistic parallels identifying chiastic arrangements are indicated by the Greek text.

A. [22a] The Lord be with (μετά) your spirit.

    B. [22b] Grace

A'. [22c] be with (μεθ') you all.

The Overall Macrochiastic Structure of 2 Timothy

The above analysis demonstrates how 2 Timothy comprises eight distinct literary units, which we have referred to as eight microchiasms. Now we consider how these eight units form an A-B-C-D-D'-C'-B'-A' structure that organizes the entire letter into a single literary unit, i.e., one macrochiasm.

The Parallel Arrangement of the A and A' Units

A Unit. 1:1–12: Do Not Be Ashamed but Share in Suffering according to the Power of God

A' Unit. 4:22: The Lord Be with Your Spirit and Grace Be with You

---

16. The pronoun "you" (σε) is italicized because it serves as a transitive word to the next A' unit. This unit also begins with the pronoun "your" (σου).

The A and A' units of the macrochiasm are connected by a set of parallel terms.

A Unit (1:1–12)	A' Unit (4:22)
χάρις (1:2; unique nom. form)	χάρις (4:22b; unique nom. form)

All of the aforementioned parallel terms are unique to the A and A' units of the macrochiasm and do not appear elsewhere in the letter.

The Parallel Arrangement of the B and B' Units

B Unit. 1:13—2:3: Guard the Commendable Entrustment in Faith like a Good Soldier for That Day

B' Unit. 4:9–21: The Lord Will Save Me from Every Evil Work

The B and B' units of the macrochiasm are connected by several sets of parallel terms and phrases.

B Unit (1:13—2:3)	B' Unit (4:9–21)
Ὀνησιφόρου (1:16)	Ὀνησιφόρου (4:19)
οἶκον (1:16)	οἶκον (4:19)
Ἔφεσον (1:18)	Ἔφεσον (4:12)

All of the aforementioned parallel terms are unique to the B and B' units of the macrochiasm and do not appear elsewhere in the letter.

The Parallel Arrangement of the C and C' Units

C Unit. 2:4–19: That They May Obtain Salvation in Christ Jesus Who Remains Faithful

C' Unit. 4:1–8: I Have Fought the Good Fight and Kept the Faith for That Day

The C and C' units of the macrochiasm are connected by multiple sets of parallel terms.

C Unit (2:4–19)	C' Unit (4:1–8)
νεκρούς (2:8)	νεκρούς (4:1)
κακοπάθησον (2:9)	κακοπάθησον (4:5)
ἑαυτοῖς (2:13, 21)	ἑαυτοῖς (4:3)
Διαμαρτύρομαι (2:14)	Διαμαρτύρομαι (4:1)
ἐνώπιον (2:14)	ἐνώπιον (4:1)
λόγον (2:15)	λόγον (4:2)
ἤδη (2:18)	ἤδη (4:6)

All of the aforementioned parallel terms are unique to the C and C' units of the macrochiasm and do not appear elsewhere in the letter.

The Parallel Arrangement of the D and D' Units

D Unit. 2:20—3:6: Reject Those Who Deny the Power of Godliness

D' Unit. 3:7–17: Remain in Salvation through Faith in Christ Jesus

The D and D' units of the macrochiasm are connected by two sets of parallel terms.

D Unit (2:4—3:6)	D' Unit (3:7–17)
διωχθήσονται (2:22)	διωχθήσονται (3:12)
ἐπίγνωσιν (2:25)	ἐπίγνωσιν (3:7)

All of the aforementioned parallel terms are unique to the D and D' units of the macrochiasm and do not appear elsewhere in the letter.

3

2 Timothy 1:1–12

Do Not Be Ashamed but Share in Suffering according to the Power of God

(A UNIT)

THIS CHAPTER EXAMINES THE first of eight microchiastic units within the 2 Timothy macrochiasm.

The First Microchiastic Unit

A. ¹ Paul, apostle of Christ Jesus through (διά ἀπόστολος Χριστοῦ Ἰησοῦ) the will of God according to the promise of life (ζωῆς) that is in Christ Jesus, ² To Timothy beloved child: Grace, mercy, peace from God the Father and Christ Jesus (Χριστοῦ Ἰησοῦ) our Lord. ³ Grace I have to God, to-the-one I (ᾧ) serve from [the way of my] forefathers in a pure conscience, as I have without-ceasing memory concerning you in my supplications night and day (ἡμέρας), ⁴ longing to see you, having-been-reminded of your tears, so-that I might become-full of joy, ⁵ taking remembrance of the without-hypocrisy faith (πίστεως) in you that housed first in your grandmother Lois and your mother Eunice, but I am convinced (πέπεισμαι) [is] also in you. ⁶ Through this reason (Δι᾽ ἥν αἰτίαν) I remind you to rekindle the gift of God, which is (ἐστιν) in you through (διά) the laying of my hands.

> B: 7 For to us God did not (οὐ) give (ἔδωκεν ἡμῖν) a Spirit of cowardice; rather of power (δυνάμεως) and love and self-control. 8a Therefore do not be ashamed of the witness of our Lord nor of me his prisoner;
>
> B'. 8b rather suffer-together for the gospel according to the power (δύναμιν) of God 9 who saved us and called to a holy calling not (οὐ) according to our works; rather according to his own purpose and grace, which was given to us (δοθεῖσαν ἡμῖν) in Christ Jesus before eternal times,

A'. 10 but now was manifested through (διά) the manifestation of our Savior Christ Jesus (Χριστοῦ Ἰησοῦ) who on-the-one-hand abolished death, on-the-other-hand brought-to-light life (ζωήν) and without-mortality through (διά) the gospel 11 toward which I-myself was appointed preacher and apostle (ἀπόστολος) and teacher; 12 through this reason (δι᾽ ἣν αἰτίαν) indeed these I suffer; rather, I am not ashamed, for I know to-the-one (ᾧ) I have faith (πεπίστευκα) and I am convinced (πέπεισμαι) that he is (ἐστιν) powerful to guard my entrustment toward *that* day (ἡμέραν).

2 Timothy 1:1–6

PAUL REMEMBERS TIMOTHY AND ENCOURAGES TIMOTHY TO REMEMBER HIM

(A ELEMENT)

2 Timothy 1:1–6: A Minichiastic Unit

The audience hears the first six verses of the letter as a minichiasm in itself. The A element centers on the theme of remembrance, Paul's remembrance of Timothy and Timothy's call to remember his calling.

> a. 1 Paul, apostle of Christ Jesus through (διά) the will of God (θεοῦ) according to the promise of life that is in Christ Jesus, 2 To

Timothy beloved child: Grace, mercy, peace from God (θεοῦ) the Father and Christ Jesus our Lord.

   b. 3 Grace I have to God, to-the-one I serve from [the way of my] forefathers in a pure conscience, as I have without-ceasing memory concerning you (σοῦ μνείαν) in my supplications night and day,

   b'. 4 longing to see you, having-been-reminded of your tears (μεμνημένος σου), so-that I might become-full of joy, 5 taking remembrance of the without-hypocrisy faith in you that housed first in your (σου) grandmother Lois and your (σου) mother Eunice, but I am convinced that [is] also in you.

a'. 6 Through (Δι') this reason I remind you to rekindle the gift of God (θεοῦ), which is in you through (διά) the laying of my hands.[1]

The first two verses, which serve as the *a* sub-element of the first minichiasm (1:1–6), themselves follow a chiastic arrangement:

(a). 1a Paul, apostle of Christ Jesus (Χριστοῦ Ἰησοῦ)

   (b). 1b through the will of God (θεοῦ) according to the promise of life that is in Christ Jesus,

      (c). 2a To Timothy beloved child:

   (b'). 2b Grace, mercy, peace from God (θεοῦ) the Father

(a'). 2c and Christ Jesus (Χριστοῦ Ἰησοῦ) our Lord.

---

1. One might ask whether the following minichiasm is valid given the cognates in ὑπόμνησιν in 1:5 and in ἀναμιμνῄσκω in 1:6. It would appear that the basis for establishing the unique parallelism between the b and b' sub-elements is unwarranted. First, we readily agree that "remembering" verbs permeate this minichiasm, but this is purposeful, reflecting from the outset of the letter one of the key themes in Paul's final words to Timothy and the believers in Ephesus. Second, the parallelism between the b and b' sub-elements is established by the unique juxtaposition and arrangements of the second-person personal pronoun "you" (σοῦ) and the cognates μνείαν and μεμνημένος:

(1) σοῦ
   (2) μνείαν
   (2') μεμνημένος
(1') σου

The letter begins with the self-identification "Paul, apostle of Christ Jesus." Although some doubt that the historic Paul authored the letter, the identification as "Paul" (Παῦλος) makes clear that the letter's recipients are to receive the words that follow as if they were the very words of the Apostle Paul.[2] Among the different ways "Paul" could have identified himself, he adopts the most common title found in the undisputed Pauline letters: "apostle of Christ Jesus" (ἀπόστολος Χριστοῦ Ἰησοῦ). An "apostle" was an emissary imbued with authority, representing the presence of the sender. A sender—in this case the resurrected and ascended "Christ Jesus"—expected the audience to receive the representative as if he were the sender himself. Thus, the opening self-identification highlights Paul's unique authority as an "apostle of Christ Jesus."[3]

Why does Paul draw attention to his apostolic authority in this intensely personal letter?[4] In 1 Timothy the apostle does so in order to contrast his legitimate authority against aspiring-but-false teachers.[5] In Titus he does so in order to empower his "true child" (1:4) with authority to complete the unfinished tasks among the churches in Crete.[6] In 2 Timothy

---

2. Towner, *Letters*, 439–40: "Whatever we make of the question of authorship, the name 'Paul' refers to the same person who authored the undisputed Pauline letters— converted Pharisee and apostle to the Gentiles."

For reasons stated in the introduction and in my commentaries on 1 Timothy and Titus, I maintain the position that the historic apostle was in fact the actual author of this letter.

3. The significant hermeneutical implications of this basic observation of Paul as apostle have been aptly summarized by Richard Gaffin. See *By Faith*, 7–8: "Our deepest concern with [Paul] is as he is an *apostle*, that is, as he is an instrument of God's revelation, authorized by the exalted Christ, for attesting and interpreting the salvation manifested in Christ . . . In our concern with Paul's teaching, then, we should want it to be said of ourselves, above all, what he himself said in 1 Thessalonians 2:13 about the church there in its response to his preaching, namely, that they 'accepted it not as the word of men,' though it was manifestly his and bore all the marks of his personality as someone living within the first-century Mediterranean world and having his roots in the Second Temple Judaism, 'but as what it truly is, the word of God.' Ultimately, and properly considered, Paul's teaching is God's word. This, I take it, is not just a pious but largely irrelevant patina on our work, to be stripped away and effectively ignored as we go about interpreting him. Rather, at stake here is a matter of sober, scientific, methodological, academic necessity for studying Paul, what, as he himself says, is 'truly' (ἀληθῶς) the case."

4. See Oberlinner, *Kommentar zum Zweiten Timotheusbrief*, 6.

5. See my related comments in *1 Timothy*, especially on the first chapter of the letter.

6. See my related comments in *To Exhort and Reprove*, especially on the first chapter of the letter.

he does so to summon his "beloved child" (1:2) not to be ashamed but to share in suffering for the gospel (1:6).[7] "The importance of faithfulness would be well grounded on the basis of apostolic authority."[8]

Indeed, one of the main goals of the letter is to foster endurance, particularly on the part of Timothy, in the face of suffering (1:6-8; 2:3, 11-12; 3:10-15; 4:1-5).[9] Given this, the phrase "apostle of Christ Jesus" alludes to Christ's sufferings and the inevitability of Paul's sufferings. The identification as "apostle" would have recalled Paul's extraordinary conversion narrative and appointment as God's "chosen instrument" (Acts 9:15).[10] But this recollection would have included the sobering words of Christ Jesus: "For I will show him how much he must suffer for the sake of my name" (Acts 9:16). Thus, the self-identification as "apostle of Christ Jesus" not only reiterates Paul's authority but also the inevitability of suffering as Christ's messenger.[11] In this sense, the phrase introduces the idea that "all who desire to live in-a-godly-manner in Christ Jesus will be persecuted" (3:12).

The two prepositional phrases, which constitute the (b) element, expand on Paul's apostleship. The first phrase reads "through the will of God." The preposition "through" (διά) has a causal sense ("on the basis of"). Paul here makes explicit what is implicit in the preceding phrase "of Christ Jesus": his apostolic authority is not of his own making but "through the will of God." Paul reiterated the source of his authority throughout his entire ministry. The most explicit example of this is found in Gal 1:1: "Paul, an apostle not from human beings nor through (δι') a human being; rather through (διά) Jesus Christ and God the Father who raised him from the dead." Paul's authority, then, is derivative authority, and any "opposition and defection from the faith"[12] declared by

7. Spicq, *Saint Paul*, 697.

8. Towner, *Letters*, 440.

9. There is a difference in opinion whether Timothy was in actual danger of turning away from the faith. It is hard to determine whether he was in danger of apostasy. But the possibility of abandoning his call was very real; otherwise, why would Paul have written the letter? And who knows if abandoning the faith itself would not have followed in a matter of time.

10. Towner, *Letters*, 440: "The reference evokes thoughts of the event in which he encountered the risen Lord and subsequently was entrusted with divine revelation."

11. Paul makes this more explicit a few verses later in 1:11-12: "toward which I-myself was appointed herald and apostle (ἀπόστολος) and teacher; through this reason indeed these I suffer."

12. Towner, *Letters*, 441.

the apostle represents a rejection of the God who willed his apostleship. Given the toxic environment created by the false teachers, Paul opens the letter by underscoring the agency of his authority.

However, as noted already, we should understand Paul's apostleship both in terms of authority *and* suffering. In a secondary but still significant sense, we are to view Christian persecution also in terms of "the will of God" (θελήματος θεοῦ): suffering is part of God's plan for our salvation. All four gospel narratives underscore the inevitability of suffering for Christ's followers. In no uncertain terms Jesus said, "Remember the word that I spoke to you: A slave is not greater than his master. If they persecuted me, they will also persecute you" (John 15:20). Such persecution does not always take the form of physical persecution. Consider the situation of Joseph, the earthly father of Jesus. Prior to his marriage, Mary was pregnant. The narrative he receives from God's angel is that what is conceived in her is by the Spirit. The angel then commands Joseph to set aside his plans to call off the engagement. We can imagine the social and religious ostracism he and Mary must have faced. Some probably thought the two were guilty of fornication; others that Mary had been unfaithful. Who, after all, would believe the narrative told by the angel? Suffering, then, in all its manifestations, is God's will for all who desire to fulfill their roles in God's plan of redemption.

The second prepositional phrase that qualifies Paul's apostleship reads "according to the promise of life that is in Christ Jesus." Some argue that the preposition "according to" (κατ') indicates that Paul's apostleship "conforms with God's promise of life" (NIV), others that it conveys purpose: Paul's apostleship is "for the sake of" proclaiming the gospel (NRSV).[13] Perhaps both senses are in view, although the latter is clearer and receives more support from the letter itself (e.g., 2 Tim 2:11). Either way, Paul's audience must view the apostle and his work as integral to the outworking of God's plan of redemption.[14] Paul views himself as an atypical person in history, one who stands in the line of prophets and is called to fulfill a unique role in God's plan of salvation. The only way to properly interpret Paul's apostleship, then, is to appreciate its divine origin ("through") and its divine purpose ("according to").

---

13. E.g., Kelly, *Pastoral Epistles*, 153; Knight, *Pastoral Epistles*, 364.

14. Towner, *Letters*, 442: "What the language does here is to describe Paul's calling to preach as being integral to the outworking of God's plan of redemptive plan—the promise of life."

The phrase "the promise of life that is in Christ Jesus" draws attention to the giver of the promise and its content. The giver of the "promise" (ἐπαγγελίαν) is the same God who has ordained Paul's apostleship. In Titus 1:2, the apostle makes the connection between God and "the promise of life" more explicit: "in hope of eternal life, which the unlying God promised (ἐπηγγείλατο) before eternal ages."[15] Similarly, in Rom 1:1-2 Paul describes the "promise of life" in terms of the "gospel of God, which he promised (προεπηγγείλατο) through his prophets in the holy writings." According to the apostle, the proper lenses for interpreting all of history is through "the promise of life," the promise given in Eden that someday an offspring of Adam would come to defeat the work of Satan and undo the effects of Adam's disobedience (Gen 3:15). History is not a random or repeating series of events but the arena in which God is providentially orchestrating all things to realize his "promise" of renewal. By connecting his apostleship with this grand "promise," Paul highlights the critical role his ministry plays in realizing God's plan to renew all things.

The phrase "promise of life," however, should not leave the impression that the "life" in view lies entirely in the future. Paul describes this "life" as "life that is in Christ Jesus" (ζωῆς τῆς ἐν Χριστῷ Ἰησοῦ). Several comments are in order. First, the "promise of life" is the promise of "eternal life" (ζωὴν αἰώνιον; 1 Tim 1:16) because it is "life" in union with the "eternal one" (Rev. 1:8). Second, it is the eternal "life" that comes as a gift of faith, not as the result of merit.[16] Finally, such eternal "life" is already realized and yet waits its full consummation at the parousia. Because it is "life that is in (ἐν) Christ Jesus,"[17] it is "right now and on into the future (1 Tim 4:8), so that God's gift of eternal life is to be understood as already in effect for those who have believed in Christ."[18] In all this we should observe that Paul cannot conceive of "life" outside of Christ.

The specification of "life in Christ Jesus" is central to Paul's self-understanding and to personal faithfulness in the face of suffering. On the one hand, Paul views all of history as the arena in which the sovereign will of God unfolds. Yet sovereignty does not preclude human responsibility.[19] The apostle recognizes that the salvation of God's elect

15. See my comments on Titus 1:3 in *To Exhort and Reprove*.

16. See my comments on 1:16 and 6:12 in *1 Timothy*.

17. For a helpful summary of the significance of the phrase "in Christ" in Paul's letters, see Ridderbos, *Paul*, 57–63.

18. Towner, *Letters*, 441.

19. See Packer, *Evangelism and the Sovereignty of God*.

depends on his faithfulness as a "preacher and apostle and teacher" of the gospel. Paul's high view of his apostleship "despite" God's sovereignty is perhaps most explicit in his first correspondence with the Thessalonians. In the opening chapter, he reiterates that the Thessalonians have been chosen by God (1:4) but then immediately underscores "what kind of men we proved to be among you for your sake" (1:5). In much of the rest of 1 Thessalonians he reminds the Thessalonians of his faithfulness in the face of persecution. Meaningless suffering is almost impossible to bear; but suffering that leads to eternal life for others empowers faithfulness, especially because it echoes the nature of Christ's own sufferings. By framing his apostleship and suffering within God's plan of redemption, Paul invites Timothy and the audience to adopt the same perspective on the suffering they experience as a result of their commitment to and union with Christ Jesus.[20]

Verse 2 progresses the chiastic movement with the (c) element by identifying the primary recipient of the letter: "To Timothy beloved child." "Timothy" (Τιμοθέῳ), identified as a coauthor in some of Paul's letters (e.g., Philemon), was one of Paul's most trusted colleagues. The descriptor "beloved child" is noteworthy when compared with the other "letters to coworkers."[21] In 1 Tim 1:2 and Titus 1:4, Paul uses the phrase "true child" (γνησίῳ τέκνῳ). The adjective "true" legitimized Paul's delegates over against the false teachers.[22] The adjective "beloved" (ἀγαπητῷ) connotes deep affection. The choice of "beloved" over "true" doesn't

20. On the impact of worldview on our experience of suffering, see Keller, *Walking with God through Pain and Suffering*, 15–16: "The crucial commonality is this: In every one of these worldviews, suffering can, despite its painfulness, be an important means of actually *achieving* your purpose in life. It can play a pivotal role in propelling you toward all the most important goals. One could say that in each of these other cultures' grand narratives—what human life is all about—suffering can be an important chapter or part of that story. But modern Western culture is different. In the secular view, this material world is all there is. And so the meaning of life is to have the freedom to choose the life that makes you most happy. However, in that view of things, suffering can have no meaningful part. It is a complete interruption of your life story—it cannot be a meaningful part of the story. In this approach to life, suffering should be avoided at almost any cost, or minimized to the greatest degree possible."

21. There are problems with the nomenclature "the Pastoral Epistles." Towner, *Letters*, 88–89: "In the final analysis, subsequent use of the term 'the Pastoral Epistles' (PE, *Pastoralbriefe*) would eventually force the letters into a restrictive interrelationship that they were never intended to have." See also Fuchs, *Unerwartete Unterschiede*; Prior, *Paul the Letter-Writer*. For this reason, I use the phrase suggested by Towner— "letters to coworkers" (89).

22. See my comments on both verses in 1 *Timothy* and *To Exhort and Reprove*.

mean that the problem of false teachers and heretical doctrines has been resolved. Rather, the adjective "beloved," coupled with the familial term "child" (τέκνῳ), reminds Timothy and the audience of the intimate and special relationship shared between the apostle and his beloved.[23] Thus, Paul expects Timothy to remain faithful—even if all prove faithless—as a son would remain loyal to his father. Or, as the chiastic progression suggests, Timothy must be faithful as a beloved child of Paul even as Paul must be faithful as a chosen "apostle of Christ Jesus."

Personal relationship and loyalty played a critical role in the apostle's ministry. This is nowhere more succinctly clear than in Philemon. As much as this is a letter on reconciliation, it is also a letter on Christian persuasion.[24] As "an old man and now a prisoner also for Christ Jesus" (9), Paul expects Philemon to be amendable to his request to "receive Onesimus" (17). This expectation is grounded on the personal relationship Paul and Philemon share, a relationship so intimate that Paul is able to make bold statements ("You owe me even your own self"; 19) and requests ("Prepare a guest room for me"; 22). In this letter addressed to Timothy, we will see how Paul adopts the same approach, using his personal relationship as the basis for his encouragements and exhortations.

The prayer "Grace, mercy, peace from God the Father and Christ Jesus our Lord" comprise the parallel (b') and (a') elements of the minichiasm of 1:1–2. The occurrence of "God" (θεοῦ) echoes its earlier occurrence in the corresponding (b) element of 1:1b—"through the will of God (θεοῦ)"; the occurrence of "Christ Jesus" (Χριστοῦ Ἰησοῦ) echoes its earlier occurrence in the corresponding (a) element of 1:1a—"apostle of Christ Jesus (Χριστοῦ Ἰησοῦ)." The repetition underscores the parallelism between the source of Paul's apostleship and the source (ἀπό) of every blessing: all good things come from "God the Father and Christ Jesus our Lord." Moreover, the identification of "God the Father and Christ Jesus our Lord" clarifies the precise meaning of the "grace, mercy, [and] peace." "Grace" (χάρις) is the "enabling power" that is "produced by God's

---

23. Towner, *Letters*, 443: "When one combines these items, the picture becomes one that involves responsibility (as of a child to a father or a disciple to a teacher) and close filial relationship. Timothy's responsibility—to continue the Pauline mission—will be spelled out through the rest of the letter; the filial obligation and relationship are underlined here as the basis for the exhortations to come."

24. For further reflection, see my *Unreconciled: The New Norm; God's Wisdom for Making Peace.*

favor."²⁵ "Mercy" (ἔλεος) is "kindness expressed for one in need."²⁶ "Peace" (εἰρήνη) describes a disposition of rest that comes from being reconciled with God.²⁷ Paul prays for all these items on behalf of his beloved child who is in a more basic sense a beloved child of "God the Father" adopted through "Christ Jesus our Lord." As a beloved child, Timothy, along with all believers, should be confident that the apostle's prayer for empowering grace, timely mercy, and abiding peace will not go unanswered.²⁸

Finally, the identification of God as "Father" (πατρός) and Christ Jesus as "Lord" (κυρίου) reminds Timothy and the audience that as much as Paul expects personal loyalty from them, on a more fundamental level the Father and Son, the source of "grace, mercy, [and] peace," merit their allegiance. Impossible to miss is the subtle alignment between loyalty to the apostle and loyalty to the one who has sent him: Christ Jesus, the sender, is "our" (ἡμῶν) Lord. Again, we see the central role relationships play in the Christian life: the Christian faith is deeply personal. It entails our relationships with other believers and ultimately our relationship to God, who is presented here in personal terms—as our "Father" and as our "Lord."

In sum, the opening two verses of 2 Timothy, which follow a chiastic pattern, focus on the source of Paul's apostleship and every blessing.

The minichiasm (1:1–6) progresses to the b sub-element, v. 3, which begins the formal body of the letter. But before we continue our analysis of the chiasm, we should make one broad observation concerning vv. 3–6. The theme of "remembrance" ties together the remaining verses in

25. Friberg and Friberg, *Analytical Greek New Testament*, s.v.

26. BDAG, s.v. Towner makes some helpful remarks on this item. See *Letters*, 443–44: "In 1 Tim 1:13 and 16, it is Paul who . . . serves as the prototypical recipient of God's mercy. And Paul's mercy-prayer for Timothy . . . places the coworker, in contrast to the false teachers, into the apostle's category. Now in this letter, the context suggests a slightly different accent. Note how the mercy-prayer is also made for Onesiphorus's household (1:16), and for Onesiphorus himself . . . because he, in contrast to 'everyone in the province of Asia,' had not been 'ashamed' of Paul (1:16, 18). Moreover, the first instructions to Timothy will urge him not to be 'ashamed' of the gospel or of Paul (1:8). Consequently, in 2 Timothy the prayer for God's mercy (or covenant-sustaining kindness and concern) is especially pointed to this danger (shame and shrinking back) that Timothy must avoid."

27. Friberg and Friberg, *Analytical Greek New Testament*, s.v.

28. Towner, *Letters*, 444: "As the letter unfolds, its relevance for all believers, especially for those facing ministry challenges, will become clear. And this suggests that we will find consolation and encouragement in the same gifts of God and in the Lordship of Christ that Paul brought directly to Timothy's attention at the outset."

this minichiasm. We have tried to highlight this already in our wooden translations, but the Greek text makes it more obvious: "I have without-ceasing memory (μνείαν) concerning you" (1:3); "having-been-reminded (μεμνημένος) of your tears" (1:4); "taking remembrance (ὑπόμνησιν) of the without-hypocrisy faith in you" (1:5); "I remind (ἀναμιμνῄσκω) you to rekindle the gift of God" (1:6). This same theme provides a usual category for interpreting the entire Bible: the various authors present God as a covenant-remembering God and they summon God's people to remember God's mercy expressed particularly in salvation. Given the dominant presence this theme has in the whole Bible, it comes as no surprise that it plays an equally important role in the opening section of this letter.

As is characteristic of most of his letters, Paul begins the body of the letter with a thanksgiving-prayer: "Grace I have to God," or, more commonly, "I thank God" (e.g., ESV). The proximity of "grace" (χάριν) to its earlier occurrence in the previous verse suggests some sort of reciprocal quality to the Christian life: as God has given us "grace" in Christ Jesus, we respond with "grace." Still, the sense of "grace" in 1:3 lacks the aspect of empowerment—given no human being can make God greater—and instead carries the sense of goodwill and thanksgiving. The present tense of the verb "have" (ἔχω) suggests an ongoing reality. Thus, perhaps what is in view is not so much a thanksgiving-prayer, although that is not entirely excluded, but a thankful disposition "to God" (τῷ θεῷ): "My disposition toward God is one of gratitude."

What is different about this thanksgiving-prayer relative to those found in the other letters is the absence of an immediate explanation for his thanksgiving. For instance, in Rom 1:8 Paul writes: "First, I thank my God through Jesus Christ for all of you, for your faith is proclaimed in all the world."[29] But in 1 Tim 1:3, the apostle goes on a tangent and then gives only an implicit explanation later in 1:5. Such a tangent is deliberate on Paul's part and gives some insight into the purpose and plan of this letter, namely remembering and keeping the faith. But before any exhortation, Paul presents himself as a model of upholding that which he has inherited.

The relative clause begins with the pronoun "to-the-one" (ᾧ). The juxtaposition to the dative form "to God" suggests the force, "Grace I have to God, to the very one I serve with my whole being." Amid all

---

29. See also 1 Cor 1:4; Phil 1:3–5; 1 Thess 1:2–3.

this talk of suffering and faithfulness, we must remember the joy and gratitude Paul experienced in his service. In the NT, the verb "I serve" (λατρεύω) describes the essence of the Christian life—wholehearted service to God.[30] This meaning derives from the LXX where the same term describes the cultic duties of the priests.[31] Paul selects this verb in order to tie his apostolic calling to the ministry and service of the priests who were also uniquely set apart.[32] Also, the present tense underscores that even up to the present suffering Paul is continuing the work carried out by his spiritual predecessors.

Paul reiterates this connection through the prepositional phrase "from [the way of my] forefathers (ἀπὸ προγόνων)," which the ESV translates "as my ancestors did."[33] This echoes Paul's defense before Felix where he declares, "I serve the God of our fathers (λατρεύω τῷ πατρῴῳ θεῷ), believing everything laid down by the Law and written in the Prophets" (Acts 24:14). "Forefathers" likely refers to the patriarchs and OT "fathers" who received the promises of divine blessing and responded in worship and service.[34] By tracing the source (ἀπό) of his own service to such "forefathers," he strengthens his own credentials. This was likely necessary given the opposition to his apostleship and gospel.[35]

But his choice of the term "forefathers" also aligns with the personal tone of the letter. As we have noted already, the first two verses make rich use of familial language: Timothy is Paul's "beloved child"; the source of all grace, mercy, and peace is God the "Father." The term "forefather" also occurs in 1 Tim 5:4 where Paul asserts that the mark of true godliness is care for one's family: "But if some widow has children or grandchildren, they must learn first to show godliness to their own household and to make repayments to their forefathers (προγόνοις); for this is acceptable

30. E.g., Rom 12:1: "Therefore, I exhort you, brothers, by the mercies of God, to present your bodies as a living sacrifice, holy and acceptable to God, which is your spiritual service (λατρείαν)." See my comments in *Introducing Romans*.

31. E.g., 1 Chr 28:13 LXX: "for the divisions of the priests and of the Levites, and all the work of the service in the house of the LORD; for all the vessels for the service (λατρείας) in the house of the LORD."

32. Towner, *Letters*, 449: "The verb thus links Paul's apostolic ministry intentionally to OT patterns of service to God."

33. BDAG, s.v.

34. Towner, *Letters*, 449: "'Ancestors' will mean not parents . . . but 'the fathers' to whom the promise of blessing was made by God and through whom the true worship of YHWH was practiced and transmitted through the generations."

35. See my comments in Jeon, *1 Timothy*.

in the sight of God." It's occurrence in 1 Tim 5:4 is literal, referring to one's actual parents or grandparents. Given these considerations, it is possible (perhaps likely) that the term προγόνων in 2 Tim 1:3 retains some familial nuance.[36] Paul's other purpose in 1:3, then, is to convey his loyalty to his spiritual fathers in hope that Timothy and the audience might do likewise by remaining loyal to Paul and his gospel.

The third part of the tripartite relative clause is the qualifier "in a pure conscience" (ἐν καθαρᾷ συνειδήσει). This exact phrase occurs in 1 Tim 3:9 to describe aspiring deacons. Among the qualifications required of them is holding to "the mystery of the faith in a pure conscience" (ἐν καθαρᾷ συνειδήσει); that is, they are to remain loyal to the gospel. In 1 Timothy, the adjective "pure" (καθαρᾷ) expresses the result of God's cleansing activity. The noun "conscience" (συνειδήσει) describes the instrument by which people apply ethical norms to concrete reality.[37] In both 2 Tim 1:3 and 1 Tim 3:9 the phrase has a dual sense. On the one hand, it conveys faithfulness to the gospel entrusted to them. Its occurrence in 1 Timothy gives an indirect challenge to Timothy: Will he also serve "in a pure conscience?" On the other hand, the phrase also conveys the "means" (ἐν) by which such faithfulness is possible. A "pure conscience" is a gift of God's cleansing grace and distinguishes true servants of Christ from false teachers.[38] In effect, Paul is saying that he has been faithful to his apostolic calling through such purifying grace. The net effect of this dual sense is that serving "in a good conscience," that is, serving loyally, indicates the possession of a "good conscience."

In sum, what does Paul convey in the tripartite relative clause "to-the-one I serve from [the way of my] forefathers in a pure conscience"? First, the apostle underscores the communal quality of his service. Whereas in other epistles he writes, "I have grace to my God" (e.g., Phlm 1:3), in 2 Tim 1:3 he highlights from the very outset that his service and worship are consistent with historic and elect Israel's service and worship. Second, as the Levitical priests were set apart to serve God, so Paul sees himself as one uniquely appointed in God's plan of redemption to bring the gospel to the Gentiles. Finally, the apostle asserts his fidelity to his calling through the means already given to him in Christ Jesus. In all this, Paul desires that his audience, Timothy and all the believers who hear the

---

36. Hence the NASB translation "forefathers."

37. Perhaps a more fitting translation would be "purified conscience."

38. See my analysis of 1 Tim 1:3-11, esp. 1:5 in *1 Timothy*.

reading of this letter, imitate his model of seeking to remain faithful to the faith they have inherited "in a pure conscience."

The remaining part of v. 3 both reiterates Paul's piety and communicates his commitment to pray for his beloved child. The adjective "without-ceasing" (ἀδιάλειπτον) and the temporal phrase "night and day" (νυκτὸς καὶ ἡμέρας) convey the depth and breadth of such piety and commitment.[39] The former implies the latter, but its inclusion is purposeful: Paul spells out what "without-ceasing" means so that Timothy knows that Paul is making regularly "supplications" (δεήσεσίν)—prayers of intercession—on his behalf.[40] The combination of the verb "have" (ἔχω) and the noun "memory" (μνείαν) carries the sense of recollection or remembrance. Negatively put, Paul has forgotten neither the God of his ancestors nor Timothy.

There is a clear connection here to the preceding relative pronoun. Paul has not forgotten his past. He remembers the worship and service of his predecessors. Similarly, Paul has not forgotten the saints in the present. He remembers them in ceaseless prayers, trusting that God will not forget his people but will shower them with grace, mercy, and peace. The implicit challenge is whether Timothy and the audience will remember Paul. Will they forget him and his gospel or will they aspire to follow his example of remembering the saints of the past and present?

Here it is important to make an observation on the need for spiritual parents in the church. When I was in seminary, I never imagined the number of spiritual "orphans" I would encounter. I am referring to people who do not have anyone praying for them on a regular basis. When I think of my parents, I am grateful for all the ways they provided for my material, emotional, and relational needs. But I am most thankful for the many nights they devoted to praying for my salvation and growth in knowledge and discernment. Now that I am a parent and pray regularly for my children, I am saddened by the number of persons who go through life confident that no one remembers them in prayer. Despite the danger of paternalism and misunderstanding, it is the duty of those who are more mature in the faith to "adopt" those who lack spiritual parents and to commit them in prayer. This challenge is especially relevant to those who are in "professional" ministry and face an unprecedented degree of temptation toward "ministry success." Our focus on making

39. Concerning the expression "night and day" (νυκτὸς καὶ ἡμέρας), see my comments on the elderly widow who prays "night and day" (1 Tim 5:5) in 1 Timothy.

40. See my comments on "supplication" (δέησις) in 1 Tim 2:1; 5:5.

bigger and better churches may come at the cost of devoting ourselves to praying for our beloved children in the faith.

The minichiasm of 1 Tim 1:1–6 progresses with the b' sub-element in which Paul continues the theme of remembrance. Verse 4 expresses loneliness, intimacy, and vulnerability: "longing to see you, having-been-reminded of your tears, so-that I might become-full of joy." The first participial phrase "longing to see you" (ἐπιποθῶν σε ἰδεῖν) conveys the apostle's deep desire to see Timothy face-to-face, a desire perhaps exasperated by his prayers on Timothy's behalf.[41] As many missionaries have said, "You can't hug a tree." We can only imagine how much Paul longed for the presence of his partners for the gospel. This phrase balances out what Paul has stated thus far in the letter. His self-identification as apostle and reiteration of intercessory prayer could leave the misimpression of authority and independence. By expressing his longing to see Timothy and thereby exposing the state of his heart, Paul makes himself vulnerable to Timothy and the audience. Such vulnerability is worth reflecting on for believers who play the role of caretaker and influencer but rarely reveal their own need and weakness. To be sure, by making statements like "longing to see you," we make ourselves vulnerable; but to do otherwise would be dehumanizing.[42]

The second participial phrase in the b' sub-element "having-been-reminded of your tears" (μεμνημένος σου τῶν δακρύων) establishes the parallel with the corresponding b sub-element "memory concerning you" (σοῦ μνείαν).[43] The mention of "your tears" progresses the theme of remembering from a general remembrance in intercessory prayer to a specific remembrance of an intimate event between the two. It is

---

41. Towner, *Letters*, 452: "The phrase describes Paul's emotional situation as he prays, generated perhaps in the course of the prayer."

42. C. S. Lewis provides compelling insight on this subject in his treatment of charity (*Four Loves*, 121): "To love at all is to be vulnerable. Love anything, and your heart will be wrung and possibly be broken. If you want to make sure of keeping it intact, you must give your heart to no one, not even an animal. Wrap it carefully round with hobbies and little luxuries; avoid all entanglements; lock it up safe in the casket or coffin of your selfishness. But in that casket—safe, dark, motionless, airless—it will change. It will not be broken; it will become unbreakable, impenetrable, irredeemable."

43. Notice the artistic layout:
σοῦ
μνείαν
μεμνημένος
σου

impossible to know the exact event (or events) Paul is referring to.[44] Still, Paul's purpose is clear: he is reminding Timothy—who has perhaps forgotten in the midst of suffering—of their unique, profound, and deep friendship.[45] This reiteration of friendship paves the way for the summons to loyalty and faithfulness that Paul will soon make.

The purpose (ἵνα) of the possible reunion is overwhelming joy: "so-that I might-become-full of joy" (χαρᾶς πληρωθῶ). The verb occurs in the passive, thus placing the onus on Timothy: Paul's experience of joy depends on Timothy's faithfulness to the gospel. Consider the contrast in Phil 1 where Paul writes: "I am hard pressed between the two. My desire is to depart and be with Christ, for that is far better. But to remain in the flesh is more necessary on your account. Convinced of this, I know that I will remain and continue with you all, for your progress and joy in the faith" (Phil 1:23–25 ESV). Now, Paul is expecting his son to endure for the sake of the apostle's joy even as Paul had endured all suffering for the joy of other believers.

Here we pause for a moment to consider the flow of the minichiasm. Paul begins by highlighting his apostolic authority: "Paul, apostle of Christ Jesus through the will of God" (1:1). But then immediately the focus shifts from his positional authority to his relational intimacy. Timothy is his beloved child upon whom he wishes grace, mercy and peace. Then Paul emphasizes how he intercedes "night and day" for his spiritual son. Finally, he expresses his longing for Timothy's presence and confesses that his joy depends on their reunion. This juxtaposition of authority and intimacy summarizes Paul's approach to ministry. We find a similar pattern in his correspondence with Philemon (esp. 8–14).[46] Paul did not have a low view of his apostolic authority, as evidenced especially in Galatians. Yet he recognized what all good leaders recognize—the importance of developing and leading through personal relationships instead of just formal authority.

The b' sub-element continues with the progression from "memory concerning you" (1:3) to "having-been-reminded of your tears" (1:4) to "taking remembrance of the without-hypocrisy faith in you" (1:5). Again, we observe the central role the theme of remembrance plays in

---

44. See Kelly, *Pastoral Epistles*, 156.

45. BDAG notes the emotive force of the verb μιμνῄσκομαι.

46. For further reflection, see Jeon, *Unreconciled; God's Wisdom for Making Peace*.

2 TIMOTHY 1:1-12 43

this letter.[47] As an aside, Paul suggests that the discipline of remembering God and his gospel is a mark of godliness. In any case, v. 5 begins with the participial phrase "taking remembrance" (ὑπόμνησιν λαβών), which can be taken passively "I am reminded of."[48] The direct object "faith" (πίστεως) can refer to the content of faith (the gospel) or the act-and-condition of faith (believing-and-being in Christ). In this case the latter is likely because of the qualifier "in you" (ἐν σοί): "it is faith that Timothy has in Christ Jesus."

Paul qualifies this faith in three ways. First, it is a "without-hypocrisy" (ἀνυποκρίτου) faith.[49] That is, it is an authentic faith that stands in contrast to the faith of the false teachers who have departed from Paul's gospel and propagated false doctrine.[50] This descriptor functions in a way similar to Paul's pronouncement of Timothy and Titus as "true child in the faith" (1 Tim 1:2; Titus 1:4):[51] Timothy's faith is "without-hypocrisy"—it is trustworthy—because it remains faithful to the apostolic teaching and does not have the divisive effects of heresies.

The second qualifier is that this faith "housed first in your (σου) grandmother Lois and your (σου) mother Eunice" (ἐνῴκησεν πρῶτον ἐν τῇ μάμμῃ σου Λωΐδι καὶ τῇ μητρί σου Εὐνίκῃ).[52] The clustering of the genitive form of "you" reinforces the continuity between Paul's remembrance of "you," his being reminded of "your tears," and his taking remembrance of the faith that dwelt first in "your" grandmother and in "your" mother. In other words, when Paul remembers Timothy, he remembers Timothy in relation to his family who transmitted the "without-hypocrisy faith" to him. Like Paul, Timothy possesses an inherited faith. Undoubtedly, Paul is strengthening the similarities between him and Timothy.[53] The verb "housed" (ἐνῴκησεν) reinforces the familial backdrop of this letter and

47. See Westfall, "Moral Dilemma," 223.

48. Friberg and Friberg, *Analytical Greek New Testament*, s.v.

49. Notice also how "without-hypocrisy" (ἀνυποκρίτου) in the b' sub-element faintly echoes "without-ceasing" (ἀπεράντοις) in the b sub-element, thus strengthening the parallelism between the two units.

50. See my comments on 1 Tim 1:5–7 in *1 Timothy* where the same phrase "without-hypocrisy faith" occurs (1:5).

51. See my comments on both verses in *1 Timothy* and *To Exhort and Reprove*.

52. Little is known about both persons other than their Jewish background (Acts 16:1). We can only speculate how they came to faith.

53. Köstenberger, *1–2 Timothy and Titus*, 213: "The opening thanksgiving in vv. 3–5 establishes continuity and antiquity by referring to Paul's 'ancestors' (v. 3) and Timothy's 'sincere faith' in continuity with that of his grandmother and mother (v. 5)."

conveys the imagery of Timothy abiding in the same household (οἶκος) of his predecessors.[54] As such, "'Faith' is thus depicted as an enduring characteristic of these three lives."[55] In contrast with our contemporary age, tradition and lineage were highly prized and marks of authenticity.

The last qualifier is the declaration "but I am convinced [is] also in you." The passive form of the verb "convinced" (πέπεισμαι) connotes certainty: Paul is so persuaded that the faith of Lois and Eunice is "also in you" (καὶ ἐν σοί) that he gives thanks to the Lord (1:3).[56] At the same time, the rest of the letter reveals some concern—to put it lightly—on the apostle's part. It appears that Timothy is cowering from his calling. Therefore, "the rhetorical effect of this statement goes beyond simple affirmation and encouragement to exhortation designed to induce Timothy to demonstrate his faith."[57] We find something similar in Paul's Letter to Philemon: "Convinced (πέποιθώς) of your obedience, I write to you, knowing that you will do even more than I say" (21). Was Paul sure that Philemon would receive Onesimus? Probably. But Paul's purpose in penning the letter was to move Philemon to prove that the apostle's confidence was not misplaced.[58] Similarly, Paul is "convinced" that Timothy has true faith. Yet, he is writing to spur Timothy to corroborate Paul's confidence that the two are indeed "cut from the same cloth."[59]

Verse 6, the a' sub-element of the minichiasm of 1:1–6, progresses the movement from Paul's remembrance of Timothy to his exhortation to Timothy to remember: "Through this reason I remind you to rekindle the gift of God" (1:6a). The phrase "through this reason (Δι' ἣν αἰτίαν)"—usually translated "For this reason" (NASB)—refers back to Timothy's inherited and sincere faith. Only because Paul is confident that Timothy already possesses the "gift of God" can he make the following

---

54. See Yarbrough's comments on 2 Tim 1:3–5 in *1–2 Timothy and Titus*.

55. Towner, *Letters*, 454. Towner also comments: "The verb translated 'to live in' . . . is Pauline and used uniformly to describe inward spiritual elements of the Christian life." See also his n41 where he observes similar Pauline language to describe indwelling sin.

56. One wonders whether the use of the preposition ἐν in 1:5 reinforces the connection between Timothy and his predecessors. Paul describes the faith of Timothy's grandmother and mother as a faith that "dwelt-*in*" (ἐνῴκησεν) first "in" (ἐν) his grandmother and mother and now "in (ἐν) you."

57. Towner, *Letters*, 455.

58. For further reflection, see Jeon, *Unreconciled*.

59. I borrow this image from Towner, *Letters*, 455.

exhortation.[60] The verb "I remind" (ἀναμιμνῄσκω) makes explicit what was implicit in the repeated use of remembrance terms— "memory" (μνείαν; 1:3), "having-been-reminded" (μεμνημένος; 1:4), "taking re-membrance" (ὑπόμνησιν; 1:5)—"As I remember, now I am summoning you to remember." The sense of reciprocity illuminates the nuance of the verb. The exhortation is akin to the challenge given to husband-and-wife to remember their vows or the warning given to Israel not to forget the Lord, their deliverer.[61] Thus v. 6 shifts the direction of the minichiasm from Paul's act of remembering to Timothy's obligation to remember.

Paul specifies that Timothy is "to rekindle the gift of God." Commentators differ on the precise meaning of both the verb "rekindle" and the object "gift of God." Some argue that the verb "rekindle" (ἀναζωπυρεῖν) means to revive what has died.[62] Others assert that the verb expresses fueling a flame until it reaches its full potential.[63] It is doubtful that the struggles of ministry have completely extinguished Timothy's faith. Still, all the interpretations agree, as the present tense of the command suggests, that Paul is summoning Timothy to be more diligent in regularly stewarding that which has been entrusted to him.

Concerning the object "the gift of God" (τὸ χάρισμα τοῦ θεοῦ), there are three main lines of interpretations. First, "the gift" refers to the special authority and ability given to ordained ministers of the gospel.[64]

---

60. Köstenberger, *1–2 Timothy and Titus*, 215: "On the basis of Paul's confidence in the faith living in Timothy, he issues a reminder and series of exhortations (δι᾽ ἣν αἰτίαν, 'therefore,' means more literally 'because of this')."

61. Towner, *Letters*, 457: "What might seem to be a gentle tone in which to touch a command is actually all the more binding, because a 'reminder' draws on shared knowledge and experience and implies that past commitments are still in effect." Especially helpful is Towner's description of Paul's approach: "the technique of obligating by reminder" (457n3).

Consider the preface of the Decalogue in which God reminds the Israelites: "I am the LORD your God, who brought you out of the land of Egypt, out of the house of slavery" (Exod 20:2 ESV). Similarly, consider Moses's exhortation: "And you shall remember the whole way that the LORD your God has led you these forty years in the wilderness, that he might humble you, testing you to know what was in your heart, whether you would keep his commandments or not" (Deut 8:2 ESV). Indeed, it is remarkable how throughout the Bible remembering is a mark of true godliness (Jas 1:24).

62. E.g., Lips, *Glaube*, 208–10.

63. E.g., Towner, *Letters*, 457.

64. E.g., Carson, *Showing the Spirit*, 20; Kelly, *Pastoral Epistles*, 159–60. See 1 Tim 4:14.

Second, "the gift" expresses one of many "gifts" of the Spirit to believers for the work of ministry and progress of the gospel.[65] Finally, "the gift" means *the* gift of the Holy Spirit.[66] While the various positions have supporting evidence and reasoning, we will see that the second half of v. 6 supports the last proposal.

Verse 6 concludes by stating that "the gift of God"—as noted by the relative pronoun "which" (ὅ)—"is in you through the laying of my hands." There is an obvious echo here ("which is in you," ἐστιν ἐν σοί) of v. 5 ("that [faith is] also in you"). The focus on the "indwelling" quality of the gift weakens the view that a visible ordination or ministry-talent is in view. Rather, it appears that Paul has in mind the Spirit, who resides in believers, gives them courage, and empowers them to persevere in all good work.[67]

The second half of the relative clause specifies that the gift came "through the laying of my hands" (διὰ τῆς ἐπιθέσεως τῶν χειρῶν μου). Both occurrences of the preposition "through" (διά) in the corresponding a-a' sub-elements denote instrumentality: as Paul's apostleship is "through" (διά) the will of "God" (θεοῦ), so too Timothy's receipt of the gift of "God" (θεοῦ) is "through (διά) the laying of my hands" (1:6). This repetition underscores the derivative nature of Christian authority. In addition, the mention of "laying of hands" supports the conclusion that "the gift of God" refers to the Spirit. For instance, in Acts 19:6 Luke indicates: "And when Paul had laid his hands (ἐπιθέντος . . . [τὰς] χεῖρας) upon them, the Holy Spirit came upon them."[68]

---

65. E.g., Knight, *Pastoral Epistles*, 370–71. See Rom 12:6; 1 Cor 12:4–31.

66. E.g., Towner, *Letters*, 458–59.

67. See esp. 1:14 and the related analysis of the verse. Still, Köstenberger suggests a "hybrid" possibility: "The 'gift of God' . . . that is in Timothy through the laying on of Paul's hands may be the pastoral ministry assigned to Timothy at his ordination service . . . Alternatively, the Holy Spirit may be in view, or a combination of the two (i.e., the Spirit as the source of Timothy's ministry assignment)."

68. The giving of the Holy Spirit through the laying of hand was not unique to Paul. For example, Acts 8:14–17 (ESV) reads: "Now when the apostles at Jerusalem heard that Samaria had received the word of God, they sent to them Peter and John, who came down and prayed for them that they might receive the Holy Spirit, for he had not yet fallen on any of them, but they had only been baptized in the name of the Lord Jesus. Then they laid their hands on them and they received the Holy Spirit." See also Acts 9:17, which indicates that Paul himself received the Spirit through the laying on of hands by Ananias.

To be sure, the witness of the NT suggests that the laying on of hands served other purposes. Sometimes it refers to commissioning an individual or group of individuals

Here we might ask whether there is any relationship between 2 Tim 1:6 and 1 Tim 4:14, which reads: "Do not be without-concern for the gift that is in you, which was given to you . . . through the laying of hands of the presbytery."[69] Both verses use the term "gift" in the singular; both share the theme of remembering the gift; both indicate that the gift came through the laying of hands. The key difference is that in one instance the laying of hands was by the apostle, the other by the presbytery. Moreover, 1 Tim 4:14 indicates that prophecy accompanied the receipt of the gift.

Two main comments are in order. First, the differences between the two verses do not necessarily imply that two distinct events are in view. It is possible that Paul participated in the laying of hands or could have prayed for him before or after the presbytery laid their hands on him. If in fact Paul did participate with the presbytery in the laying of hands, the specification of "my (μου) hands" in 2 Tim 1:6 might be intentional, reiterating the personal nature of the letter.[70] Second, contextual considerations suggest that two distinct events are in view. In 1 Tim 4:14, the mention of "the gift" is preceded by the "ministerial gifts" of reading Scripture, exhorting, and teaching (4:13). In this context, "the gift" seems to refer to the various *charisma* given for the edification of the saints. In 2 Tim 1:6, "the gift" is immediately qualified as "a spirit of . . . power and love and self-control" (1:7). This qualification echoes what Paul says of the "sons of God" who are led by "the Spirit of God" (Rom 8:14), namely, that they "have received the Spirit of adoption" (8:15). Thus, in this second context, "the gift" seems to refer to "*the* Spirit." In sum, 2 Tim 1:6 probably refers to Timothy's receipt of the Spirit, whereas 1 Tim 4:13 refers to a special congregational commissioning service.[71]

for a specific work (e.g., Acts 6:6; 13:3; 1 Tim 5:22), but even in these instances we cannot rule out that the laying on of hands did not entail an extra outpouring of the Spirit. In other instances, the laying of hands goes hand-in-hand with prayer (e.g., Matt 19:13–15) and healing (e.g., Mark 6:5; Luke 4:40). The different functions of the laying of hands warns us from being dogmatic about our conclusion in 2 Tim 1:6, although the evidence seems to point to the Holy Spirit.

69. See my comments on the verse in *1 Timothy*.

70. See Knight, *Pastoral Epistles*, 209.

71. Towner, *Letters*, 460: "Given Timothy's resume, which included service as Paul's mission coworker and occasional assignment within established congregations (e.g., 1 Cor 4:17), separate references to a congregational commissioning (1 Tim 4:14) and to an apostolic commissioning in conjunction with his conversion/initiation present no great problem."

In the end, it is impossible to ascertain with complete certainty the precise historical event behind this "laying of my hands." Nevertheless, the rhetorical purpose of v. 6 is clear: Timothy is to follow Paul's example of remembering the faith of his predecessors and the special fellowship shared between the two by remembering his unique receipt of the Holy Spirit that came through the laying of hands by his spiritual father.

2 Timothy 1:7–8a

A Spirit of Power, Love, and Self-control

(B Element)

Verse 7, which initiates the B element, gives a pneumatological basis ("for"; γάρ) for the summons to "rekindle the gift of God": all believers have received the Spirit—not of "cowardice" (δειλίας)—but of "power (δυνάμεως) and love and self-control."[72] The verse echoes Rom 8:15 with some modification to fit the context of the letter. We find similar echoes in Luke 24:49 and Acts 1:8, which speak of the Spirit's clothing Jesus's followers with power.[73] One could go back even further and note parallels with Josh 1:9: "Have I not commanded you? Be strong and courageous. Do not be cowardly (δειλιάσῃς), and do not be dismayed, for the LORD your God is with you wherever you go." While the linguistic tie is not as strong here as in some of the other texts, the command to be courageous and the reminder of God's empowering presence establish a clear

---

72. Contra Köstenberger, *1–2 Timothy and Titus*, 216n36: "The anarthrous πνεῦμα would seem to make the lowercase rendering more likely." If, as Köstenberger himself suggests, the *charisma* in 1:6 likely refers to the Holy Spirit, it is hard to see why 1:7 would refer to a human spirit instead of the Spirit who abides "in us." See esp. 1:14.

73. A comparison of the Greek between these verses highlights the point:

- 2 Tim 1:7: οὐ γὰρ ἔδωκεν ἡμῖν ὁ θεὸς πνεῦμα δειλίας ἀλλὰ δυνάμεως καὶ ἀγάπης καὶ σωφρονισμοῦ.

- Rom 8:15: οὐ γὰρ ἐλάβετε πνεῦμα δουλείας πάλιν εἰς φόβον ἀλλ᾽ ἐλάβετε πνεῦμα υἱοθεσίας ἐν ᾧ κράζομεν· αββα ὁ πατήρ.

- Luke 24:49: καὶ [ἰδοὺ] ἐγὼ ἀποστέλλω τὴν ἐπαγγελίαν τοῦ πατρός μου ἐφ᾽ ὑμᾶς· ὑμεῖς δὲ καθίσατε ἐν τῇ πόλει ἕως οὗ ἐνδύσησθε ἐξ ὕψους δύναμιν.

- Acts 1:8: ἀλλὰ λήμψεσθε δύναμιν ἐπελθόντος τοῦ ἁγίου πνεύματος ἐφ᾽ ὑμᾶς καὶ ἔσεσθέ μου μάρτυρες ἔν τε Ἰερουσαλὴμ καὶ [ἐν] πάσῃ τῇ Ἰουδαίᾳ καὶ Σαμαρείᾳ καὶ ἕως ἐσχάτου τῆς γῆς.

echo.[74] All of these texts remind their audiences of their possession of the Spirit and thus their unique ability to face suffering with power, love, and self-control.

Verse 7 moves from one negative descriptor to several positive descriptors. It begins with the declaration "For to us God did not give a Spirit of cowardice." In the context, "to us" (ἡμῖν) likely refers to Paul and Timothy, although clearly all believers—especially those in the audience with Timothy—are also included.[75] Concerning the "Spirit" (πνεῦμα), we observe that the "Spirit" comes from God: "God gave" (ἔδωκεν ἡμῖν ὁ θεός) to us this "Spirit," the same "God" (θεοῦ; 1:1) who willed Paul's apostleship and the "God" (θεοῦ; 1:2) who gives grace, mercy, and peace. Given this, it is inconceivable for the "Spirit," then, to be correlated with "cowardice" (δειλίας), a "shameful state of fear from lack of courage."[76] This term gives some insight into the current situation. As my analysis of 1 Timothy demonstrates,[77] Timothy was already combating the rise and spread of heterodoxy. By the time Timothy received 2 Timothy, the false teachers had gained the upper hand. It appears that Timothy, already a timid person (1 Cor 16:10), was tempted to distance himself from Paul and his gospel. Like any normal person, he did not want to suffer, at least not to the degree the apostle suffered.[78] The negative statement "God did not give a Spirit of cowardice" was Paul's indirect but forceful way of conveying the dissonance between Timothy's fears and the fearless Spirit in him.

There are three contrasting ("rather"; ἀλλά) positive descriptors that further qualify the gift of the "Spirit." Timothy has received the Spirit of "power and love and self-control." The first descriptor "power" (δυνάμεως) likely refers to the supernatural strength given for gospel ministry and specifically for endurance in suffering. Its mention here with the Spirit is almost gratuitous, given the way "power" always accompanies

---

74. Towner, *Letters*, 461: "The verbal echo, if present is admittedly faint. But the tone, narrative setting, and intention of the instructions create a plausible match. The effect would be to call on the image of Joshua, who in his commissioning was urged to be strong and courageous and not timid because God would be present." See also his linguistic support for the parallelism between 2 Timothy and Joshua text in n20.

75. For the inclusion of all believers with ἡμῖν, see Cranfield, "Changes of Person and Number in Paul's Epistles."

76. Friberg and Friberg, *Analytical Greek New Testament*, s.v.

77. See my comments in *1 Timothy*, esp. ch. 3.

78. Contra Hutson, "Was Timothy Timid?"

an outpouring of the Holy Spirit. Perhaps the most notable example is the transformation of Jesus's disciples post-Pentecost. At Gethsemane, despite lofty talk of undying faithfulness, in the end all the disciples fled to save themselves. Later, when a servant-girl accuses Peter of following Christ, he adamantly denies him. Yet, following an outpouring of God's Spirit, the disciples—perhaps most notably for Peter—transform. The bestowal of the Spirit is so profound that Luke comments, "Now when [the rulers and elders and scribes in Jerusalem] saw the boldness of Peter and John, and perceived that they were uneducated, common men, they were astonished" (3:13). This same Spirit of "power" abides in Timothy and can grant him courage for all endurance.

In 1 Timothy, the second descriptor "love" (ἀγάπης) usually describes the service rendered to others through the power of the Spirit.[79] Love is a mark of genuine faith, evidence of the Spirit's empowering presence. However, in this context "love" may also express the confidence that the Spirit gives to believers that they are children of God. Romans 8:15 describes how Christians "did not receive the spirit of slavery to fall back into fear, but . . . the Spirit of adoption as sons, by whom we cry, 'Abba! Father!'" This reality leads to the lofty conclusion that "nothing in all creation is able to separate us from the love of God that is in Christ Jesus our Lord" (Rom 8:39). With this confidence—mediated through the Spirit—Timothy and believers are able to love others even in the face of persecution and rejection.

The third descriptor is "self-control" (σωφρονισμοῦ). Its cognates occur regularly in 1 Timothy to describe all who profess godliness.[80] The popular translation "self-control" or "self-discipline"[81] might leave the impression of "Christian asceticism," but this sense doesn't fit the context. The general meaning of the word is moderation or sobriety. Also, the descriptors "power and love and self-control" are stated in contrast to "cowardice." In Paul's estimation, "cowardice" stems from a warped view of reality, from an outlook that fails to take seriously Christ's first and second coming. In short, it is the fruit of unbelief. In this regard, "self-control" represents a theologically modified version of moderation; it refers to a general equanimity and a tempered response to all of life, but

---

79. See my comments on 1 Tim 1:5 and 2:15 in *1 Timothy*.

80. See my comments on 1 Tim 2:9, 15 and 3:2 in *1 Timothy*.

81. See the ESV translation of "self-control" and translations in the NIV, NLT, and NRSV of "self-discipline."

especially to suffering, in view of the promise of eternal life.[82] Paul himself will exhibit such "self-control" in his tone and reflections throughout the letter.

Verse 8a follows in response (οὖν) to Timothy's possession of the Spirit. The twofold command of v. 8 begins with, "do not be ashamed of the witness of our Lord nor of me his prisoner." The verb "be ashamed" (ἐπαισχυνθῇς) expresses fear and embarrassment and possibly even alienation. Timothy and the audience would have felt the force of the verb, given "the values of honor and shame . . . were central to that culture."[83] But the precise meaning of the command is somewhat ambiguous. The more obvious interpretation is that Timothy is experiencing shame and so has distanced himself from his calling, the gospel, and Paul. The apostle, then, is summoning Timothy to stand firm in his faith and to fulfill his call to proclaim the gospel.[84]

But perhaps we have the order wrong. Is it that Timothy is ashamed and is therefore not bearing witness to the gospel and associating with Paul? Or is it the other way around? Is it that because he is not bearing witness to the gospel, Timothy is bringing shame and embarrassment to Paul and the witness? The flow of the text so far supports the latter, although we do not want to be so binary in our thinking. We know that Paul and his beloved child are separated and that the former longs to see the latter (1:4). But there is a sense that this feeling is not fully reciprocated. Could it be that Timothy was already distancing himself from Paul, leading to alienation on the apostle's part? Similarly, the very command to remember his spiritual lineage (1:5) suggests some distancing on Timothy's end from his inherited faith. Finally, the summons "to rekindle the

82. Towner, *Letters*, 462: "It depicts control over one's actions and thoughts that prevents rash behavior and aids a balanced assessment of situations. In this context, it would apply to Timothy's appraisal of the situation of opposition and confrontation and allow him the clarity of thought necessary to trust in the invisible God despite the threats of very visible opponents."

83. Towner, *Letters*, 463. Towner adds: "Honor was accorded to a person or a group on the basis of public acknowledgement that one's family was honorable or had inherited honor, or that virtuous deeds had been done. Often values like strength, courage, wisdom, and generosity were associated with honor. Shame, on the other hand, was the absence of these virtues or the refusal to accord them to someone. Weakness, selfishness, and foolishness were the negative counterparts that were despised." For further reflection on the related subjects of shame and honor, see deSilva, "Honor and Shame," 518–22; Malina, *New Testament World*, 28–62; Moxness, "Honor and Shame," 19–40.

84. Marshall, *Pastoral Epistles*, 703.

gift of God" leaves little question that Timothy is cowering in ministry. The command, then, not to "be ashamed" likely means that by neglecting his call to preach and distancing himself from his spiritual predecessors, Timothy is dishonoring Paul and the gospel.[85]

Typical of Paul is his complete identification between the gospel and himself.[86] The command could read, "do not be ashamed of the message of our Lord nor of me his messenger." Here, he describes the gospel as "the witness of our Lord" (τὸ μαρτύριον τοῦ κυρίου ἡμῶν). The term "witness" also occurs in 1 Tim 2:6. There, the preceding verses summarize the apparent incongruity of the gospel. On the one hand, it is inclusive because "God our Savior . . . desires all people to be saved and to come to the knowledge of the truth" (1 Tim 2:3-4). This good news includes even the worst of sinners who once persecuted the church (1 Tim 1:12-16). On the other hand, the gospel is exclusive because "there is one God, and there is one mediator between God and man, the man Christ Jesus, who gave himself as a ransom for all" (1 Tim 2:5-6a). Paul concludes 1 Tim 2:6 by asserting that this "is the witness" (μαρτύριον) given at the "proper time."[87] Such is "the witness (μαρτύριον) of our Lord."

It is possible that the specification of "our Lord" (κυρίου ἡμῶν) is recalling Paul's opening prayer where "Christ Jesus" is also identified as "our Lord" (κυρίου ἡμῶν). If this is the case (which it most likely is), Paul is highlighting a specific nuance about the "testimony," namely that it comes as a personal entrustment from the resurrected and exalted "Lord."

Paul is a "prisoner" (δέσμιον) in order to preserve and promote this "witness." Paul's self-identification as "prisoner" has a variety of effects. It evokes a personal response from Timothy and the believers with him as they hear the reading of the letter and reflect on the apostle's example of suffering for the gospel. It inspires Timothy from "cowardice" and toward courage. Finally, Paul's self-identification as "his prisoner" communicates that the apostle is suffering according to the sovereign will of his Lord.

---

85 Towner, *Letters*, 463-64: "By his failure he is discrediting or shaming the ones mentioned. Timothy is cast in the role of one who, on the basis of his own identification with or distancing from the gospel, accords either honor or shame to the testimony about Christ and to Paul himself."

86. See esp. Gal 1. For Paul, the rejection of his apostleship was equivalent to a rejection of his gospel, and the rejection of his gospel was identical to rejecting his apostleship.

87. For further reflection, see my comments on these verses in *1 Timothy*.

Ultimately, he is not a prisoner of Caesar but of the Lord.[88] Therefore, he has no reason to be afraid. The same holds true for Timothy who is a child of God through the receipt of the Spirit.

We might pause for a moment and ask why the gospel and its witnesses elicit shame and scorn. This question seems especially relevant today, given "gospel-centered" and "gospel-driven" ministries have become so popular. While the gospel is good news for sinners, it inevitably offends because it asserts that all have sinned and all are saved by grace alone through faith in Christ. To an individual that takes pride in his autonomy or in his moral achievement, the whole notion of being dependent on God's mercy and unworthy of divine favor is repulsive. The declaration that God has come to save is good news only to those who believe they need saving. Otherwise, the message and its messengers are viewed as objects of ridicule and offense.

2 Timothy 1:8b–9

SHARE IN SUFFERING FOR THE GOSPEL OF GRACE

(B' ELEMENT)

The B' element begins with the complementary command "rather suffer-together for the gospel according to the power of God" (1:8a). The disjunction "rather" makes clear that being ashamed and suffering-together represent two opposite responses to the situation Timothy is facing. The command in 1:8b suggests why Timothy was struggling with "a spirit of cowardice": proclaiming the "witness of our Lord" always leads to suffering "for the gospel." The call to "suffer-*together*" (συγκακοπάθησον) recalls not just Paul's imprisonment but also the deep fellowship between the apostle and Timothy (1:3–4). In this regard, v. 8b represents the climax of everything Paul has said thus far: Paul summons Timothy to remember their bond and to respond by suffering with the apostle for the "gospel."[89]

---

88. See my related comments on Phlm 1:1 in *Unreconciled*.

89. In passing, it is worth noting how Paul's command to "suffer-together" for the gospel runs counter to modern sensibilities. Paul views Timothy as a "beloved child" (1:2). The instinct of every parent—at least in contemporary culture—is to minimize suffering for their children. Against such a cultural milieu the call to share in suffering is especially jarring—but also especially noteworthy. At the very least it is a sobering reminder that there are things in life far worse than suffering. Paul's rehearsal of

The term "gospel" (εὐαγγελίῳ) occurs only once in the corresponding letter of 1 Timothy (1:11). In this first letter, Paul asserts that the "gospel" reveals "the glory of the blessed God." The term "mercy" best captures the essence of this gospel. Paul reflects on how Christ Jesus appointed him to be a preacher of the gospel even though formerly he "was a blasphemer, persecutor, and insolent opponent" (1 Tim 1:13). God responds to this foremost of sinners by flooding him with grace, faith, and love in Christ Jesus (1 Tim 1:14). After reflecting on his own conversion, Paul concludes that if God could save and call him, surely this same grace is available to all "those who were to believe in him for eternal life" (1 Tim 1:16). This is the "gospel" for which Paul, Timothy, and all believers must suffer.[90]

First Timothy is essentially a polemic against the false teachers whose heterodoxy was threatening to overturn the church, God's missional-household.[91] This same struggle seems to persist in 2 Timothy. For this reason Paul reiterates the need to depend on the Spirit-given "power" (δυνάμεως) that God has bestowed upon Timothy and all believers. It is this power—not Timothy's own resolve—that will enable him to suffer with the apostle for the gospel: "suffer-together . . . *according to* the power of God (κατὰ δύναμιν θεοῦ)."

Here we have the coming together of human responsibility and divine sovereignty, which we find throughout the Bible and especially in Paul's letters. Timothy is called to partake in suffering. In this sense, he must do so with all his might and focus. Still, the ability to do so comes from God who gave the Spirit of "power and love and self-control." Paul says something similar in Phil 2:12–13 (ESV): "Therefore, my beloved, as you have always obeyed, so now, not only as in my presence but much more in my absence, work out your own salvation with fear and trembling, for it is God who works in you, both to will and to work for his good pleasure." Again, we see the interplay of human responsibility and divine empowerment that precludes either passivity or autonomy in life and ministry.

Verse 9 rehearses the gospel, which at its core is a message of salvation by grace in Christ Jesus. God is the author of salvation, as the paired

Timothy's own lineage (1:5) suggests that that something is apostasy—forfeiting the salvation that has been passed from one generation to another and therefore forfeiting "the promise of life that is in Christ Jesus" (1:1).

90. For further reflections on these verses, see my comments in *1 Timothy*.

91. See comments in *1 Timothy*.

participles "saved us and called to a holy calling" (τοῦ σώσαντος ἡμᾶς καὶ καλέσαντος κλήσει ἁγίᾳ) make clear. The exact relationship between the two verbs is difficult to determine, in large part because of the ambiguity of the latter. Is this an instance of epexegesis where the two verbs reflect the same reality? If so, "called *to* a holy calling" means "called to be like God, the fountain of all life, in his holiness."[92] First Tim 6:12 supports this meaning: "Take hold of the eternal life to which you were called (ἐκλήθης)." This "eternal life (ζωῆς)" is the "life (ζωῆς) that is in Christ Jesus" (2 Tim 1:1). Thus "called to a holy calling" could mean "called to eternal life." Alternatively, we could interpret the verbs sequentially: "The sequence of the first two participles . . . probably corresponds to a description of the event and the application of it to people."[93] Here, "calling" seems to have an instrumental force— "called *with* a holy calling," that is, called by God through the gospel of his Son. Either interpretation is possible, although 1 Tim 6:12 suggests the first.[94] But the main point is clear: God has already accomplished salvation.[95] Timothy and all believers are to live out of this newly established reality.

Paul immediately qualifies this salvation through a contrast of works and grace. The decision to begin with the "non-reason"—"not (οὐ) according to our works"—seems intentional, jarring the audience and leaving them with the impression "definitely not by works." This sequence recalls the corresponding B element where Paul highlights that "God did not (οὐ) give us a Spirit of cowardice." In this earlier occurrence, the emphasis also falls on what is not the case in order to establish what is. However one understands "our works," whether it is a general reference to all human works or a specific reference to works of the Mosaic law, the meaning is clear: God's salvations is not at all "according to" (κατά) human effort, good or bad (Rom 9:11-12); rather, as we will see, it rests entirely on God's kindness.[96]

92. E.g., 1 Cor 1:2; see also Fee, *1 and 2 Timothy, Titus,* 229.

93. Towner, *Letters,* 467; see also Towner, *Goal of Our Instruction,* 95-96.

94. Köstenberger suggests a variation of the second interpretation (*1-2 Timothy, Titus,* 218): "Once saved by grace, we've been 'called with a holy calling' (NASB; cf. Eph 4:1), 'not according to our works'—the holy God has set us apart for ministry." His interpretation focuses less on salvation and more on vocation, the good works that God has prepared in advance for believers to complete (Eph 2:10).

95. Notice that both participles occur in the aorist.

96. This interpretation of the phrase "not according to our works" accords with Paul's previous summary of the gospel in 1 Tim 1:11-16. Paul makes abundantly clear that his apostolic commission was not the result of his "works": "I was a blasphemer,

The disjunction "rather" (ἀλλά) conveys a strong contrast, namely that it is "not according to *our* works" but much "rather according to *his own* purpose and grace." The repetition of the preposition "according to" (κατά) strengthens the force of the contrast. "Purpose" (πρόθεσιν) refers to God's "design" or "will," and "grace" (χάριν) to his "goodwill" or "favor."[97] Coupled with the adjective "own" (ἰδίαν), these terms reiterate the sovereignty of salvation: God planned to save "us" entirely on his own accord—without any external obligation to human effort—because of his "own" unmerited kindness.[98]

Verse 9 elaborates on the subject of "grace" through the participial phrase "which was given to us (δοθεῖσαν ἡμῖν) in Christ Jesus before eternal times." The participle is a "divine passive," drawing the audience's attention to the source of every good gift. The phrase echoes v. 7 in the corresponding B element: "For to us God did not give (ἔδωκεν ἡμῖν) a Spirit of cowardice; rather of power." Also, the idea of God's giving is clearly present even in the A element: God has given "the promise of life that is in Christ Jesus" (1:1); God gives "grace, mercy, peace" to Timothy and the believers with him (1:2); God has given his *charisma* ("the gift of God") to Timothy for endurance (1:6). All this underscores God's munificence and nuances our understanding of human faithfulness: all our suffering for the gospel cannot compare with what God has already given and what he will reveal on the Day of Glory.[99]

Paul specifies that God's grace was given "in Christ Jesus" (ἐν Χριστῷ Ἰησου), that is, by virtue of a believer's faith-union with the risen Lord.[100] Again, this echoes Paul's earlier phrase that sourced "the promise of life . . . in Christ Jesus" (1:1). For Paul there is no divine blessing outside

persecutor, and insolent opponent. But I received mercy because I had acted ignorantly in unbelief" (1 Tim 1:13).

97. Friberg and Friberg, *Analytical Greek New Testament*, s.v.

98. This dynamic gives insight into Paul's self-identification as "his prisoner" (1:8a). If salvation results from a mix of human "works" and God's "grace," human beings owe something to God but not everything. If, however, salvation is entirely "according to his own purpose and grace," all that we are and have belong to him. In this sense, all believers are prisoners—albeit joyful and thankful prisoners—owing everything to him.

99. See a similar description of God's generosity in 1 Tim 1:14. Note especially the use of the verb "overflowed." The apostle is not just saying that God gives to sinners more than they deserve, but *so* much more; see my comments in *1 Timothy*.

100. For a brief but helpful discussion of "union in Christ," see Ridderbos, *Paul*. For a more extended discussion, see *"In Christ"* in *Paul*.

of Christ.[101] The closing phrase "before eternal times" conveys "when" God conceived and worked out the plan of salvation. Rooted in Hebrew thought, the phrase describes the "eternal" mode of God's existence, which contrasts the finitude of creation.[102] Thus, the phrase "expresses to the audience the 'transhistorical' framework for understanding God's [gift of grace]."[103] Understood against the rest of v. 9, the phrase reiterates God's sovereignty in saving sinners through Christ Jesus.

2 Timothy 1:10–12

Paul Is Not Ashamed of the Revealed Gospel

(A′ Element)

Verse 10 begins the A′ element by contrasting ("but"; δέ) the "a-temporal" setting of salvation in God's volition (1:9b) with its historical revelation in Christ. The "grace" that was previously hidden in "eternal times" "now was manifested through the manifestation of our Savior Christ Jesus." This contrast underscores the significance of the "now" (νῦν): the revelation of that which was hidden signals "the inauguration of the age of salvation in Christ."[104] That is, the coming of Christ represents an eschatological event that begins the "last days," given the prophecies and promises of the OT have "now" been realized. The verb "manifested" (φανερωθεῖσαν) also occurs in the contrasting declarations "who was manifested (ἐφανερώθη) in flesh, justified in Spirit" (1 Tim 3:16). In both verses, the verb refers to Christ's incarnation—his life, death, and resurrection.

101. See my comments on 1 Tim 1:14; 3:13 in *1 Timothy*.

102. Towner, *Letters*, 470: "The time phrase itself, literally 'before eternal times,' drawn from Hebrew thought, distinguishes between the timelessness of God's existence and the temporality of his creation . . . at this point in the text, the theological poem tells us that the plan to save through the work of Christ was made, and in God's mind worked out, prior to creation."

103. Jeon, *To Exhort and Reprove*, 27. I add: "The phrase also provides the framework for appreciating further the special place of Paul's apostolic ministry. God's divine plan to give life was hidden from human perception and understanding since it was conceived of 'before eternal times.' No person could possibly have known God's purposes through his own efforts. For this reason a representative—in this instance the apostle Paul—had to be sent in order to disclose God's eternal will."

104. Towner, *Letters*, 471: "Here the past tense (aorist participle) indicates that the decisive event of revelation has occurred and, as defined by the term 'now,' that this event of revelation is particularly relevant to the condition of the present age."

The preposition "through" (διά), like its occurrences in 1:1 and 1:6 of the A element, is instrumental: the manifestation of grace has come by means of "the manifestation of our Savior Christ Jesus." There is an obvious but intentional redundancy here. Paul makes singularly clear that the manifestation of divine grace and the manifestation of Christ Jesus are one and the same. Also, Paul just stated in 1:9 that God's grace was given *in Christ Jesus* (ἐν Χριστῷ Ἰησοῦ). Now in 1:10 Paul says that grace was manifested *through Christ Jesus* (Χριστοῦ Ἰησοῦ). As we have noted elsewhere, for Paul there is no divine favor outside of Christ; every blessing comes "in Christ Jesus" or "through Christ Jesus."[105]

Epiphany language in Paul (e.g., "manifested/appeared," "manifestation, appearance") refers to either Christ's first or second coming. In 1 Tim 6:14, Paul summons believers to remain obedient until the "manifestation (ἐπιφανείας) of our Lord Jesus Christ." Here, in 2 Tim 1:10, the "manifestation (ἐπιφανείας) of our Savior Christ Jesus" refers to Christ's first coming. Taken together, Christ's first and second manifestations form the boundaries of Paul's "elliptical eschatology," which, in turn, serves as the basis for the Christian life.[106] The shift from "Lord" (1:2, 8) to "Savior" (σωτῆρος) may be arbitrary, but it accords with Paul's preoccupation with "life" (1:1) and salvation (1:9) in this first microchiastic unit.[107] Finally, the genitive form of "Christ Jesus" (Χριστοῦ Ἰησοῦ) corresponds to it earlier occurrences in 1:1 and 1:2 where Paul presents Christ as the means of eternal life and present grace, mercy, and peace. None of these blessings would have been possible had Christ not stepped into history to save sinners.

Through a pair of contrasting participles, Paul explicates what "Christ Jesus" accomplished as "Savior." "On the one hand" (μέν), he defeated death; "on the other hand" (δέ) he brought to light immortality. This juxtaposition echoes typical Pauline language which contrasts the age of darkness/death with the age of light/life.[108] First, Paul declares that the "Savior" "abolished death" (καταργήσαντος . . . τὸν θάνατον). The verb means "to bring to naught," that is, to render ineffective and

---

105. See esp. Eph 1:3–14.

106. See Gaffin, *By Faith*, 30–32, 65–66, 69, 72.

107. Indeed, this juxtaposition of titles reminds us that Christian salvation is Lord Salvation: Christ is our Savior insofar as he is also our Lord; see Horton, *Christ the Lord*; Frame, *Salvation Belongs to the Lord*.

108. See Vos's treatment of these "two ages" in *Pauline Eschatology*, 13–18.

useless.[109] "Death" continues in the sense that people still die. Yet, the aorist tense underscores the certainty of Christ's victory over "death." Believers, then, live certain of their own death and certain of the death of death in the death of Christ. There is no reason, then, for Timothy and all believers to live gripped by the fear of "death." Its reign has come to an end.

Second, Christ "brought-to-light life and without-mortality." The verb "brought-to-light" (φωτίσαντος) means to expose fully or to facilitate complete understanding. Its use here may echo Gen 1:3 where light signals the dawn of a new era of life out of darkness.[110] The "life" (ζωήν) in view is the "life (ζωῆς) that is in Christ Jesus," which Paul qualifies in 1 Tim 1:15 and 1 Tim 6:12 as "eternal life" (ζωὴν αἰώνιον; αἰωνίου ζωῆς, respectively). The same idea is present here in 2 Tim 1:10 where Paul juxtaposes "life" with "without-mortality" (ἀφθαρσίαν).[111] This is striking, given Paul uses the adjectival cognate in 1 Tim 1:17: "To the King of the ages, immortal (ἀφθάρτῳ), invisible, the only God, be honor and glory forever and ever." The overall impact of v. 10, then, is that the immortal one has appeared, defeated mortality, and shown how mortals can now participate in God's eternal mode of existence.

Verse 10 concludes with the important prepositional phrase "through the gospel." This second occurrence of "gospel" (εὐαγγελίου) forms bookends with the first occurrence in 1:8b. Everything in between summarizes its content, namely that God saves not according to works but according to his grace in Christ Jesus. This salvation is the promise of eternal life, the opportunity to share in God's everlasting mode of existence. The prepositional phrase, however, does not focus on the glory of this promise, but on the way God has made it known, namely *through* (διά) the gospel." Thus, Paul comes full circle, reminding Timothy why

109. Friberg and Friberg, *Analytical Greek New Testament*, s.v.

110. Gen 1:3 LXX: And God said, "Let there be light (φῶς), and there was light." Towner, *Letters*, 472: "It is therefore proper, as well as poetic, that the language of 'illumination' ('*brought* life and immortality *to light*') should be used to portray the unveiling of eternal life in the midst of darkened humanity. The focus is on triumph over death and the shining forth of eternal life. Such language, belonging as it does to a well-defined network of imagery for depicting the apprehension of invisible realities (especially 'through the gospel'), would call to mind the contrasting images of sin as darkness and God as light (cf. 1 Cor 4:5; Eph 3:9; 1 Tim 6:16)."

111. Some commentators suggest that "life" and "immortality" are best understood as a hendiadys ("immortal life"); see Marshall, *Pastoral Epistles*, 708; Mounce, *Pastoral Epistles*, 485.

it is necessary for him to suffer-together for the "gospel." Outside of the "gospel" and therefore outside of the perseverance of its messengers, the world cannot know this alternative—and higher—mode of existence made available through Christ.[112]

Paul immediately grounds his calling (1:11) and reason for suffering (1:12) in this gospel ("toward which I-myself was appointed"; εἰς ὃ ἐτέθην ἐγώ). The gospel, in other words, becomes the grid through which he understands his identity, mission, and even suffering. Paul uses the verb "appointed" somewhat regularly to describe his apostolic commission. In 1 Tim 1:12, he writes, "I thank him who has given me strength, Christ Jesus our Lord, because he judged me faithful, appointing (θέμενος) me to his service." Similarly, in 1 Tim 2:7 he notes: "For this I was appointed (ἐτέθην) a preacher and an apostle (I am telling the truth, I am not lying), a teacher of the Gentiles in faith and truth." The sense of the verb is authoritative appointment: Paul is not an apostle by choice or ambition. Rather, he is an "apostle of Christ Jesus through the will of God" (1:1); hence, the passive voice. The only fitting response is to remain faithful to his divine appointment by preserving the truth of the gospel and enduring all suffering.

The three titles Paul uses to describe his office are "preacher and apostle and teacher" (κῆρυξ καὶ ἀπόστολος καὶ διδάσκαλος). This is almost an exact echo of 1 Tim 2:7 except that Paul does not include the parenthetical comment "I am telling the truth, I am not lying" and the specification "teacher of the Gentiles in faith and truth." This may be incidental, but it could also point to a key difference between the two letters. Whereas in 1 Timothy Paul is concerned to assert his apostolic authority within God's household, in 2 Timothy his aim is to inspire Timothy toward endurance. The repetition of "apostle" (1:1) may convey that Timothy's spiritual father has not forgotten his appointment but remains clear about his identity and purpose even in the face of suffering. Most notably, v. 11 is brief, giving way to the more extended discussion of suffering in v. 12. Paul's main concern is not to reiterate his position as "preacher and

---

112. Towner, *Letters*, 473: "Thus in a subtle way the closing phrase of v. 10 redirects the theology back to the point (made by Paul) that gave rise to it—'join with me in suffering for the gospel' (v. 8)—and delivers a reason anticipated by the earlier point—Why join in suffering for the gospel? Because preaching it is the divinely chosen means by which God's salvation, crafted in and through the Christ-event, may be made available to the world."

apostle and teacher" but to establish the tie between faithfulness to the gospel and his suffering.

Verse 12 concludes the A' element (1:10–12) and the A microchiasm (1:1–12). It expresses Paul's view on his suffering, his response to his suffering, and a brief explanation of his response. First, he states "through this reason indeed these I suffer," that is, because of his appointment as preacher, apostle, and teacher of the gospel he suffers. The prepositional phrase "through this reason" (δι᾽ ἣν αἰτίαν) parallels its corresponding occurrence in 1:6 where Paul exhorts Timothy to "rekindle the gift of God" because of the faith he has inherited. Also, the verb "suffer" (πάσχω) recalls the earlier summons to "suffer-together" (ἐπαισχυνθῇς) for the gospel. These echoes seek to reiterate the bond between Paul and his spiritual son: "Through this reason be faithful in suffering, even as through this reason I remain faithful in my suffering for the gospel." But what is Paul referring to by "these" (ταῦτα)? The most obvious answer is his imprisonment. But the plural form of the demonstrative suggests more. As Paul indicates in the corresponding A element, he is also suffering separation from his "beloved child" (1:3–4). He is also suffering because he longs to experience the eternal life that God has promised in Christ.[113]

Paul, however, makes emphatically clear his response to his suffering: "rather, I am not ashamed" (ἀλλ᾽ οὐκ ἐπαισχύνομαι). This declaration is an obvious echo of Paul's command "not [to] be ashamed (ἐπαισχυνθῇς) of the witness of our Lord nor of me his prisoner" (2:8a). The absence of an object to Paul's declaration (e.g., "I am not ashamed of the gospel") communicates Paul's overall resolute disposition.[114] Thus, Paul is setting an example for his spiritual son of how to respond to the suffering that inevitably follows from a call to gospel-ministry.[115] He then provides a twofold explanation (γάρ) for his confidence.

First, he states, "for I know to-the-one I have faith." The verb "know" (οἶδα) does not refer to just a conceptual knowledge of God. Rather, the verb includes a personal understanding built out of experience. The relative pronoun "to-the-one" (ᾧ) recalls its earlier occurrence in 1:3 where the apostle describes his robust prayer-life: Paul knows God not just through revelation but also through intimate relationship. The verb "I

113. See Phil 1:23; 2 Cor 5:8.

114. Towner, *Letters*, 475: "In Paul's case, this is a determined mind-set; his condition of suffering has not moved him to feel ashamed for the gospel he has proclaimed."

115. See Clarke, "'Be Imitators of Me,'" 354–57.

have faith" (πεπίστευκα) echoes the noun cognate "faith" (πίστεως) in 1:5 of the A element where Paul describes Timothy's genuine faith. The sense of the verb is likely that Paul too has genuine faith in God, a sincerity reflected in his faithful service as a preacher, apostle, and teacher of the gospel. Such faith is possible because God has first shown his kindness and trustworthiness throughout Paul's life and ministry. In 1 Tim 1:11, Paul indicates that "I was-counted-faithful" (ἐπιστεύθην) with the message of the gospel. That is, despite his previous record as a persecutor, God appointed him to be the chief ambassador of the gospel to the Gentiles. Later in 2 Timothy, Paul reminds Timothy of how Christ rescued him time and time again (3:11) and stood by him even when everyone else had abandoned him (4:17). Thus, when Paul says, "for I know to-the-one I have faith," he is expressing a deep trust in the One who has proven to be trustworthy.

Second (καί), Paul is also confident because he is "convinced (πέπεισμαι) that he is powerful to guard my entrustment toward that day." Here too we have an echo of Paul's earlier statement in the corresponding A element regarding Timothy's faith: "I am convinced (πέπεισμαι) [is] also in you" (1:5). In other words, Paul is just as "convinced" of Timothy's inherited faith as he is of God's power. One can imagine how that must have been both unnerving and inspiring for Timothy. In the second instance, the object of Paul's confidence is God's ability ("power"; δυνατός) to "guard my entrustment" (τὴν παραθήκην μου φυλάξαι).[116] This declaration recalls Paul's final summons in 1 Tim 6:20: "O Timothy, guard the entrustment" (τὴν παραθήκην φύλαξον). This "entrustment" to Timothy is described in 1 Tim 1:12 as "my entrustment," that is, the gospel that has been entrusted to Paul. Paul, Timothy, and Christ, then, are "partnering" for the one gospel, and because God is "involved" and because "he is powerful," Paul and Timothy can rest assured that their work will not be in vain.[117] As Paul prepares for his departure, he is entrusting that which

---

116. Towner, *Letters*, 475: "The verb/noun combination, literally, 'guard the deposit,' alludes to the practice of entrusting a commodity of some sort with a person who is to protect it and eventually return it to the owner."

117. There may be an echo of 1 Tim 6:15 where Paul exalts God as the "blessed and only Power" (δυνάστης). Timothy can find comfort because this Power has given to him, and all believers, a spirit of "power (δυνάμεως) and love and self-control" to suffer and endure for the gospel.

was first entrusted to him, namely the gospel, and the fruit of his labors to God.[118]

"That day" (ἐκείνην τὴν ἡμέραν) refers to that final "day," a real and historical day as real as the supplications Paul lifts for Timothy "night and day" (ἡμέρας), when the "promise of life" (1:1) will be fully realized. The apostle is not ashamed and is able to endure all sufferings as a preacher, apostle, and teacher of the gospel because his outlook on life is bracketed by the first "manifestation of our Savior Christ Jesus" (1:10) and "that day." This is the "day" when Paul will no longer suffer any separation (1:3-4); when Jesus will declare that he is not ashamed of those who were not ashamed of him (1:8a); when all suffering for the gospel will be vindicated (1:8b); when the life marked by "without-mortality" will materialize; and when Paul's work as an apostle will be rewarded. Indeed, Paul sees this as a day so glorious that all suffering will be undone and relativized (Rom 8:18). Even Paul's longing to see Timothy "so-that I might become-full of joy" (1:5) pales in comparison to his longing for "that day" when his joy will be made complete. In expressing such hope, Paul seeks to "rekindle the gift of God" (1:6) that is in Timothy and to move him from cowardice and shame toward a renewed resolve to "suffer-together for the gospel" (1:8b).

---

118. Some commentators argue that "the deposit" is something Paul has received from God; see Kelly, *Pastoral Epistles*, 165–66; others that it is something Paul has entrusted to God; see Marshall, *Pastoral Epistles*, 710–11; Swinson, *What Is Scripture*, 81–82. Most translations favor the latter. Towner, *Letters*, 476: "Probably most decisive for a solution is the fact that God is the one who is to guard the deposit, which would normally imply that he is the recipient of the deposit entrusted by Paul (thus TNIV's 'what I have entrusted'). There is also some evidence that in related discussions the one to whom the deposit originally belongs is identified in the genitive (as Paul is here in the pronoun 'my')."

4

2 Timothy 1:13—2:3

Guard the Commendable Entrustment in Faith like a
Good Soldier for That Day

(B Unit)

THIS CHAPTER EXAMINES THE second of eight microchiastic units within
the 2 Timothy macrochiasm. Having presented himself as a model of confidence and endurance and—more significantly—having underscored
God's own power and commitment to guard the gospel, Paul returns to
explicitly encouraging Timothy to faithfulness. He does so through a mix
of exhortations, negative and positive examples, and the rich imagery of
a soldier.

The Second Microchiastic Unit

The second of eight microchiasms within 2 Timothy is carefully composed of four elements (A-B-B'-A'). Linguistic parallels are indicated by
the Greek text.

A. ¹³ Have the pattern of sound words that you heard from me
(παρ' ἐμοῦ ἤκουσας) in the faith and love that are in Christ Jesus
(τῇ ἐν Χριστῷ Ἰησοῦ). ¹⁴ The commendable entrustment guard
(καλὴν παραθήκην) through the Holy Spirit who is housed in us.

¹⁵ You know this, that all that are in Asia turned-from me, among whom are Phygelus and Hermogenes.

B: ¹⁶ May the Lord give mercy (δῴη ἔλεος ὁ κύριος) to the household of Onesiphorus, that often he refreshed me and was not ashamed of my chain; ¹⁷ rather, being in Rome, earnestly he sought me and found (εὗρεν) [me]—

B': ¹⁸ may the Lord give (δῴη . . . ὁ κύριος) to him to find mercy (εὑρεῖν ἔλεος) from the Lord (κυρίου) on that day— and the-many-things in Ephesus he served, you know well.

A': ²:¹ You, therefore, my child, be-strengthened in the grace that is in Christ Jesus (τῇ ἐν Χριστῷ Ἰησοῦ) ² and what you heard from me (ἤκουσας παρ' ἐμοῦ) through many witnesses, these entrust (παράθου) to faithful human beings, who also will be able to teach others. ³ Share-in-suffering as a commendable (καλός) soldier of Christ Jesus.

2 Timothy 1:13–15

GUARD THE WORDS OF THE APOSTLE UNLIKE THOSE WHO HAVE TURNED

(A ELEMENT)

Verse 13 begins the second microchiastic unit (1:13—2:3) and the A element. Paul exhorts Timothy: "Have the pattern of sound words that you heard from me." Like its previous occurrence in 1:3 (I have [ἔχω] without-ceasing memory concerning you), the verb "have" (ἔχε) means to hold steadfastly; hence "retain" (RSV) or "keep" (NIV). The noun "pattern" (ὑποτύπωσιν) also occurs in 1 Tim 1:16. In this previous instance, Paul describes his conversion as a paradigm for all who would come to trust in Christ Jesus. Similarly, the "pattern (ὑποτύπωσιν) of sound words" must remain as the standard of belief for all believers.[1] Finally, although here he qualifies the "sounds words" as "that [which] you heard from me" (παρ' ἐμοῦ ἤκουσας), in 1 Tim 6:3 these "sounds words" are

---

1. Towner, *Letters*, 478: "Paul does not have in mind his message as a general pattern, but, in this context of false teaching, the main point is the specific standard of accuracy his words represent . . . Consequently, maintaining the Pauline form and nature of the gospel has become Timothy's obligation."

those "of our Lord Jesus Christ." For Paul there is no difference, given he is an apostle of Christ Jesus. Viewing himself on the same trajectory as the OT prophets who declared, "Thus says the Lord," he sees his words as being the very words of God (2 Thess 2:13). This reality is also why Paul uses the qualifier "sound": it is the Word of the Lord given through the words of his apostle that give life to the people of God.

The phrase "sound words" (ὑγιαινόντων λόγων) would have been familiar to Timothy and the believers with him. In 1 Timothy, Paul uses the phrases "sound teaching" (ὑγιαινούσῃ διδασκαλίᾳ; 1:10) and "sound words" (ὑγιαίνουσιν λόγοις; 6:3) to refer to his gospel. The qualifier "sound" is polemical. It does not refer just to the life-giving quality of Paul's gospel. Rather, it distinguishes his gospel from the teaching of the heretics and troublemakers. The relative clause "that you heard from me" indicates both Timothy's embrace of this "pattern of sound words" and the continuity between Paul's ministry and Timothy's. Just as Timothy is to recall and retain his inherited faith, so too he must hold fast to Paul's gospel in the face of heresy. Altogether, then, the command has the force of stating, "Have constantly this pattern of sound words before you that you received from me."

Timothy is to do so "in the faith and love that are in Christ Jesus" (ἐν πίστει καὶ ἀγάπῃ τῇ ἐν Χριστῷ Ἰησοῦ). The phrase "in faith" occurs regularly in 1 Timothy.[2] But perhaps the most helpful parallel is 1 Tim 1:14 where the apostle speaks of the overabundance of God's grace that was poured out in Christ Jesus: "the grace of our Lord overflowed for me with the faith and love that are in Christ Jesus" (πίστεως καὶ ἀγάπης τῆς ἐν Χριστῷ Ἰησοῦ). Through their union with Christ Jesus, believers obtain "a pure heart and a good conscience and a without-hypocritical faith (πίστεως ἀνυποκρίτου)" (1 Tim 1:5). A "without-hypocritical faith" is how Paul describes the faith that Timothy has inherited (2 Tim 1:5). Similarly, according to 2 Tim 1:7 God has given Timothy a "Spirit of power and love (ἀγάπης) and self-control." The false teachers have swerved from these "union blessings" by wandering into vain discussions (1 Tim 1:6). It would seem that Paul is summoning Timothy to hold to the pattern of sound teaching by making every effort to maintain the "faith and love" that he, on the one hand, inherited from his grandmother and mother, on the other hand, received by virtue of his union with Christ Jesus. In short, Timothy must do the work of maintaining the pattern of sound

2. 1 Tim 1:2; 1:4; 2:7, 15; 3:13; 4:12.

doctrine by attending to his relationship with the risen Lord, the source of all "faith and love."[3]

Paul follows v. 13 with a parallel command in 1:14: "The commendable entrustment guard." The apostle uses the adjective "commendable" (καλήν) because the "entrustment" (παραθήκην) comprises the "sound words" that come from the Lord and give life to the church.[4] Just as the pursuit of a quiet and godly life is "commendable" (καλήν) in the sight of the Lord (1 Tim 2:2–3), so too is Paul's gospel. We know this is the case because the "entrustment" is the very thing that God himself guards (1:14). Verse 14, then, is a call to participate in the very activity of God, to "guard" (φύλαξον) what God is guarding and to do so confidently because God is involved in the work.

The second half of v. 14 parallels the second half of v. 13. As Timothy is to uphold the pattern of sound words through Christ Jesus, so too he is to guard the commendable entrustment "through the Holy Spirit who is housed in us." The implication is that being "in Christ Jesus" is tantamount to having the "Holy Spirit" (πνεύματος ἁγίου), the same Spirit (πνεῦμα) who is the source of "power and love and self-control" (1:7).[5] In Christ we possess the Spirit whose very presence enables believers to uphold the pattern of sound words and guard the entrustment. In both vv. 13 and 14, Paul underscores the divine means by which human faithfulness is possible. In this way, he indicates that even our faithfulness ultimately is the result of God's gracious empowerment.[6]

The verb "housed" (ἐνοικοῦντος) first appeared in 1:5: "taking remembrance of the without-hypocrisy faith in you that housed (ἐνῴκησεν) first in your grandmother Lois and your mother Eunice." In 1:14, Paul

---

3. Towner, *Letters*, 478: "'Faith and love' serve as an abbreviation for the authentic life of faith, combining into a unity the dimensions of one's relationship to God and the lifestyle of service produced by that faith-relationship (see on 1 Tim 1:5, 14). In short, for Timothy to 'keep' the apostolic message and proclaim it he must at the same time pay careful attention to his own faith in Christ."

4. The adjective "commendable" occurs frequently in 1 Timothy (1:8, 18; 2:3; 3:1, 7, 13; 4:4, 6*; 5:10, 25; 6:12*, 13, 18, 19) to underscore the inherent worth and goodness of an activity or object.

5. Explicit reference to the "Holy Spirit" occurs only here in Paul's letters to Timothy (though there are several references to "the Spirit"); see also Titus 3:5. For further reflection on the Spirit in these several letters, see Marshall, "Holy Spirit in the Pastoral Epistles," 291–305; Trebilco, "Significance and Relevance of the Spirit," 241–56.

6. Köstenberger, *1–2 Timothy and Titus*, 220: "Human effort thus is imperative, albeit in reliance on divine enablement."

adds "in us" (ἐν ἡμῖν). This final link in this spiritual chain is of special importance. It is as if Paul is saying, "The same Spirit who lives in me lives in you. Therefore, as I have guarded the commendable entrustment as preacher, teacher, and apostle, so too you, my spiritual child, can—and must—do the same."

Paul's exhortation to Timothy is not said in a vacuum. In v. 15 Paul states, "You know this, that all that are in Asia turned-from me, among whom are Phygelus and Hermogenes." Paul describes the situation as something Timothy "knows" (οἶδας) but perhaps does not fully appreciate, namely that others have ceased to partner with Paul for gospel-suffering.[7] In fact, the numbers are significant—"all who are in Asia" (πάντες οἱ ἐν τῇ Ἀσίᾳ). Paul is exaggerating somewhat, given he names Onesiphorus a few verses later as a paradigm of loyal friendship. Still, the impact of the statement is clear: "All" in the sense of "most" have abandoned Paul. A literal translation of the verb "turned-from" (ἀπεστράφησάν) is "turned away the ear, i.e., stopped listening."[8] Thus, most have "turned-from" him. This is disconcerting given Paul's unique status as preacher, apostle, and teacher (1:10). Moreover, it is worth remembering that for Paul there was no difference between turning from him or his gospel; denial of one was tantamount to rejecting the other.[9] More significantly, rejection of Paul and his gospel ultimately represented a rejection of the one that sent him. The verb, then, is perhaps best understood as an expression of apostasy; and the net message is, "Most in Asia have apostatized." The implied question for Timothy and those with him is, "All have turned a deaf ear to me—will you do the same?"

Paul names two specific individuals among those who have turned away—"Phygelus and Hermogenes" (Φύγελος καὶ Ἑρμογένης). This

---

7. Some suggest that Timothy was not aware of the situation Paul describes; see Towner, *Letters*, 480. The phrase "you know this" may serve as a transition to a new (but related) topic or could be rhetorical, conveying, "You are aware of this" (even if Timothy was not aware). But given Timothy likely ministered in Ephesus or near Ephesus, the most important city in Asia, a Roman province, it is unlikely that Timothy was unaware of this mass abandonment. Köstenberger, *1–2 Timothy and Titus*, 222–23: "In keeping with the customary pattern for moral exhortation, the emphasis isn't on telling Timothy something he doesn't already know but of reminding him of the importance of acting on what he does know and of encouraging him to continue to do what he's already been doing."

8. Friberg and Friberg, *Analytical Greek New Testament*, s.v.

9. Contra Köstenberger, *1–2 Timothy and Titus*, 223: "'Deserted' doesn't necessarily imply that these former coworkers left the faith entirely (but cf. Titus 1:14); what is clear is that they no longer partner with Paul in ministry."

parallels what Paul does in 1 Timothy when he names Hymenaeus and Alexander as two notable individuals that have abandoned the faith.[10] Little is known about Phygelus and Hermogences, but their very mention suggests that at some point they played critical roles in the work of the gospel.[11] Given 2 Timothy was read aloud before all the believers, we can imagine the impact of hearing the apostle single out these individuals. They embody the antithesis of what Paul commends in the preceding two verses—upholding sound doctrine and guarding the commendable entrustment. By naming them, Paul presents negative models that Timothy and the audience are to reject.

2 Timothy 1:16–17

ONESIPHORUS, AN EXAMPLE FOR TIMOTHY AND ALL BELIEVERS

(B ELEMENT)

Paul presents Timothy not just with a negative example (1:15) but also a positive example of not being ashamed but joining in suffering (1:8).[12] Verse 16, which begins the B element, is a prayer of blessing upon the household of Onesiphorus: "May the Lord give mercy . . ." The verb "give" (δῴη) occurred already in 1:7 and 1:9 with God and/or Christ Jesus as the subject. Here in 1:15, Paul reiterates the obvious point that from the "Lord" (κύριος) comes all good things. From a rhetorical perspective, "the wish is intended as a prayer expressed indirectly to the Lord (Jesus) but directly to the one or ones to be blessed, showing a sense of solidarity and immediacy of concern."[13] In this sense, the prayer functions similarly

10. See my comments on 1 Tim 1:19–20 in *1 Timothy*.

11. Towner, *Letters*, 481: "Yet both the language of Paul's description ('deserted') and the logical demands of the illustration suggest that the reason they are mentioned is their former association with Paul in some capacity (noteworthy colleagues or church leaders) and their disappointing betrayal either when Paul was in need of moral support (4:14) or as part of an apostasy."

12. Van Neste is correct in asserting, "There is practically universal agreement that there is a break between 1:14 and 1:15"; see "Cohesion and Structure," 149. Nevertheless, the chiastic arrangement that we have adopted illustrates the relationship between these separate structures and Paul's overall rhetorical purpose.

13. Towner, *Letters*, 482. Similar prayers occur in the OT (e.g., Gen 27:28; Num 6:26; Ruth 1:9). Here too the prayer-blessings reinforce camaraderie between different

to Paul's opening blessing in 1:2. Along this line, "mercy" (ἔλεος) explicitly recalls Paul's prayer for grace, mercy (ἔλεος), and peace from God the Father and Christ Jesus our Lord (κυρίου). As in the former instance, "mercy" is divine help for a person in need or trial. The implication is that Onesiphorus will require aid in his continued effort to labor and even suffer for the gospel.

The specification of "the household (οἴκῳ) of Onesiphorus" is not insignificant and may give some insight into the role he played among believers.[14] The household imagery is pervasive in 1 Timothy, both implicitly and explicitly.[15] An aspiring overseer or deacon must be known for managing his own "household" (οἴκου) in a commendable manner (3:4, 12). The reason for this is spelled out in 3:5: "For if someone does not know how to manage his own household (οἴκου), how will he care for God's church," which is "the household (οἴκῳ) of God" (3:15)? Against the backdrop of this pervasive use of "household," the specification of "household" here in 1:16 suggests that Onesiphorus was a man leading his own household well and possibly a person of influence and means among the believers (e.g., an aspiring deacon if not a deacon already).

More to the point, Onesiphorus is highlighted at this point in the letter because he models what Timothy should also do, for "often he refreshed me and was not ashamed of my chains." This summary echoes Paul's earlier command "not to be ashamed . . . of me his prisoner" (ἐπαισχυνθῇς, 1:8) and Paul's declaration that he himself is not "ashamed" (ἐπαισχύνομαι, 1:12). The sense of not being "ashamed" takes on special significance, given "all who are in Asia turned-from me." It is one thing for Onesiphorus to stand by the apostle when everyone else is doing likewise; it is another matter when he does so in isolation. In this way, Onesiphorus serves as a unique paradigm of faith and mercy.

Paul highlights the impact of Onesiphorus's actions. The adverb "often" (πολλάκις) indicates that there was a regularity and sincerity to Onesiphorus's kindness. The verb "refreshed" (ἀνέψυξεν) literally translates "make cool." Such kindness likely entailed practical needs, including

individuals.

14. Köstenberger, *1–2 Timothy and Titus*, 223: "(The fact that the man had a family—as well that he was able to travel to track Paul down in Rome—suggests he was a freedman rather than a slave; slaves were usually unable to marry or have children of their own.)" See also Thomas, "New Testament Characters," 116–17.

15. See my comments in related sections of *1 Timothy*; see also Poythress, "Church as Family."

food, drink, and personal company.[16] The verb reminds us of the opening verses of the Letter. While Paul was not ashamed of his sufferings, we should not suppose that Paul was not "often" discouraged. The opening words, "longing to see you, having-been-reminded of your tears, so-that I might become-full of joy" (1:4), make clear his loneliness and despondency. Indeed, the verb "refreshed" implies that Paul was in need of renewal. Therefore, Timothy's decision to identify with or disassociate from the apostle—his decision to cower from or partake in suffering for the gospel—would impact the state of Paul's soul.

Paul details what it meant for Onesiphorus "not [to be] ashamed of my chains." According to v. 17, "rather, being in Rome, earnestly he sought me and found [me]."[17] The use of the disjunction "rather" (ἀλλά) accentuates that which follows in v. 17, which represents the antithesis of being ashamed. The term that best summarizes Onesiphorus's actions is grit: taken together, the adverb "earnestly" (σπουδαίως) and verbs "sought" (ἐζήτησέν) and "found" (εὗρεν) convey the image of an obsessed person who will not stop his search until he has found what he has been looking for. In one sense, Paul presents Onesiphorus as a shadow of Christ, who came to seek and save the lost (Luke 19:10), even to the point of death. This gospel-imagery is strengthened by the fact that Paul was in prison. Onesiphorus's resolve to find Paul at all costs might have very well reminded Paul of his own salvation.[18]

---

16. Towner, *Letters*, 483.

17. Note that the participle "being" is ambiguous, that is, there is no reason to believe that Onesiphorus intentionally came to Rome to find Paul. Rather, it seems that while he was in Rome, he learned of Paul's circumstances and therefore sought him out.

18. The use of the phrase "at all costs" is intentional. Towner, *Letters*, 483: "The cost involved for Onesiphorus is hinted at in the second part of the reason: he 'was not ashamed . . . of my chains,' that is, of Paul's imprisonment. It was no light thing for a person to be associated with a criminal. In doing so, one ran the risk of being regarded by the authorities (as well as by family members, friends, neighbors, and business associates) as a sympathizer and possibly an accomplice and, therefore, deserving imprisonment or punishment . . . Paul wore the chains on his hands, a mark of shame in society, as a badge of honor earned by his solidarity with Jesus Christ and refusal to 'be ashamed' of the cross. Onesiphorus's wholehearted solidarity with Paul in his circumstances demonstrated the same refusal to categorize imprisonment for the cause of Christ as a social stigma."

2 Timothy 1:18

MERCY FOR ONESIPHORUS ON THE DAY OF THE LORD FOR ALL HIS SERVICE

(B' ELEMENT)

Verse 18 begins the B' element and clearly echoes elements of 1:16 of the B element:

1:16: May the Lord give mercy (δῴη ἔλεος ὁ κύριος) to the household of Onesiphorus

1:18: may the Lord (ὁ κύριος) give (δῴη) to him to find mercy (ἔλεος) from the Lord (κυρίου) on that day

Paul's explicit recollection of Onesiphorus's kindness may have triggered the repetition of the prayer-wish. The force of this repetition may have been, "*Indeed*, may the Lord grant him mercy . . ." The main difference is that the recipient of "mercy" shifts from "the household of Onesiphorus" to "him" (αὐτῷ). But we should not read too much into this as Onesiphorus was the head of his household; thus any blessings on "him" would have been enjoyed by his entire "household."[19]

What is noteworthy, however, is the use of the verb "find" (εὑρεῖν), which is a clear echo of its occurrence in 1:17. Earlier, the apostle explicitly stated that salvation is not of human works but solely of God's own purpose and grace (1:9). This might have left the impression that human endeavor is inconsequential. However, Paul offers a corrective through this chiastic movement, suggesting that Onesiphorus's ability "to find mercy" is directly tied to his merciful work of finding Paul. This apparent contradiction seems somewhat unsettling. Perhaps rather than trying to fully reconcile the two, we should accept the antinomy: on the one hand, salvation is entirely the work of the Lord; on the other hand, though in no way human beings contribute to their salvation, the mercy they receive "from the Lord on that day" is related to the mercy they have extended.[20]

---

19. Some suggest that at this point Onesiphorus has passed away and that Paul is praying for his postmortem salvation; see Bassler, *1 and 2 Timothy and Titus*, 137; esp. Oberlinner, *Kommentar zum Zweiten*, 63–64. Others contend that he was still alive; see Guthrie, *Pastoral Epistles*, 148–49; Knight, *Pastoral Epistles*, 386. Whether he is alive or dead is difficult to determine from the text and ultimately irrelevant because Paul is praying for mercy on the Day of Judgment, not for postmortem salvation.

20. Jesus himself suggests the same; see esp. Matt 25:34–40.

The phrase "on that day" (ἐν ἐκείνῃ τῇ ἡμέρᾳ) recalls Paul's declaration just a few verses earlier: "I am convinced that he is powerful to guard my entrustment toward that day (ἐκείνην τὴν ἡμέραν)." The repetition here is deliberate: the apostle seeks to reiterate the central role "that day" should play in the life of all believers. Any suffering in this life pales in comparison to the glory believers will enjoy "on that day" when the Lord will remember and honor every good work. The message could not be clearer for Timothy: Onesiphorus was not ashamed of Paul but sought him out to refresh him; consequently, he can be assured of finding mercy. Timothy likewise can have this confidence if he too shares in Onesiphorus's courage and participation in suffering for the gospel.

Paul also brings to attention "the-many-things in Ephesus he [Onesiphorus] served." The verb "served" (διηκόνησεν) occurs twice in 1 Timothy (3:10, 13) to describe the office of the deacon. Its occurrence here suggests that Onesiphorus might have been a deacon, though the verb can also be used to describe general service. His life must have been so devoted to good works ("the-many-things," ὅσα) that it was evident to all ("you know well"; βέλτιον σὺ γινώσκεις). The inclusion of the personal pronoun "you" (σύ) is likely intentional to express, "You *yourself* know!" Thus, Timothy is not left without an exemplar of profound and consistent loyalty.

2 Timothy 2:1–3

Be Strengthened to Suffer as a Solder of Christ Jesus

(A′ Element)

Verse 2:1 begins the A′ element, which concludes the second microchiastic unit (1:13—2:3) by recalling key phrases and ideas introduced in the A element (1:13–15). Having presented negative (Phygelus and Hermogenes) and positive (Onesiphorus) examples, Paul now brings the focus back to Timothy through the personal pronoun "You" (σύ). This focus is reinforced through the personal reference "my child" (τέκνον μου). The use of "child" as a descriptor for Timothy is common.[21] What is unique is the inclusion of "my," which heightens the personal tone of the letter and reminds Timothy and the audience of the special relationship shared between Paul and Timothy. This relationship, in turn, serves as

21. See 1 Tim 1:2, 18; 2 Tim 1:2.

the basis for Timothy's authority to carry out the commands given by the apostle. The command that follows ("therefore"; οὖν) proceeds from Paul's presentation of various examples and of the Lord's judgment that will take place "on that day" (1:18). Paul expects his spiritual son to consider the summons to not be ashamed but to share in suffering through the concrete examples set before him and the inevitable reality of final judgment. Moreover, if Onesiphorus was able to show such kindness and faithfulness toward Paul, how much more should Timothy, given his special status as "my child."

To guard the commendable entrustment—especially in the face of apostasy—is a challenging task. For this reason, Paul exhorts Timothy to "be-strengthened in the grace that is in Christ Jesus." The verb "be-strengthened" echoes Paul's self-description of his apostolic calling: "I have grace to the one who strengthened (ἐνδυναμώσαντί) me, Christ Jesus our Lord" (1 Tim 1:12). Paul's desire is for his spiritual son to imitate him. The repetition of the verb strengthens this bond. The apostle specifies that strength is found "in the grace (χάριτι) that is in Christ Jesus (ἐν Χριστῷ Ἰησοῦ)."[22] This phrase also echoes Paul's apostolic calling: "But the grace (χάρις) of our Lord overflowed with the faith and love that are in Christ Jesus (ἐν Χριστῷ Ἰησοῦ)" (1 Tim 1:14). As Elijah assured Elisha, so now Paul assures Timothy that the same grace that has empowered Paul is fully available to Timothy.[23] This is the "grace" that Paul prays for on Timothy's behalf and has already been given to all believers in Christ Jesus: God "saved us . . . according to his own purpose and grace (χάριν), which was given to us in Christ Jesus (ἐν Χριστῷ Ἰησοῦ)" (2 Tim 1:9).[24] The exhortation, then, is for Timothy to continue in the "grace" that is already his via union with Christ Jesus.[25] Endurance in ministry is directly

---

22. This is already implied in the passive voice of the command, which suggests that power comes from God. The middle voice is possible, but the immediate context makes clear that strength for endurance in ministry comes from above, not from within.

23. 2 Kgs 2:1–14.

24. The term "grace" (χάρις) may also recall the power given by the "gift" (χάρισμα) of the Holy Spirit. Towner, Letters, 489: "In 1:6 'grace' (charis) language occurs in the discussion of the 'gift (charisma) of God.' If we make the connections, the charisma of God (= the gift of the Holy Spirit) will be understood as the means by which God manifests his grace (charis) among his people. The perspective in 2:1 may have shifted slightly, but the connections are similar. In this case, power is linked with 'grace,' which is further defined as being 'in Christ Jesus.'"

25. This seems to be an echo of Jesus's own exhortation in John 15:4–5: "Abide in

tied to the empowering grace that comes from regular communion with the risen Lord.[26]

In addition to ("and"; καί) finding strength in Christ Jesus, Timothy must "entrust" the gospel to others. Paul begins v. 2 by specifying the object of entrustment: "what you heard from me through many witnesses." There are two parts to the "what" (ἅ). First, it comprises the things Timothy has heard directly from Paul (ἤκουσας παρ᾽ ἐμοῦ). This recalls Paul's earlier statement in 1:13 of the corresponding A element: "Have the pattern of sound words that you heard from me (παρ᾽ ἐμοῦ ἤκουσας)." "What you have heard from me," then, is "the pattern of sound words that you heard from me," namely the gospel. Second, Paul is referring to things he has taught in the presence of many.[27] The term "witnesses" (μαρτύρων) refers to persons who can give ascertainable facts. It occurs twice in 1 Timothy, once in relation to any accusations raised against elders (5:19), the other to Timothy's own calling (6:12). Both instances reflect public activities or events.[28] Similarly, here in 2:2a, attention is drawn to Paul's public proclamation of the gospel, which many "witnesses" could authenticate.

Timothy must entrust "these" (ταῦτα) things, that is, "what you heard from me through many witnesses," to reliable and capable persons. There appears to be a play on words between the command "entrust" (παράθου) and the object "the commendable entrustment" (παραθήκην; 1:14). The net effect would have been, "Entrust the entrustment to trustworthy persons." The imperative "entrust" recalls its only occurrence in 1 Tim 1:18: "This charge I entrust (παρατίθεμαι) to you, Timothy, my child." Taken together, these verses convey the image of one runner passing the baton to another. Paul had received the gospel and exhorted

---

me, and I in you. As the branch cannot bear fruit by itself, unless it abides in the vine, neither can you, unless you abide in me. I am the vine; you are the branches. Whoever abides in me and I in him, he it is that bears much fruit, for apart from me you can do nothing."

26. Note the present tense of the verb "be-strengthened" (ἐνδυναμοῦ).

27. The preposition διά can have two different senses—"in the presence of" or "through." This may lead some to suppose that two distinct interpretations are in view—"in the presence of many witnesses" and "through many witnesses." The former means that the "witnesses" authenticate the message; the latter that the "witnesses" relay the message. See Towner on the letter in 1-2 Timothy and Titus, 153–215. I maintain the translation "through many witnesses" but take it to mean that they attest to what Paul taught and preached before many.

28. See my comments in Jeon, 1 Timothy.

Timothy to hold to "the pattern of sound words that you heard from me."
Now, Timothy must do likewise by entrusting "what you heard from me
through many witnesses" to others. This was necessary and urgent, given
"all that are in Asia" had already turned from Paul and his gospel. A new
crop of faithful servants had to be raised.

Both the modifier "faithful" (πιστοῖς) and the noun "human beings"
(ἀνθρώποις) occur regularly in 1 Timothy. The noun rotates from referring to believers and unbelievers; but the modifier refers solely to true
converts.[29] Thus, "faithful human beings" in 2 Tim 2:2 is another way
of expressing "genuine believers." But, given the polemical context, the
phrase probably includes the nuance of those that have remained loyal
to Paul's apostolic message even in the face of widespread apostasy. Such
individuals have already demonstrated their reliability and therefore
should be considered first in Timothy's selection of prospective leaders.

Timothy, however, must select men who are marked not only by
character but also competence.[30] Specifically, these same persons ("who";
οἵτινες) "will be able (ἱκανοί) also to teach (διδάξαι) others." The verb
"teach" plays a critical role in 1 Timothy.[31] Teaching and authority go
hand-in-hand in God's household. Paul, then, is not concerned merely
with the ability to teach. Rather, he is concerned with raising men who
will "teach" with authority because they are holding fast to the apostolic
message.[32] In this sense, Paul's command to "entrust to faithful human
beings, who also will be able to teach others" sounds similar to his instructions on appointing elders who must be "able to teach" (διδακτικόν;
1 Tim 3:2).

In sum, the command of 2 Tim 2:2 reminds Timothy to prioritize
succession planning in his overall efforts to preserve and promote the
gospel. Given Timothy's many responsibilities and the pressures he faced,
this reminder would have been anything but gratuitous.

---

29. See esp. 1 Tim 4:10, 12; 5:16; 6:2.

30. Given Paul prohibits women from teaching in liturgical contexts (1 Tim 2:12),
he likely has men in view by "human beings." This is confirmed by the parallelism
between 2 Tim 2 and 1 Tim 3:2, where Paul describes the office of elder, an office that
is limited to men.

31. See 1 Tim 2:12; 4:11; 6:2; and my comments in Jeon, 1 Timothy.

32. Köstenberger, 1-2 Timothy and Titus, 228: "While ἀνθρώποις is probably gen-
der inclusive . . . it is nonetheless likely that the term here refers to men, presumably
present or potential elders."

Verse 3 concludes the second microchiasm (1:13—2:3) by harkening back to Paul's earlier summons to "share-in-suffering (συγκακοπάθησον) for the gospel" (1:8). In 2:3, the same command to "share-in-suffering" (συγκακοπάθησον) follows Paul's note that "all who are in Asia" turned from him. This note deepens Timothy's understanding of Paul's loneliness (1:3–4). Similar to its first occurrence, the command to "share-in-suffering" has a very personal quality: "Timothy, don't abandon me as well. Rather, like Onesiphorus, share-in-suffering by continuing the work of propagating the gospel. Do so by the grace that is in Christ Jesus." The first instance of the command focused on suffering for the gospel, the second for Paul. Thus, as is typical of Paul's letters, we observe a strong identification between the apostle and his gospel.

To better Timothy's understanding of what it means to suffer for the gospel Paul uses several metaphors. The first is that of a soldier (στρατιώτης): Timothy is to "share-in-suffering as a commendable soldier of Christ Jesus." The parallelism between "commendable (καλός) soldier" and "commendable (καλήν) entrustment" in 1:14 suggests that Timothy's status derives in part from the "commendable" quality of that which he preserves and represents. The use of military language is not surprising, given the verb "guard" in 1:14 describes the activity of a watchman. The qualifier "of Christ Jesus" (Χριστοῦ Ἰησοῦ) reiterates that Timothy is a soldier under the command of Christ, even as Paul is "an apostle of Christ Jesus (Χριστοῦ Ἰησοῦ)" (1:1): both are under authority. This means that Timothy must carry out his "commendable" work through "the grace that is in Christ Jesus" (τῇ ἐν Χριστῷ Ἰησοῦ; 2:1). As such, any fighting for the faith must reflect both the paradoxical strength and gentleness of the commander.

5

2 Timothy 2:4–19

That They May Obtain Salvation in Christ Jesus Who Remains Faithful

(C Unit)

THIS CHAPTER EXAMINES THE third of eight microchiastic units within the 2 Timothy macrochiasm. Paul continues his effort to spur Timothy to faithfulness by employing rich imagery, strong warnings, and wisdom for discerning the times.

The Third Microchiastic Unit

The third of eight microchiasms within 2 Timothy is composed of four elements (A-B-B'-A'). Linguistic parallels are indicated by the Greek text.

A. 4 None (οὐδεὶς) who-is-a-soldier gets-entangled in the affairs of life, that he might please the one-who-enlists-soldiers. 5 But if someone (τις) also competes-as-an-athlete, he is not crowned unless (ἐὰν μὴ) lawfully he competes-as-an-athlete. 6 It is necessary for the laboring farmer to first partake of the fruits. 7 Understand what I am saying (λέγω); for to you the Lord (κύριος) will give insight in all-things.

B. ⁸ Remember (μνημόνευε) Jesus Christ raised from the dead, from the seed of David, according to the gospel of mine, ⁹ in which I am suffering-as-an-evildoer until bonds; rather the word of God has not been bound; ¹⁰ for this [reason] all-things I endure (ὑπομένω) for-the-sake of the elect, that they themselves might also obtain the salvation that [is] in Christ Jesus with eternal glory. ¹¹ Faithful is the word; for if we died-together, also we will live-together.

B'. ¹² If we endure (ὑπομένομεν), also we will reign-together; if we will deny [him], he also will-deny-us; ¹³ if we are-without-faith, he remains (μένει) faithful, for he is not able to deny himself. ¹⁴ᵃ These things remind (ὑπομίμνῃσκε),

A'. ¹⁴ᵇ charging before God not (μὴ) to word-fight, upon no (οὐδέν) usefulness, upon catastrophe of-those-who-hear. ¹⁵ Strive to present yourself approved to God, a worker without-shame, handling-orthodoxly the word of truth. ¹⁶ The profane empty-sounds avoid; for upon more irreverence they will progress, ¹⁷ and the word of theirs like gangrene will have increase. Among whom are Hymenaeus and Philetus, ¹⁸ the-someones-who (οἵτινες) regarding the truth have swerved, saying (λέγοντες) the resurrection already has happened, and they are overturning the faith of some (τινων). ¹⁹ However, the strong foundation of God has stood, having this seal: "The Lord (κύριος) knows the-ones-who-are of him," and, "From without-righteousness must withdraw all that-name the name of the Lord (κυρίου)."

2 Timothy 2:4-7

PORTRAITS OF DISCIPLINE AND ENDURANCE

(A ELEMENT)

Verse 4 underscores a soldier's focus: "None who-is-a-soldier gets-entangled in the affairs of life, that he might please the one-who-enlists-soldiers." Paul indicates elsewhere that all believers are soldiers of Christ (Eph 6:10-20). Thus, the phrase "None who-is-a-soldier" could be generalized to read "None who-is a believer." Still, the repetition of the verb (see 1 Tim 1:18) makes clear that Paul is applying the metaphor primarily to Timothy. The verb ἐμπλέκεται expresses immersion, entanglement, perhaps even obsession. It is impossible for any person to completely detach from "the affairs of life" (ταῖς τοῦ βίου πραγματείαις). Nevertheless, as any soldier in any place at any time can attest, a soldier's life is marked by simplicity: his involvement in civilian affairs is minimal. He is not overly preoccupied with what he will eat or wear; he does not obsess over money and material possession. He is disentangled from such things so that he might focus on his mission.[1]

Simplicity and focus stem from "that Day" (1:18) when all will stand before God to receive their judgment. Here, Paul conveys the same idea by indicating that a soldier pursues disentanglement "that he might please the one-who-enlists-soldiers" (τῷ στρατολογήσαντι ἀρέσῃ). This notion of gracious enlistment likely reminds Paul of his own calling: "I thank him who has given me strength, Christ Jesus our Lord, because he judged me faithful, appointing me to his service" (1 Tim 1:12). Jesus enlisted Paul even though formerly he was a blasphemer, persecutor, and rebel. In response to such grace, Paul's single purpose in life was to please his commander: "For am I now seeking the approval of man or of God? Or am I trying to please (ἀρέσκειν) man? If I were still trying to please (ἤρεσκον) man, I would not be a servant of Christ" (Gal 1:10).

Paul adds two more illustrations (2:5 and 2:6) to reiterate the same basic point, namely that a distinct lifestyle should accompany a person committed to Christ. Verse 5 begins on an interesting note, given the backdrop of 1 Timothy. The pronoun "someone" (τις) has at best an ambiguous connotation in the previous letter. More often than not, Paul uses it in a pejorative way to refer to the false teachers. Perhaps the disjunction "But" (δέ) serves as a subtle contrasting marker with the soldier of Christ. The adverb "lawfully" (νομίμως), which only occurs one other time between 1 and 2 Timothy in 1 Tim 1:8, further supports that Paul might have the false teachers in view: "But we know that the law is commendable, if someone (τις) lawfully (νομίμως) uses it." In the previous instance found in 1 Timothy, Paul is condemning the false teachers who have deviated from the gospel because of their inadequate understanding of his gospel (1 Tim 1:8–11) and because of their devotion to controversies (1 Tim 1:4) and greed (1 Tim 6:5).[2]

1. Köstenberger, *1–2 Timothy and Titus*, 229: "For first-century Roman soldiers, this could mean refraining from marriage and serving as a soldier for twenty-five years or more." See also his related note (69).

2. See my comments on these sections in Jeon, *1 Timothy*. Concerning the adverb

The echoes in 2:5 to 1 Tim 1:8, coupled with the use of athletic imagery, conveys to Timothy that he must train as an athlete (ἀθλῇ, ἀθλήσῃ) would in his study of and instruction in the gospel. Bible study, in other words, is not a passive affair but requires the discipline and zeal of elite athletes. Moreover, a harsh warning is given through the pivot of the following minichiastic structure:

a. But also if (ἐάν) someone competes-as-an-athlete (ἀθλῇ),

b. he is not crowned (στεφανοῦται)

a.́ unless (ἐάν) lawfully he competes-as-an-athlete (ἀθλήσῃ).

Paul's words could not be clearer (or, harsher): desire alone is insufficient. To receive the crown, which is presumably shorthand for "the crown of life" (4:8), requires unyielding dedication, particularly in the face of suffering. The warning of this minichiasm certainly applies to the "some-ones" who, according to 1 Timothy, have missed the mark with respect to the faith (6:21).

The third image is that of "the laboring farmer" (τὸν κοπιῶντα γεωργόν).[3] Here too the backdrop of 1 Timothy is instructive. The verb "labor" occurs in 1 Tim 4:10 and 5:10 to describe those who "labor" in the proclamation of the word. To be sure, here in 2 Tim 2:6 Paul is describing a "farmer" who works steadfastly to produce a fruitful yield. Nevertheless, the image focuses on the same concern for discipline and endurance that Paul has already raised regarding the soldier and athlete.[4]

Concerning this "laboring farmer," Paul says that "it-is-necessary (δεῖ) . . . to first partake of the fruits." The same form of the verb "it-is-necessary" occurs in 1 Tim 3:2, 7, and 15, all of which describe the necessary character and work of leaders in God's household. Its occurrence

---

νομίμως, Towner, Letters, 494: "In the actual competitions from which this metaphor is drawn the stipulated condition or requirement ('according to the rules') referred either to the rules of the face or to the ten-month period of disciplined training that professional athletes had to complete to qualify for the games."

3. Köstenberger, 1-2 Timothy and Titus, 230: "In antiquity, 'somewhere around 85 or 90 percent of the whole population was directly involved with growing or getting food as their primary occupation . . . [so that] Paul's analogy . . . would have been much more alive to his original readers than to many of us."

4. Paul's repeated emphasis on discipline reminds me of the resolutions of Jonathan Edwards; see Jonathan Edwards Resolutions. His discipline in all aspects of life but especially in his study of the Bible makes clear why he became such a theological phenom!

here in 2:6 suggests that Paul has in view the life and ministry of leaders. Paul draws on the somewhat universal principle that a person should enjoy the "fruit" (καρπῶν) of his labors (e.g., Prov 27:18). To be the "first" (πρῶτον) to "partake" (μεταλαμβάνειν) is to enjoy a position of honor. Paul is reminding Timothy that God's justice will not pass those who have kept the faith even in the face of suffering and persecution. Although individuals like Paul currently occupy the bottom rung of society, in the end God will exalt the faithful as the "first" to share in Christ's glory. Moreover, the overall sense of 2:6 is that despite hardship, there will undoubtedly be fruit. For Paul, this must have been especially important to keep in mind given his imprisonment. Similarly, for Timothy this inevitable outcome echoes what Paul said earlier in 1:12: "I am persuaded that he is able to guard until that day what has been entrusted to me." No good endeavor will fail to bear a multitude of fruit on "that day."[5]

Paul concludes this first A element both with a command and a promise. He begins with the exhortation: "Understand what I am saying" (νόει ὃ λέγω).[6] The use of the verbs "understand" and "I am saying" is striking, given Paul's description of the false teachers in 1 Tim 1:7 as those who are "neither understanding (νοοῦντες) what they are saying (λέγουσιν) nor what they are asserting." Undoubtedly, Paul is summoning Timothy and all the believers with him to consider the interconnections and implications of being like a soldier, athlete, and farmer. But in another sense the command is a backhanded way of expressing, "Don't be like the false teachers who lack understanding." Either way, especially in the face of suffering Timothy must be thoughtful, remembering his calling and the hope of eternal life by reflecting on this rich imagery.

Verse 7 concludes with the promise "for to you the Lord will give insight in all-things." The verb "give" (δώσει) emphasizes again what Paul has underscored throughout, namely that Christ gives generously to his people.[7] The word order here may be significant: "for to *you* (γάρ

5. Though on the surface some may view these heavenly rewards as a mere transactional motivation for pursuing godliness, C. S. Lewis helpfully rebuts this suggestion: "We are afraid that heaven is a bribe, and that if we can make it our goal we shall no longer be disinterested. It is not so. Heaven offers nothing that a mercenary soul can desire. It is safe to tell the pure in heart that they shall see God, for only the pure in heart want to. There are rewards that do not sully motives" (Lewis, *Complete C. S. Lewis Signature Classics*, 639).

6. Towner observes that this was "a well-known didactic formula"; see *Letters*, 496.

7. See 2 Tim 1:7, 9, 16, 18. At the risk of speculative exegesis, it appears that Paul is suggesting to Timothy and all with him, "Consider all that God has given us—far more

σοι)"—in contrast to the false teachers—"the Lord will give insight in all-things" (ὁ κύριος σύνεσιν ἐν πᾶσιν).[8] Finally, the "Lord" who gives grace, mercy, and peace (1:2); the "Lord" who is the center of God's revealed gospel (1:8); the "Lord" who will give Onesiphorus mercy—it is this same "Lord" who is actively at work here and ready to give "insight in all-things." "All-things" is likely referring specifically to all the suffering and the related questions that will arise as Timothy faces persecution and rejection.

2 Timothy 2:8-11

REMEMBER THE MODELS OF JESUS CHRIST
AND THE APOSTLE PAUL

(B ELEMENT)

Verse 8, which initiates the B element of the third microchiasm, renews the theme of remembrance, something that was also pronounced in the opening verses (1:3–6). Paul indicates "I have remembrance (μνείαν) of you" (1:3), "I remember (μεμνημένος) your tears" (1:4), and "I am reminded (ὑπόμνησιν) of your sincere faith" (1:5). He concludes this section with the exhortation, "I remind (ἀναμιμνήσκω) you to fan into flame the gift of God" (1:6). Also, implicit throughout the letter so far is an appeal to remember Paul even when all have abandoned him. Now, in 2:8, Paul summons Timothy to "remember" (μνημόνευε) both "Jesus Christ" (Ἰησοῦν Χριστόν) and his spiritual father.[9] The context of this command is the suffering that inevitably entails the life of a soldier of Christ.

---

than anything we could ever ask or imagine. What would be the only fitting response? To persevere in every good work."

8. Drawing a loose parallel between 2 Tim 2:7 and Prov 2:6 LXX, Towners observes: "There we notice the contrast between the one (sg. 'you'; '[my] son,' Prov 2:1, 2, 3, etc.), who diligently pursues wisdom, and 'those who have forsaken the upright way' (pl.; *hoi enkataleipontes*, 2:13). In the wider discussion of 2 Timothy, this latter group could correspond to the opponents and to those who have forsaken the apostle, whose desertion is described with the language of Prov 2:13 (4:16: 'all have forsaken me': [*pantes me enkatelipon*]; 4:10: 'Demas deserted me' [*Dēmas me enkatelipen*]; cf. 1:15)." See *Letters*, 495–96.

9. Many translations (e.g., NIV) break up the single sentence of 2:8–11 into shorter and more manageable sentences. In doing so, the impression may be that the command to "remember" is limited to "Jesus Christ." As we note below, this is mistaken because Paul is setting forth both himself and their shared Master as models of faithfulness.

It is doubtful that Paul's concern here is for Timothy to recall a theological truth, namely Christ's dual natures. Rather, the contrasting phrases "risen from the dead" and "from the seed of David" convey the redemptive-historical significance of Christ's resurrection.[10] The perfect tense of the participle "risen" (ἐγηγερμένον) indicates a past event, the significance of which spills over into the present.[11] Christ's resurrection "from the dead" (ἐκ νεκρῶν) marks a decisive shift from the aeon of darkness and death. In stark contrast stands life immortal that has been brought to light through the gospel. That Jesus came "from the seed of David" represents both the fulfillment of God's promise to David and Jesus's participation in man's fallen condition. Timothy is to ponder the new reality that has come through the endurance of Christ who shared fully in mankind's suffering but was ultimately vindicated in his resurrection. In this sense, Paul presents Christ as a worthy model to imitate.

Verse 8 concludes with the prepositional phrase "according to the gospel of mine" (κατὰ τὸ εὐαγγέλιόν μου). The basic sense is that the apostle endorses these affirmations concerning "Christ Jesus."[12] But given the term "gospel" has occurred several times now (2 Tim 1:8, 10), some summary comments are in order. First, Paul's gospel has as its center "Jesus Christ" (Ἰησοῦν Χριστὸν)—who he is and what he has done. Second, there is no "good news" apart from Christ's resurrection from the dead. If he was not raised, death's reign continues.[13] Third, the gospel finds its root in the OT story of covenant promises made to key figures, including David. Fourth, the gospel implies a movement in history. As noted above,

10. For a fuller treatment of this idea, see Gaffin, *By Faith*, 21–26.

11. Towner, *Letters*, 499: "[The perfect participle 'having been raised'] perhaps opens up for the reader the way to think more immediately of the lasting significance of Jesus' resurrection—that is, it is not just a historical event to be remembered but a truth holding promise for believers to be rehearsed over and over again (1:10)." Towner also contrasts the sequence here in 2 Tim 1:8 with that of Rom 1:3–4, which inverts the order. He proposes that if we assume the Romans passage lies in the background, "Paul's reason for leading off with the thought of Jesus' resurrection in 2:8 must be to anchor firmly in Timothy's mind the accompanying concept of vindication: the resurrection must imply the thought of Jesus' suffering that culminated in his crucifixion, but that whole complex of events recalls equally his ultimate vindication and victory over death."

12. Towner, *Letters*, 499: "This authentication might be regarded as a polemical response to a competing heretical message (2 Tim 2:18), but its basic sense was to endorse the message as apostolic and characteristic of the proclamation Paul directed to the Gentiles (Rom 2:16; 16:25)."

13. See my comments on this topic in *A New King*.

in Christ a new age of eternal life has begun and will be consummated when he returns. Finally, Paul's gospel is his gospel, that is, it stands in contrast to any other supposed gospel propagated by the false teachers. The "mine" here is likely polemical: "my gospel in contrast to theirs."

The relationship between 2:8 and 2:9 parallels that of 1:11 and 1:12. In the earlier instance, Paul roots his calling as a preacher, apostle, and teacher in the gospel and asserts that his suffering is directly rooted in his call to proclaim the gospel. Here, in 2:9, Paul also roots his suffering in gospel-proclamation. The language, however, is different. In 1:12, Paul uses the language "for this reason" (δι᾽ ἣν αἰτίαν); here, Paul writes, "in this (ἐν ᾧ) I am suffering." The sense of the preposition "in" is that Paul is suffering because he is remembering and remaining in the gospel even as all turn away from it (1:15). Concretely, this fidelity takes on the form of fulfilling his apostolic calling even in the face of persecution. The mention of "suffering" (κακοπαθῶ) comes as no surprise, given the frequent mention of it already in the letter.[14]

The apostle does not hesitate to detail his own suffering. He writes, "until [as far as] bonds as an evildoer." The language here appears deliberate, recalling Christ who himself was arrested and treated like a criminal.[15] The implication is that the apostle has identified so deeply with Christ and his mission that he now suffers in the way Christ suffered.[16] By giving Timothy some insight into his interpretation of his suffering as an apostle, Paul hopes that Timothy will find comfort knowing that he too—like his spiritual father—now bears the marks of Christ. Whereas in 1:16 Paul uses the term "chain" (ἅλυσίν), here he uses "bonds" (δεσμῶν). Perhaps no significant nuance is in view.[17] But the latter does carry the connotation of impediment. Paul's point is that he is being treated like an "evildoer" (κακοῦργος) whose work as an apostle, preacher, and teacher of eternal life must be checked. As Towner suggests, "The term translated

14. 2 Tim 1:8, 12; 2:3.

15. Köstenberger, *1–2 Timothy and Titus*, 235: "The phrase 'like a criminal' (κακοῦργος) may constitute a deliberate attempt to tie Paul's fate to Jesus's . . . Jesus's accusers before Pilate called similarly, 'If this man weren't a criminal (κακὸν ποιῶν), we wouldn't have handed him over to you' (John 18:30)."

16. Towner, *Letters*, 502–3: "Although Paul has defined the character of his ministry in terms of 'suffering' in previous sections, at this point he reflects on the actual nature and extent of his hardship and connects this experience closely with that of Jesus . . . Paul, who has followed his Lord in that same faithfulness, suffers the same fate."

17. For further reflection on chains in Roman imprisonment, see Rapske, *Book of Acts*, 206–312.

['evildoer'] is used only here outside of Luke's references to the criminals crucified alongside of Jesus (Luke 23:32, 33, 39); it often designated the worst sort of criminals, those headed for crucifixion."[18] If this was the case, we can understand why all in Asia disassociated with Paul (1:15) and why Paul longs for fellowship with those who are not ashamed of his shameful state (1:3–8).

Nevertheless, Paul's story does not end in imprisonment. There is a faint echo of 1:12 where Paul declares "I am convinced that he is powerful to guard my entrustment toward that day." In other words, no matter what happens to the apostle, the gospel will go forth because God himself is committed to its progress. For this reason, v. 9 concludes with the declaration, "rather the word of God is not bound." To be sure, the messenger is "bound" (δέδεται), but in stark contrast (ἀλλά) the message is not![19] In fact, this odd juxtaposition is perfectly consistent with God's general pattern of showing his power through human weakness.[20] The singular form of "the word" (ὁ λόγος), in contrast to its plural form (1:13), recalls the repeated trustworthy sayings in 1 Tim 1:15, 3:1, and 4:9: "Faithful is the word (ὁ λόγος)." This "word" is the gospel, the success of which does not depend on human beings because it is "the word of *God* (τοῦ θεου)." It will continue to go forth to achieve God's salvific purposes. Thus, Timothy, like a good soldier, persevering athlete, and laboring farmer, can and must endure all suffering.

Verse 10 seems to have both a retrospective and prospective quality. Does "for this [reason]" (διὰ τοῦτο) refer to what he has just said, namely that "the word of God is not bound," or, what he is about to say, namely the salvation of "the elect"? It may be both.[21] Paul is asserting that "all-

18. Towner, *Letters*, 503.

19. Köstenberger, *1–2 Timothy and Titus*, 234–35: "The apostle here expresses his confidence in the sovereignty of God and in the effective power of his word in the face of mounting [Neronic] persecution . . . While Paul's fate was closely tied to the progress of the gospel in early Christian history (Acts 9–28), he was convinced that the power of the gospel far transcended his own preaching of it. Ultimately, the fate of the gospel doesn't rest on any one human messenger, no matter how important or influential; its victory is assured by its own inherent power (cf. Rom 1:16)."

20. This is Paul's main thesis in the letters of 1 and 2 Corinthians.

21. Contra Towner, *Letters*, 504n25: "Some have taken ['for this reason'] to refer forward to 'the elect' and the purpose clause (ἵνα) that follows . . . However, while this is possible (especially if the reference is solely to the purpose clause that is then the reason for Paul's action), it is awkward and repetitive and actually obscures the force of the point Paul has just made about the emergence of the gospel's power through (or in spite of) human weakness."

things I endure" (πάντα ὑπομένω) because even his bonds cannot thwart God's commitment to advance the gospel.[22] Again, his ability to hold fast in "all-things"—not just in suffering—stems from his conviction that God will guard the good deposit (1:12). But Paul also ties his endurance directly to the salvation of God's people—"for the-sake of the elect" (διὰ τοὺς ἐκλεκτούς).[23] God's sovereignty does not preclude human responsibility. Just because God has elected some to salvation does not mean that they will "automatically" be saved. Election and Paul's apostolic work, which includes suffering and endurance, are tied together. In other words, God's sovereignty in salvation does not lead to human passivity. Rather, it results in exactly the opposite—the determination to work hard and remain faithful out of full conviction that such labors are not in vain.

By "all-things" Paul is referring to his isolation (1:3-5); his anxiety for Timothy (1:6-7); his imprisonment (1:8, 16); complete abandonment (1:15); and his treatment as a criminal (2:9).[24] Paul's intention here is not to list all his actual suffering but to make the point that there is nothing he would not endure for the sake of fulfilling his apostolic calling. The precise meaning of the verb "endure" is clear from the context of what Paul has said so far in the letter. In a general sense, it means upholding the faith one has received even in the face of widespread apostasy. But in the case of Paul, it is likely referring to the faithful execution of his calling as a preacher, apostle, and teacher (1:11) despite the inevitable suffering that follows as a result.[25] It is not by accident that he uses this verb, given the rich imagery of soldier, athlete, and farmer he referenced earlier.

The goal (ἵνα) of Paul's suffering—and, more so his endurance—is the salvation of the elect. There does appear to be an emphasis on the elect ("they themselves might also," καὶ αὐτοί); that is, Paul endures

---

22. Marshall, *Pastoral Epistles*, 737.

23. Commentators differ on the meaning of "the elect." Some argue that it refers to those who have been chosen by God but have yet to come to faith (e.g., Knight, *Pastoral Epistles*, 399). Others reject this narrower theological interpretation and argue from the OT that it refers generally to "the people of God" (e.g., Towner, *Letters*, 504-5). Such a distinction may be unnecessary, given "the people of God" includes those that have been chosen but remain unconverted in a given moment.

24. See also 2 Cor 11.

25. Towner, *Letters*, 504: "'Endurance' (3:10) describes an attitude of determined 'holding on' in times of struggle; in the NT it is linked with the severest trials (Rom 5:3) and comes to be seen as a sign of apostleship (2 Cor 6:4; 12:12). Moreover, as the present context confirms, 'endurance' looks beyond the present trials to a victorious outcome in resurrection."

so that they *too* might share in the salvation that he and Timothy already possess. The verb "obtain" (τύχωσιν) with the genitive means to "experience something."[26] The context makes clear that the prospective recipients have yet to "obtain" or "experience" God's gift of salvation. The obtainment and experience of salvation, then, is a future reality that depends directly on the faithfulness of Paul and Timothy. This "condition" heightens the need for endurance, especially on the part of Timothy.

The exact phrase "in Christ Jesus" (ἐν Χριστῷ Ἰησοῦ) occurs somewhat regularly in 1 and 2 Timothy. "In Christ Jesus" come grace, faith, and love (1 Tim 1:14; 2 Tim 1:9, 13). In the letter opening, Paul roots eternal life "in Christ Jesus" (2 Tim 1:1). Empowering grace to endure all things also comes "in Christ Jesus" (2 Tim 2:1). The "salvation (σωτηρίας) that [is] in Christ Jesus," then, is more than just future blessing. It includes blessings here and now that come by virtue of a believer's union with Christ. But such divine blessings are possible for the elect only through the endurance of the Lord's servants who opt to partake in suffering for the gospel.

Paul elaborates further on the "salvation that [is] in Christ Jesus" through the prepositional phrase "with glory eternal." Given all the focus on present suffering, the rich imagery implicit in the phrase "glory eternal" is jarring. Both terms "glory" (δόξης) and "eternal" (αἰωνίου) occur regularly in 1 and 2 Timothy to describe God's mode of existence. The gospel is that which reveals the "glory (δόξης) of the blessed God" (1 Tim 1:11); to God alone be "honor and glory (δόξα)" (1 Tim 1:17); Christ Jesus was raised "in glory (δόξῃ)" (1 Tim 3:16). Similarly, to God "be honor and eternal (αἰώνιον) power" (1 Tim 6:16); God gave us grace in Christ before the "eternal (αἰώνιον) ages" (2 Tim 1:9). "Eternal" is also regularly used to qualify the "life" that Christ has brought (1 Tim 1:16; 6:12). Thus, God's gift of salvation offers to believers the privilege of participating in God's glorious and eternal mode of existence.[27] Paul's perspective—which he wants Timothy to ponder—is that they must suffer for the everlasting joy of "the elect" even as Christ endured all suffering to bring many into glory.

26. Friberg and Friberg, *Analytical Greek New Testament*, s.v. See also Acts 24:2; Heb 11:35.

27. Towner adds that the salvation in view represents the recovery of that which was lost (*Letters*, 506): "Paul especially depicts the state of humankind in terms of a loss of glory (Rom 3:23; 8:19–21). Consequently, salvation means a regaining, through God's gracious gift, of (or a sharing in) God's glory."

Within the broader context of 1 and 2 Timothy, v. 11 represents the fourth and final occurrence of the trustworthy saying: "Faithful is the word" (πιστὸς ὁ λόγος). In all three earlier instances (1 Tim 1:15; 3:1; 4:9), the statement occurs near a salvific declaration. In 1 Tim 1:15 it precedes the declaration "that Christ came into the world to save sinners"; 1 Tim 3:1 follows on the heels of the controversial statement that "a woman will be saved through childbearing" (2:15); 1 Tim 4:9 precedes the statement that God "is the Savior of all people" (4:10). Thus, it is not always clear whether the faithful saying pertains to what comes before or after. Here in 2 Tim 2:11, if taken with what precedes, the trustworthy saying suggests that the endurance of the Lord's faithful servants will lead to the salvation of many. If taken with what follows, Paul is saying that the proceeding contrasting statements in 2 Tim 2:11–13 are worthy of all trust in the face of suffering. Either way, v. 11 concludes the B element and therefore should be understood in view of Paul's broader concern to command Timothy toward remembrance and faithfulness.[28]

Verse 11 initiates four somewhat symmetrical conditional statements.[29] These follow the basic pattern of human decision and divine reaction. Towner takes note of this: "In combination with the solemn introductory formula, this genre emphasizes the certainty of the promises and warnings spelled out for Timothy."[30] Consistent with his focus on union with Christ in 2:10 ("in Christ Jesus"), the verbs in the first contrasting statements of 2:11 detail further the implications of this union. Paul writes, "for if we died-together, also we will-live-together." The use of the prefix σύν is especially notable, further highlighting the idea of union. According to this first pair, true union entails full participation

28. Towner, *Letters*, 506–7: "As we approach what appears to be a theological affirmation, it is important to bear in mind that we are still in the middle of a section of parenesis. The theological material that follows in vv. 11–13 is both supportive and illustrative of the command 'remember' given in v. 8 . . . this insertion of theological affirmations makes the obligation to join in suffering impossible to miss and too serious to dismiss . . . Paul is not inserting the traditional material simply to remind himself why he 'endures' (v. 10a), but to provide a theological basis for the behavior Timothy must seek to emulate."

29. Scholars differ on whether the sayings are original to Paul. Köstenberger insists that they are (*1–2 Timothy and Titus*, 236). Yarbrough insists the opposite, namely that Paul used preformed traditions (*Paul's Utilization of Preformed Traditions*, 42). Either position bares little relevance to the clear rhetorical function the sayings serve in the immediate context.

30. Towner, *Letters*, 508. See also Johnson, *Letter's to Paul's Delegates*, 66.

in pain and glory, in death and life.[31] The mention of "mutual death" (συναπεθάνομεν) suggests that for Paul, dying on account of his call as apostle, teacher, and preacher was a real possibility that he had already accepted. At the risk of exalting Paul, he had calculated the cost in advance.

Yet, death for Paul was not the final word. The conditional statement concludes with the apodosis "also we will live-together." The theme of eternal life is prominent in this letter. Paul is an apostle according to the promise of life that is in Christ Jesus (1:1). Christ has abolished death and brought life to light through the gospel (1:10). For believers, eternal life via union with Christ Jesus is the grid for interpreting death.[32] What is the "word" upon which Paul, Timothy, and all believers should build their lives and pursue endurance? The "faithful word" is that if we suffer for the gospel even to the point of death, then death will not be the final word. Because Jesus Christ has risen from the dead (2:8), we too will live. For this reason, Timothy, along with all believers, can remember his calling and endure in every good work.

2 Timothy 2:12–14a

HE WILL NOT DENY HIMSELF

(B′ ELEMENT)

Verse 12 initiates the B′ element by reiterating a prominent theme in the letter—endurance. Echoing Paul's declaration "for this [reason] all-things I endure" (ὑπομένω; 2:10) in the corresponding B element, v. 12a indicates: "If we endure (ὑπομένομεν), also we will-reign-together." The use of the plural is appropriate given Paul is stating a general principle. However, its use may also convey a movement from the first person singular in 2:10, which includes only Paul, to the first person plural, which includes Paul and Timothy. Also, the second conditional statement specifies the meaning of the first, namely what it means to identify with Christ in his suffering. For Paul this takes on the form of enduring everything for the

31. Köstenberger, *1–2 Timothy and Titus*, 237: "'Died with him' likely refers to the believer's spiritual union with Christ rather than to martyrdom (though readiness to martyrdom may be implied on a secondary level)."

32. Contra the view that Paul has in view the believer's present experience in Christ; see, e.g., Fee, *1 and 2 Timothy, Titus*, 249; Köstenberger, *1–2 Timothy and Titus*, 237–38.

elect, including unjust imprisonment. Like his spiritual father, Timothy must not be ashamed of the gospel but share in suffering by raising faithful men who also will be able to teach others.

The protasis gives way to the apodosis: "also we will reign-together (συμβασιλεύσομεν)." As Paul indicated in the first conditional statement, eternal life will follow present suffering. Again, the apostle brings to focus the meaning of the first statement by indicating what this life will entail—the privilege of "reigning together."[33] Indeed, God's kingship is highlighted twice in 1 Timothy, both at the beginning and conclusion of the letter: "To the King of eternities . . . be honor and glory" (1:17); "the King of those who-are-kings and Lord of those-who-are-lords . . . be honor and eternal sovereignty" (6:15). To "reign-together" means to share in the eternal honor and glory of the King. This outcome of endurance puts all suffering in perspective. As Paul writes elsewhere, such present sufferings pale in comparison with the glory that will be revealed for those that have believed (Rom 8:18).

The second half of v. 12 reflects a shift in mood: "if we will deny (ἀρνησόμεθα) [him], he-also will deny (ἀρνήσεται) us." The nuance of the controlling verb "deny" in 1 and 2 Timothy is a denial expressed not by profession but inaction. The obvious example is 1 Tim 5:8, "But if someone does not provide for his own and especially his household, he has denied (ἤρνηται) the faith and is worse than an unbeliever" (1 Tim 5:8). The person in view professes the faith, but his failure to tangibly meet the needs of his own household reveals that his faith is counterfeit. In 2 Timothy, denying the faith takes the form of not enduring in the faith and not completing the task that has been given. For Timothy, this would entail abandoning the faith he has inherited from his predecessors and failing to fan into flame the gift of God (1:5-6). For Paul, this would entail neglecting his call as preacher, apostle, and teacher (1:11). For Phygelus and Hermogenes, this entailed turning from Paul and his gospel (1:15). To "deny [him]" is to refuse to share in suffering for the gospel.

A difficult question arises at this point. It appears that salvation is conditional.[34] Paul clearly states that the consequence of denying Christ

33. This appears to be an obvious echo of Jesus's own teaching. For instance, Matt 10:22b reads: "But the one who endures (ὑπομείνας) to the end will be saved." Later in this same Gospel, Jesus makes clear that those who will be saved will share in his reign by sitting on the twelve thrones and judging the twelve tribes of Israel (19:28).

34. Yet, the witness of Scripture suggests a more nuanced view. Peter's repeated and severe denial of Christ only served to underscore Christ's mercy to him

is Christ's denial of us "on the day" (1:18). We must be careful not to minimize the force of the statement: to some degree, eschatological blessing and curse depend on present human decision and action. The future tense of both occurrences of the verb brings the focus again to the Day of Judgment (1:16–18). This appreciation of the future is also evident in Paul's rich images of soldier, athlete, and farmer, all of whom anticipate a day of glory. In no ambiguous way, Paul makes clear that as glory awaits those who endure, judgment awaits those who turn from the gospel. Jesus himself gave some clue as to what this divine denial will look like in Matt 7:23: "And then will I declare to them, 'I never knew you; depart from me, you workers of lawlessness.'"

Verse 13 contains the last conditional statement: "if we are-without-faith, he remains faithful." To "be-without-faith" (ἀπιστοῦμεν) means to act disloyally or prove false.[35] This fits the context of 2 Timothy well, given Paul has emphasized the need to uphold one's faith and calling despite pervasive apostasy. This entails remembering the gospel and its representatives and enduring all things for the saints. The apodosis bears this out by highlighting "he remains (μένει) faithful." This echoes Paul's self-declaration: "for this [reason] all-things I endure (ὑπομένω) for-the-sake of the elect" (2:10). Thus, v. 13 could be read as "if we do not endure, he nevertheless endures." Or, given the qualifier "faithful" (πιστός), "if we are faithless, he remains faithful." Here, Paul is reiterating what he has already said in 1:12 and 2:10, namely that God is so committed to glorifying himself that he will preserve and promote the gospel irrespective of the faithfulness (or faithlessness) of his servants.

The reason (γάρ) for God's enduring faithfulness is that "he is not able to deny himself." In 1 and 2 Timothy, the verb "be able" (δύναται) relates to what is possible. First Timothy 5:25 indicates that some good

(Matt 26:69–75). Also, Paul has already underscored that "God saved us and called us to a holy calling, not according to our works" (1:9). Such "works" would certainly include the "work" of endurance. Finally, Paul has reiterated that even endurance is possible only through the grace that comes from being "in Christ Jesus" (2:1). It seems unlikely, then, that v. 12b is teaching that a genuinely saved person can lose his salvation. Rather, it appears that the lack of endurance ultimately reveals the lack of genuine faith.

For further reflection on this important topic—classically described as the "perseverance of the saints"—see Boice and Ryken, *Doctrines of Grace*. See also Steele et al., *Five Points of Calvinism*.

35. Friberg and Friberg, *Analytical Greek New Testament*, s.v. Towner, *Letters*, 513: "More likely the verb refers here to lapses in loyalty to Christ that amount to unfaithfulness."

works are conspicuous, but even those that are not "are not able" (οὐ δύνανται) to remain hidden, and will ultimately be revealed on the Day of Judgment. Echoing Job 1:21, Paul declares: "For nothing we brought into the world, nor 'are we able' (δυνάμεθα) to bring anything out" (1 Tim 6:7). Finally, Paul describes God as that "irreproachable light" whom no one has seen or "is able" (δύναται) to see (1 Tim 6:16). The emphasis is on what is possible versus impossible. Thus, at the conclusion of 2:13, Paul is underscoring that it is impossible for God to deny himself. The verb "deny" (ἀρνήσασθαι), taken with 2:12, conveys we can deny God; he can deny us, but he *cannot* deny himself. The first two are possibilities; the last is not because faithlessness contradicts God's nature.

Again, Paul's ultimate concern here is not abstract theological reflection but spurring faithfulness on the part of Timothy and all who are with him. Endurance for the sake of the elect is most reasonable because God remains faithful to himself, which means he will be faithful to those who remain faithful to him. This is the "faithful word" that Timothy can take hold of. In the face of challenging circumstances, the one thing Timothy can be absolutely sure of is God's covenant-keeping character: he remains faithful to himself, his mission, and his servants.[36]

The B' element concludes with the exhortation, "These things remind."[37] While it is not entirely clear what "these things" (ταῦτα) might be referring to, most likely it is the trustworthy sayings that Paul has

36. Towner, *Letters*, 513: "The language of faithfulness is used to describe God and Christ in reference to keeping promises related to the covenant, especially in the context of the trials that make human faithfulness so difficult to maintain." Some suggest that what Paul has in mind in v. 13 is hope even for apostates. For instance, Köstenberger, *1–2 Timothy and Titus*, 239: "At the same time, the closing line may anticipate the reference to Hymenaeus and Philetus in v. 17, asserting that some people's faithlessness will not take away God's faithfulness to those he has chosen, especially church leaders. This holds out hope for those who were swayed by the preaching of Paul's opponents and fell into ungodliness, and even for the opponents themselves (cf. vv. 19, 24–26)." While this is possible given what follows in the second half of 2 Tim 2, Paul's main concern is to spur personal faithfulness on the part of Timothy. This line of interpretation "works" if what Paul is trying to say is, "God hasn't given up on those who have fallen away, so neither should you." But this interpretation may be too specific. The likely interpretation is that in a general sense God is faithful to himself and the gospel; therefore, Timothy should also remain faithful.

37. Paul probably has in view the "faithful human beings" in 2:2 as the recipients of Timothy's reminders, although there is no reason to limit the reminder just to them. Köstenberger, *1–2 Timothy and Titus*, 241: "Paul now urges him to 'remind' . . . the people in his church (esp. the 'faithful men' in vs. 2) of 'these things' (see vv. 3–13 and following verses)."

just rehearsed, although they could also include the overall paraenesis contained in the B element (2:8–11). The verb "remind" (ὑπομίμνῃσκε) echoes the exhortation to "remember (μνημόνευε) Jesus Christ" (2:8). Verse 8 is an exhortation to "remind yourself"; v. 14 shifts to reminding others. Most likely, by reminding others Timothy will simultaneously remind himself. Here again we see how central the theme of remembrance is in 2 Timothy and for the difficult task of endurance. The ὑπο-prefix likely serves as an intensifier: "Cause to remember and ponder regularly and deeply." Apart from these disciplines of remembrance and reflection, Timothy and those under the care of his ministry will likely not endure.

2 Timothy 2:14b–19

WHAT BELIEVERS MUST BE PURPOSEFUL
ABOUT PURSUING AND AVOIDING

(A' ELEMENT)

The A' element follows the exhortation "These things remind" with a complementary summons: "charging in-the-presence of God not to word-fight." Two key features stand out. First, the participle "charging" (διαμαρτυρόμενος) recalls Paul's own charge to Timothy: "I charge (διαμαρτύρομαι) you . . ." (1 Tim 5:21). Again, we see a parallelism between the activities of the apostle and his spiritual child. The precise repetition of the phrase "in-the-presence of God" (ἐνώπιον τοῦ θεοῦ) in 1 Tim 5:21 and 2 Tim 2:14 strengthens this parallelism.[38] As Paul did in 2 Tim 1:18, here he is broadening Timothy's outlook beyond the immediate circumstance to include the "presence of God." Both the verb and the perspective convey a sense of solemnity: all of life must be lived in the presence of God, but especially the work of instruction. Second, the infinitive "to word-fight" (λογομαχεῖν) recalls Paul's descriptor of the agitators in 1 Timothy. Such troublemakers exhibit a proclivity toward controversy and "word-fights" (λογομαχεῖ; 1 Tim 6:4). As 2 Tim 2:5 recalled the false teachers who do not use the law lawfully, 2:14b, which parallels 2:5 through the repetition of μή, again focuses on these heretics. Verse 14b could be heard as a solemn charge to the faithful not

---

38. See my related comments on the verb and phrase as they occur in 1 Tim 5:4; 5:21; and 6:13 in Jeon, *1 Timothy*.

to be like the false teachers: "Consider them and do not be like them."[39] This pedagogical approach may not be popular today, but it was a regular practice for Paul to present positive and negative examples and to exhort his followers, "Be like me, not like them."

The final part of v. 14 recalls both the soldier-imagery Paul uses in 2:4 of the corresponding A element and key descriptors of the false teachers in 1 Timothy. Soldiers, athletes, and farmers do not get entangled in civilian affairs; that is, they do not waste time and resources on things that are "to no usefulness" (2:14b). The term "usefulness" (χρήσιμον) means "profitable, beneficial." As Towner notes, "Practical 'usefulness' was the traditional test of any teaching's quality, and the polemics Paul prohibits do not measure up."[40] Rather, soldiers, athletes, and farmers focus their limited time only on that which will yield benefits for their ultimate goal. The parallelism between 2:4 of the A element and 2:14b of the A′ element yields the overall sense, "None (οὐδεὶς) who is a soldier of Christ" (2:4) will engage in activity that leads to "no (οὐδέν) usefulness" (2:14b).

The contrast, "to no usefulness, at the catastrophe of-those-who-hear" also echoes similar statements in 1 Tim 1:3–4: "Charge certain persons not to teach any different doctrine, nor to devote themselves to myths and endless genealogies, which promote speculations rather than the stewardship from God that is by faith." By entering into useless debates, these false teachers were hurting the life and work of God's household. Similarly, toward the end of 1 Timothy, Paul says of these false teachers: "He has an unhealthy craving for controversy and quarrels about words, which produce envy, dissension, slander, evil suspicions, and constant friction" (1 Tim 6:4–5). In 2 Tim 2:14b, Paul is more explicit, indicating that word-fighting leads to the "catastrophe of-those-who-hear" (καταστροφῇ τῶν ἀκουόντων).[41] "Catastrophe" can also mean ruin, perversion, or leading astray,[42] which is the exact description of those who have swerved with respect to the faith (1 Tim 6:21; see

---

39. Towner, *Letters*, 518: "The fact that all verbal forms in v. 14 are in the present tense may suggest the implication 'stop quarreling about words,' in which case the emphasis of this command is remedial rather than preventive."

40. Towner, *Letters*, 519.

41. Whereas the first ἐπί coupled with the accusative "no usefulness" (οὐδὲν χρήσιμον), the second ἐπί occurs with the dative (καταστροφῇ). The latter use introduces a result clause as the parallels with the 1 Tim text; see Köstenberger, *1–2 Timothy and Titus*, 242n91: "The term refers to God's bringing about physical destruction at the end-time judgment (Gen 19:29 LXX; 2 Chr 22:7 LXX; cf. *1 Clem.* 7.7); cf 1 Tim 6:9."

42. Friberg and Friberg, *Analytical Greek New Testament*, s.v.

also 1 Tim 1:19).[43] The effect of persistent word-fighting is the opposite of what happens when Timothy persists in the "sounds words that you heard (ἤκουσας) from me" —"For by doing this, you will save yourself and those-who-hear (ἀκούοντάς) you" (1 Tim 4:16).

Instead of getting entangled in useless word-fights, Timothy must "strive to present yourself approved to God, a worker without-shame, handling-orthodoxly the word of truth." The main verb "strive" (σπούδασον), which means "to make haste, to do your best,"[44] recalls the mindset and work ethic of soldiers, athletes, and farmers. Timothy is to work with all his might to gain mastery of the "word" just as a professional athlete labors to become a champion. The qualifier "approved" (δόκιμον) recalls the apostle's instructions regarding deacons: "these also must-be-approved (δοκιμαζέσθωσαν) first, then they-must-serve-as deacons" (1 Tim 3:10).[45] Timothy must remember that someday he will have to "present" (παραστῆσαι) himself to God, that is, he will have to give an account as one entrusted to propagate the "word."[46] Given this future reality, he must "strive" not for the approval of man but of God.

The perspective implicit in the words "to present yourself approved to God" also reiterates the "that day" mindset pervasive in this letter. Paul is confident that God will guard until "that day" what was entrusted to him (2 Tim 1:12). Paul prays that the Lord may grant Onesiphorus mercy on "that day." The sayings all assume "that day" when all will be judged and vindicated (2:11–13). Given this perspective, like the soldier in the corresponding A element that avoids worldly affairs in order to please his commander (2:4), Timothy is to live for the approval of "God" (θεῷ), the God who appointed him and Paul to service.

The phrase "a worker without-shame" functions almost as a summary of what Paul has said so far in the letter. "Worker" (ἐργάτην) also translates as laborer or toiler. The image echoes Paul's metaphor of "the laboring farmer" in 2:6 of the corresponding A element. The term also recalls Paul's instruction in 1 Tim 5:18 to compensate sufficiently those who

---

43. See my comments in Jeon, *1 Timothy*.

44. Friberg and Friberg, *Analytical Greek New Testament*, s.v.

45. For further comments on the verb and adjectival cognate, see Jeon, *1 Timothy*.

46. Köstenberger, *1–2 Timothy and Titus*, 242: "Teaching God's Word is no task to be performed in a cavalier manner . . . This is the case all the more because teachers are accountable to God, as those who should present themselves (παραστῆσαι—in a cultic sense in Rom 12:1, but here probably to God as a judge) to him on judgment day as tested and approved."

labor in teaching: "For the writings says... 'The worker (ἐργάτης) is worthy of his wages.'" More so, the adjective "without-shame" (ἀνεπαίσχυντον) recalls the verbal cognate ἐπαισχύνομαι, which occurs in 1:8, 12, and 16: Timothy is summoned not to "be ashamed" (ἐπαισχυνθῇς); Paul declares that he is not "ashamed" (ἐπαισχύνομαι) of his suffering for the gospel; and Onesiphorus was not "ashamed" (ἐπαισχύνθη) of Paul's chains. Indeed, shame—specifically not being ashamed—plays an important role in 2 Timothy. The "worker without-shame" finds its archetype in Paul, who focuses on preserving the gospel in hope of receiving God's approval. Indeed, "that day" will redeem those who have suffered from human beings while shaming those that have been ashamed of the gospel and its representatives. Verse 15 could be viewed as an indirect—but clear—exhortation to be like Paul in his courage and especially in his handling of the gospel. This is fitting, given in 2:14b he has presented the false teachers and agitators as negative examples to avoid.

The precise meaning of "a worker without-shame" is teased out in the closing participle phrase "handling-orthodoxly the word of truth." Loosely, the participle "handling-orthodoxly" (ὀρθοτομοῦντα) means to "teach accurately"; more literally, "cutting a straight road through difficult terrain, making straight paths."[47] This call to preserve and promote orthodoxy must be heard in contrast to the false teachers who engage heterodoxy (1 Tim 1:3).[48] These supposed teachers are notorious for "desiring to be teachers of the law, without understanding either what they are saying or the things about which they make confident assertions" (1 Tim 1:7). Thus, the participle phrase carries a polemical quality: "Don't be like the false teachers."

The phrase "the word of truth" (τὸν λόγον τῆς ἀληθείας) supports this recollection of the false teachers. In 1 Tim 6:3 Paul describes the heretic as one who "teaches-heterodoxy and is not given to the healthy words (λόγοις) of our Lord Jesus Christ and the teaching that accords with godliness." A few verses later Paul says of these false teachers that they have become "deprived of the truth (ἀληθείας)" (1 Tim 6:5). To

47. Friberg and Friberg, *Analytical Greek New Testament*, s.v. Köstenberger, *1–2 Timothy and Titus*, 243: "The word 'correctly teaching' (ὀρθοτομέω) conveys the notion of 'cutting straight' (rather than crooked), whether cutting a road in order to forge a straight path (cf. Prov 3:6 LXX; 11:5 LXX) or some other setting. In an age when Roman roads were masterful examples of skilled engineering, this metaphor would have communicated well."

48. For further reflection on the identity and activity of the heretics, see Jeon, *1 Timothy*.

rightly handle "the word of truth" is to rightly interpret and teach the words of the Lord Jesus Christ that were entrusted to the apostle and now stand as the authoritative teaching among all believers. Again, we see that v. 15 is a summons to do the opposite of the false teachers who have abandoned orthodoxy by engaging in heterodoxy: "Strive to be otherwise."[49]

The command in 2 Tim 2:16a to avoid "profane empty-sounds" (τὰς δὲ βεβήλους κενοφωνίας) recalls 1 Tim 6:20, "Swerve from profane empty-sounds (τὰς βεβήλους κενοφωνίας)."[50] Here, in 2:16a, Paul makes explicit what has been implicit thus far—a charge to "avoid" (περιΐστασο) the practices and waywardness of the false teachers. "Profane" refers to what is "strictly open and accessible to all."[51] In 1 Tim 1:9 it is coupled in Paul's vice-list with "unholy" (ἀνοσίοις καὶ βεβήλοις). Paul could be saying that Timothy is not to involve himself with common matters. This fits well, given Paul's comparisons to focused and disciplined soldiers, athletes, and farmers. However, the immediate context (2 Tim 2:15) and the similar command in 1 Tim 6:20 suggest that "profane" refers to teaching that contradicts divine revelation, i.e., Paul's gospel.[52] Any such talk is aptly coined by Paul as "empty-sounds" (κενοφωνίας), hollow-utterings that do not even merit the title of "words."

Paul uses a rich variety of words to convey the sense "avoid" (περιΐστασο). In 1 Tim 4:7 he uses the term "refuse" (παραιτοῦ), which also connotes "disdain, reject, spurn." In 1 Tim 6:20, he used the term "turn-from" (ἐκτρεπόμενος). The verb in 2 Tim 2:16 draws the image of "going around something so as to keep aloof."[53] Earlier, Paul indicated that all in Asia turned from him. Given this, v. 16a could be understood as an exhortation for Timothy to shun such "empty-sounds" and their proponents in the same way that all in Asia avoided Paul. Again, we observe the theme of identification, which is expressed not only relationally (e.g., 2 Tim 1:4–6) but also "propositionally": identification with Paul and

49. Köstenberger, *1–2 Timothy and Titus*, 242: "Second, unlike the false teachers, Timothy must make every effort . . . to teach God's Word accurately."

50. See my comments in related sections of *1 Timothy*. See also my comments on 1 Tim 4:7 ("But irreverent (βεβήλους) and silly myths refuse").

51. Friberg and Friberg, *Analytical Greek New Testament*, s.v.

52. Towner, *Letters*, 523: "The sense of 'profane' or secular', that is, 'distant from and foreign to (and even 'in opposition to') God', should be retained in this discussion of false doctrine and the manner in which it is dispensed. The point is that the heretical nonsense threatens to bring the teaching of the church down to the level of base human teaching."

53. Friberg and Friberg, *Analytical Greek New Testament*, s.v.

his gospel entails creating distance from the "empty-sounds" that stand in opposition.

The second half of v. 16 delineates the consequences of giving any attention and tacit allegiance to profane empty-words: "for upon more irreverence they will progress." The term "irreverence" (ἀσεβείας) recalls Paul's vice list in 1 Tim 1:9, which includes the adjective "irreverent" (ἀσεβέσιν). All the listed vices stand in contrast to the quality of "righteous" (δικαίῳ): they describe those who are outside of Christ. Paul is lifting Timothy's eyes to consider the final destination of those that perpetuate and devote themselves to "empty-sounds" that contradict the gospel. The verb "advance" (προκόψουσιν) depicts a person moving "increasingly"—"upon more" (ἐπὶ πλεῖον)—toward a particular end.[54] Here, it is toward destruction, the antithesis of the eternal life to which Christ has called his followers.

That Paul is concerned not primarily with individual piety but corporate vitality is made clear in v. 17: "and the word of theirs like gangrene will have increase." We should hear "the word of *theirs*" (ὁ λόγος αὐτῶν) in stark contrast to "the word of *God*" (ὁ λόγος τοῦ θεοῦ; 2:9), "the *faithful* word (πιστὸς ὁ λόγος; 2:11)," and "the word of *truth*" (τὸν λόγον τῆς ἀληθείας; 2:15). Whereas divine, faithful, and truthful words nourish because they are "sound/health/life-giving words" (ὑγιαινόντων λόγων; 1:13), "the word of theirs" is "like gangrene" (ὡς γάγγραινα), "spreading ulcers" or "cancer."[55] Continuing the imagery of progress from 2:16, Paul asserts that the words of false teachers "will have increase" (νομὴν ἕξει). The term "increase" occurs figuratively to describe "an ulcerous growth that spreads and eats the flesh."[56] Through such graphic imagery in 2:17a, Paul recalls 2:14b where he made clear that the words of the false teachers

54. Towner, *Letters*, 524: "Irony and contrast serve to strengthen the force of this reason. On the one hand, the concept of 'progress' employed in this verse (3:9, 13), here emphasized with the addition of the preposition phrase 'more and more,' was frequently associated with moral and spiritual growth. Here Paul turns the concept into sharp irony to denounce the teaching and methods (and perhaps the claims to godliness) of the opponents as 'progress' in ungodliness (see also 3:13)." Köstenberger, *1–2 Timothy and Titus*, 244: "Literally the latter phrase reads 'progress more and more in ungodliness,' involving a wordplay: those given to irreverent, empty speech—self-styled doctrine 'progressives,' perhaps—will indeed 'progress (προκόπτω) but entirely in the wrong direction (cf. 3:9, 13; see also 1 Tim 4:15)."

55. Friberg and Friberg, *Analytical Greek New Testament*, s.v.

56. Friberg and Friberg, *Analytical Greek New Testament*, s.v. For further reflection of the use of medical terminology in Paul's writings, see Malherbe, "Medical Imagery in the Pastorals," 19–35; Köstenberger, *1–2 Timothy and Titus*, 244.

are of "no usefulness" and lead only to "catastrophe" (2:14b). Thus the health of God's household depends directly on what Timothy and those under him heed.

Characteristic of Paul, he names representative figures who muddy themselves in senseless controversies and function like viruses among the believers: "Among whom are Hymenaeus and Philetus."[57] The identification of specific individuals is notable because Paul's letters were read aloud before all the believers.[58] More than likely "Hymenaeus and Philetus" (Ὑμέναιος καὶ Φίλητος) were among the congregation at the time of the reading or known to all the believers. Paul mentions "Hymenaeus" in 1 Tim 1:20; there is no reason to assume that he is speaking of someone else here.[59] His repeated reference to Hymenaeus suggests that the latter's heretical activites have persisted despite Paul's public condemnation in the previous letter. There is no other mention of "Philetus" in the NT, but we can assume that Timothy and the audience were well acquainted with him.

In v. 18, Paul pejoratively refers to these persons as "the-some-ones-who regarding the truth have swerved." Paul's use of the pronoun "the-someones-who" (οἵτινες) echoes the "someone" (τις) in 2:5 of the corresponding A element. In 2:5, Paul depicts the athlete somewhat ambiguously: he is not crowned unless he competes lawfully. As we noted, 2:5 is likely a subtle recollection of the false teachers who do not know how to use the law lawfully (1 Tim 1:8). What was subtle previously is now made explicit in 2:18: these "someones" have deviated from the truth of the gospel. The verb "swerved" (ἠστόχησαν) may be *the* defining verb Paul uses in 1 and 2 Timothy to describe the agitators. Twice in 1 Timothy, at the bookends, Paul says of the false teachers: "someones swerving (τινες ἀστοχήσαντες) from [a pure heart and good conscience] have strayed toward empty-word" (1:6); "someones (τινες) . . . have swerved (ἠστόχησαν) regarding the faith (περὶ τὴν πίστιν)" (6:21). Verse 21 is also instructive for understanding the phrase "regarding the truth" (περὶ τὴν ἀλήθειαν) in 2 Tim 2:18. The "truth" is the "truth" (ἀληθείας) of the gospel by which a person can be saved (1 Tim 2:4); it is the "word of truth (ἀληθείας)" (2 Tim 2:15), which must be handled properly for preservation and promotion. In other words, it is the content of "faith."

57. See, e.g., 1 Tim 1:20; 2 Tim 1:16; see also the use of the identical construction ὧν ἐστιν in these verses.

58. See esp. related sections in Jeon, *1 Timothy*, that detail this practice.

59. For more information on Hymenaeus, see Jeon, *1 Timothy*.

Thus, from the perspective of truth and faith, these agitators have gone astray and therefore do not merit attention from believers.

Paul then proceeds to explain how Hymenaeus and Philetus have deviated from the truth. They are guilty of "saying the resurrection has already happened." What they are "saying" (λέγοντες) has the effect of gangrene, the opposite effect of what Paul "says" (λέγω) in 2:7 of the corresponding A element. Whereas Paul calls Timothy to ponder what he "says," Timothy is to avoid the empty-words of such persons who claim that "the resurrection already has happened" (ἀνάστασιν ἤδη γεγονέναι). This claim would have unsettled the believers with Timothy because it would have suggested that they have not become united with Christ (2:11) or that "resurrection" was just spiritual, not bodily.[60] Moreover, in this letter, Paul speaks of "the promise of life in Christ Jesus" (1:1) that has *not* "already happened." Paul knows that "that day" of "resurrection" glory when his labors vindicated remains in the future (1:12). Similarly, the Lord has yet to extend mercy to Onesiphorus on "that day" (1:18). To claim that the "resurrection already has happened" is to suggest that "the day" has come and gone. This, of course, does not square with the present situation Paul and the believers find themselves in.

Verse 18 concludes by reiterating the dire consequence of this heretical claim.[61] These agitators "are overturning the faith of some." The verb "overturning" (ἀνατρέπουσιν) expresses to "upset, overthrow, ruin."[62] This statement underscores the profound consequence of human words and actions: they have the capacity to "overturn" the faith of "some." Here, it is not entirely clear whether "faith" (πίστιν) is referring to the content of belief or the act of belief. But such a fine distinction may not be necessary

60. Towner, *Letters*, 529: "The implication of such a teaching for the average believer would have been that the resurrection hope was completely spiritualized into some presently attainable mode of living. In essence, however, it meant the deflation of hope in a substantial resurrection, and meant that salvation became a totally spiritual (as opposed to material) affair. In any case, it marked a confusion of the relation of this temporal stressful existence and future perfection in salvation. For those in the community who could not quite see through the present curtain of distress to the traditional Pauline hope of resurrection, the doctrine of present resurrection offered a compelling substitute, but at the cost of the disruption to their faith." Köstenberger, *1–2 Timothy and Titus*, 245: "Asserting that believers experienced the full reality of Christ's resurrection already in the present, the opponents may have proceeded to maintain that it therefore didn't matter how they lived (cf. 1 Cor 4:8)."

61. The conjunction καί ("and") can introduce a result; see BDAG, s.v.

62. Friberg and Friberg, *Analytical Greek New Testament*, s.v. See also my comments on the verb and its use in Titus 1:11 in Jeon, *To Exhort and Reprove*.

as the two are related: believers are called to have faith in sound faith. The use of the pronoun "some" (τινων), which again in 1 and 2 Timothy tends to have a pejorative connotation, suggests that the persons most impacted by the heretical teachings are those who were not well-established in the faith but immature or ambivalent.

Even in the face of widespread apostasy ("however"; μέντοι) "the strong foundation of God stands" (2:19). Building imagery, as suggested by the term "foundation" (θεμέλιος), recalls different parts of 1 Timothy. Paul writes in hope that Timothy and the believers with him might know how "to behave in the household of God, which is the church of the living God, a pillar (στῦλος) and buttress (ἑδραίωμα) of the truth" (1 Tim 3:15). The term "foundation" itself occurs in 1 Tim 6:19 where Paul encourages generosity as a "good foundation (θεμέλιον) for the future." Thus, household/structural imagery plays a critical role in understanding 1 and 2 Timothy. The assertion here that "the strong (στερεός) foundation of God has stood (ἕστηκεν)" contrasts the "overturning [of] the faith of some" (2:18). Timothy can persist as a good soldier of Christ because in the end nothing can overturn God's household.[63]

But what is "the strong foundation" referring to? The answer is suggested in what follows: "having this seal: the Lord knows the-ones-who-are of him.'" A "seal" indicates authenticity: it is a "way to recognize."[64] Assuming this definition, v. 19 suggests that there are two ways to recognize authentic faith. On the one hand, "the Lord knows the-ones-who-are of him."[65] The mention of the "Lord" (κύριος) recalls its earlier occurrence in 2:7 of the corresponding A element. In this first instance,

63. Concerning the OT background to the *themelios* imagery, Towner observes: "An echo of [LXX] Isa 28:16 is probable . . . In the early church, this OT text became an important OT christological testimony (Rom 9:22; 1 Pet 2:6) . . . Paul responds to the turbulent situation facing Timothy by drawing on the part of the well-known OT statement that emphasizes the certainty of God's acts, and applies it to the stability of the church. Yet, as the context suggests (2:8, 11), it is precisely the truth of the resurrection of Jesus Christ that anchors this 'foundation' and that can stabilize the tottering 'faith of some' (v. 18); and the application of the Isaiah text elsewhere allows its fainter christological echo here to be heard." See *Letters*, 530–31. See also Towner, "Use of the Old Testament in the Letters to Timothy and Titus," 71.

64. Friberg and Friberg, *Analytical Greek New Testament*, s.v. See also Molina and Eck, "Σφραγίς (*sfragis*)," 1–4.

65. This is an obvious echo of Num 16:5 LXX: "And he spoke to Korah and all his assembly, saying, God has visited and known those that are his (ἔγνω ὁ θεὸς τοὺς ὄντας αὐτοῦ) and who are holy, and has brought them to himself; and whom he has chosen for himself, he has brought to himself."

the mention of the "Lord" comes after Paul's exhortation to consider the discipline of a soldier, athlete, and farmer. The first A element reflects a dynamic interplay between human responsibility and divine sovereignty. Something similar seems to be taking place in 2:19b. Paul underscores the sovereignty of God by asserting that only the "Lord knows the-ones-who-are of him" (ἔγνω κύριος τοὺς ὄντας αὐτοῦ). Although Hymenaeus and Philetus overturn the faith of some, Timothy can rest assured that such apostasy does not surprise the Lord. God already knows who truly belong to his household.[66]

Paul, however, does not allow for any passivity. Already, in the A' element, he has underscored the need for Timothy to pursue a different path from that of the agitators. Bringing this third microchiasm to a conclusion, Paul summarizes what he has said already: "From without-righteousness must withdraw all that-name the name of the Lord." The relationship to what Paul just said is obvious. The statement "the Lord (κύριος) knows those who are of him" is another way of indicating that the Lord knows those who belong to him—he knows their names. If this is the case, then those who know the Lord, that is, "the one-that-names the name of the Lord" will seek to live out covenant-faithfulness by withdrawing from all unrighteousness.[67] There is some echo here of Paul's ex-

---

66. The use of different OT texts reinforces this point. Commenting on the echo of Num 16:5 LXX, Towner, *Letters*, 533: "Both the OT content and the present context must be compared to appreciate the full weight of the citation's claim that 'the Lord knows those who are his.' In both cases authority is disputed. Then there is the issue of loyalty—to God in the OT context and to Christ in the present setting (vv. 9-13), and to their appointed servants . . . Korah presented a challenge to Moses' and Aaron's authority, and in so doing rebelled against God; God confirmed his choice of Moses and Aaron by the destruction of Korah and all who sided with him. The reader familiar with the OT background is compelled to view the present situation in a similar light: characters such as Hymenaeus and Philetus with their false teaching present the apostolic ministry with a leadership challenge . . . Positively, for Timothy and other readers the force of the citation comes in the reminder that the Lord knows his people personally and will distinguish between true and false followers and preserve the community of faith formed around him . . . The parenetic force of this reminder for Timothy (cf. 1:6-8) should not be missed." See also Köstenberger, *1-2 Timothy and Titus*, 246.

67. This last portion of 2 Tim 2:19 echoes various LXX texts, including Num 16:26-27; Lev 24:16; Isa 26:13; Ps 6:9. For the significance of these OT connections, see Towner, *Letters*, 534-37. Noteworthy is Towner's final comment: "The parallels are obvious: challengers to God's/the Lord's representatives (Moses/Paul) have been named, and the people must choose sides, thereby establishing their identity. Consequently, the verbal contact in 'turn away'/'depart from' should be taken seriously as an echo of the Korah story's climax: the OT story provides a narrative illustration of the concept of 'wickedness' (*adikia*) and the narrative source that gives meaning to the command in v. 19d."

hortation to bondservants. Paul summons those under a yolk to esteem their masters "so that the name (ὄνομα) of God and the teaching may not be reviled" (1 Tim 6:1). Here, Paul generalizes that specific exhortation to include "all that-name the name of the Lord (ὁ ὀνομάζων τὸ ὄνομα) of the Lord."

For Timothy, however, this does not entail serving an earthly master. Rather, it requires taking intentional steps to depart from unrighteousness. The language here, as we have seen already, seems deliberate, recalling important terms from 1 Timothy. First, the imperative "must withdraw" (ἀποστήτω) occurs in 1 Tim 4:1. Here, Paul explicitly states: "Now the Spirit truly says that in later times some will depart (ἀποστήσονταί) from the faith by devoting themselves to deceitful spirits and demonic teachings." Second, the description "without-righteousness" (ἀδικίας) stands in clear contrast to Paul's characterization of believers in 1 Tim 1:9 as "righteous" (δικαίῳ). In sum, the force of 2 Tim 2:19 is that those who are known by God and know God—that is, those who name the name of the Lord—must withdraw from those that have withdrawn from the faith. Again, this echoes what Paul says in 2:16 about avoiding the gangrene-words of agitators who have swerved from the truth. In sum, "the strong foundation" is referring to genuine believers who are known by God and who know God as evidenced in their deliberate choice to depart from wickedness.[68]

The idea of departing from those that have departed from the faith accords with the overall thrust of this third microchiasm. Soldiers, athletes, and farmers are all alike in that they set themselves apart. Soldiers of Christ, in particular, are distinct because they hold on to the true gospel and endure in the face of suffering. They do so because they are hopeful of the future glory that God will assuredly give to those that remain in Christ and trust in God's faithfulness. The practical outworking of being a devoted soldier is to avoid the senseless talk of false teachers and to focus on maturing as an adept handler of God's revealed word. In the end, endurance as a soldier of Christ is the marker of genuine faith.

---

68. Marshall, *Pastoral Epistles*, 755–56; Towner, *Goal of Our Instruction*, 132.

6

2 Timothy 2:20—3:6

Reject Those Who Deny the Power of Godliness

(D UNIT)

THIS CHAPTER EXAMINES THE fourth of eight microchiastic units within the 2 Timothy macrochiasm. Paul continues his effort to spur Timothy to endure suffering and fulfill his calling. Timothy is to do so by heeding Paul's main exhortation in the previous section to set himself apart from the false teachers who spread empty-talk and upset the faith of some.

The Fourth Microchiastic Unit

The fourth of eight microchiasms within 2 Timothy is composed carefully of four elements (A-B-B'-A'). Linguistic parallels are indicated by the Greek text.

A. ²⁰ But in a great house (οἰκίᾳ) there are not only golden and silver vessels; rather [there are] wooden and clay [vessels], and on-the-one-hand some toward honor, but on-the-other-hand some toward without-honor; ²¹ therefore, if someone purifies himself from these (τούτων), he will be a vessel toward honor, sanctified, useful for the master, toward all good work ready. ²² But youthful desires (ἐπιθυμίας) flee, but pursue righteousness, faith, love, peace with those who invoke the Lord from a pure heart.

B. ²³ But moronic and without-instruction (ἀπαιδεύτους) controversy disregard, knowing that (εἰδὼς ὅτι) they birth fights (μάχας);

B'. ²⁴ But it is necessary for the slave of the Lord not to fight (μάχεσθαι); rather to be gentle to all, able-to-teach, forbearing, ²⁵ in respectfulness instructing (παιδεύοντα) those who oppose—perchance to them God may give repentance toward a knowledge of truth ²⁶ and they may become-sober-again from the snare of the devil, having-been-captured by him toward that will. ³:¹ But this perceive that (ὅτι) in the last days there will come difficult times; ² For human beings will be lovers-of-self, lovers-of-money, boasters, arrogant, blasphemous, without-obedience to their parents, without-gratitude, without-holiness, ³ without-feeling, without-reconciliation, devilish, without-self-control, without-tameness, without-loving-good, ⁴ treacherous, reckless, puffed-up, lovers-of-pleasure rather than lovers-of-God, ⁵ª having the form of godliness but the power of it denying;

A'. ⁵ᵇ and these (τούτους) turn-from. ⁶ For from these (τούτων) are those-who-slip into the households (οἰκίας) and captivate foolish-women who-are-weighed with sins, led by many desires (ἐπιθυμίαις)

2 Timothy 2:20–22

Becoming a Useful Vessel

(A Element)

The third microchiasm ends with a subtle reference to God's household: "However, the strong foundation of God has stood . . ." (2:19). Paul now picks up on this imagery and begins the fourth microchiasm and the A Element with the declaration: "But in a great house there are not only golden and silver vessels; rather [there are] also wooden and clay [vessels]." Here, what was implicit becomes explicit, namely the imagery of a "great house" (μεγάλῃ . . . οἰκίᾳ). The adjective "great," which can mean "large" or "wealthy" (or possibly both), underscores that this given "house" is unique through its possession of multiple "vessels." "Household" imagery plays a significant role in Paul's first letter.[1] Here, the underlying principle pertaining to this "great house" holds equally true for the "household of God" (οἴκῳ θεοῦ; 1 Tim 3:15).[2]

What Paul says in 2:20 comes as little surprise. The contrast between "golden and silver vessels" (σκεύη χρυσᾶ καὶ ἀργυρᾶ) and "wooden and clay [vessels]" (ξύλινα καὶ ὀστράκινα) parallels the contrast between himself and Timothy and the false teachers respectively.[3] The implication is made explicit in the rest of v. 20, namely that the former are "toward honor" (εἰς τιμὴν) while the latter are "toward without-honor" (εἰς ἀτιμίαν).[4] The μὲν . . . δὲ structure could not make the contrast clearer.[5] Moreover, it is worth noting the earlier references of "honor" in 1 Tim 1:17 and 1 Tim 6:16.[6] In the first instance, Paul ascribes "honor (τιμή) and glory" to "the king of eternities"; in the second, Paul similarly declares "eternal honor (τιμή) and dominion" to the immortal and invisible God. Thus, there appears to be alignment between the "golden and silver vessels" set apart

1. See my comments in related sections of *1 Timothy*.

2. Contra Köstenberger, *1–2 Timothy and Titus*, 248n103.

3. A contrast is clearly in view between objects of superior material makeup and those of lesser quality; contra Köstenberger, *1–2 Timothy and Titus*, 248: "In the picture of a large house (presumably owned by a wealthy individual) with a variety of articles, the point is not so much that utensils made of gold and silver are intrinsically superior to those made of wood or clay (note the arrangement in decreasing order of value). All fulfill a useful function . . . but some tools serve nobler purposes than others."

4. There appears to be some echo of Rom 9:21 where Paul mentions the potter who has the right to "make one vessel on-the-one-hand toward honor, but on-the-other-hand [some] toward without honor" (ποιῆσαι ὃ μὲν εἰς τιμὴν σκεῦος ὃ δὲ εἰς ἀτιμίαν). The subtle implication could be that while "golden and silver vessels" will last into eternity, "wooden and clay [vessels]" are destined to destruction.

Note also that my interpretation assumes that the attributions of "honor" and "shame" apply completely to each category, that is, all the "golden and silver vessels" are "toward honor" while all the "wooden and clay [vessels]" are "toward without-honor." Towner, *Letters*, 540: "Having in these parallel statements just separated the implements into two groups, first based on material value and second according to use, the latter twofold division should almost certainly be taken as a further specification of the two categories in the sense 'the former . . . the latter . . .' instead of as further defining only the second common category of vessel in the sense 'some . . . some.' To each category in v. 20a belongs a purpose in v. 20b, and these are not to be confused."

5. Towner, *Letters*, 538: "The real reason for introducing the image of the house is to describe the 'articles' within it. Paul does this by explicit contrast ('not only . . . but also . . .') to heighten the distinction already apparent in the materials from which the articles are made."

6. See also 1 Tim 5:17; 6:1.

"toward honor" and the God who will receive all "honor" throughout eternity. But perhaps what is more important to note than the nuances of the types of material in view—or, even the purpose of the articles—is Paul's abiding preoccupation with Timothy's need to distinguish himself from the false teachers.

Paul proceeds then to explain how "someone" (τις) can become a "vessel toward honor" (σκεῦος εἰς τιμήν): "therefore, if someone purifies himself from these, he will be a vessel toward honor." The conjunction "therefore" (οὖν) indicates that the reality expressed in 2:20 demands a response. The pronoun "someone" tends to have a pejorative connotation in these related letters;[7] thus, its occurrence here suggests that even the "someones" that have deviated from the truth have hope if they repent. But its use may be more neutral to express a general principle. The verb "purifies" (ἐκκαθάρῃ) recalls Paul's descriptions of a converted person in 1 Tim 1:5: "The purpose of the charge is love from a pure (καθαρᾶς) heart and good conscience and sincere faith." All this is the work of the Lord; that is, the heart has been purified, the conscience is functioning, and faith is sincere through the working of the Holy Spirit. The sense of 2 Tim 2:21 appears to be describing the continued effort of a believer to make in "himself" (ἑαυτὸν) what is already true in Christ. "These" (τούτων) may be referring to the wood and clay vessels (which represent the false teachers and troublemakers) or, more generally, to the gangrene words and even rebellious attitudes of Hymenaeus and Philetus (2:17–18).[8] Timothy and all who follow him must cleanse themselves from such corroding influences.

By doing so, Timothy will become "a vessel toward honor." Paul further explains what he means by this in the threefold descriptor "sanctified, useful for the master, toward all good work ready." The first participle "sanctified" (ἡγιασμένον) recalls the verb's earlier occurrence in 1 Tim 4:5, where Paul declares that everything in creation is to be received with thanksgiving because it "is sanctified (ἁγιάζεται) through the word of God and prayer." A similar idea is present in 2 Tim 2:21 where "someone" has become "sanctified" through the synergistic efforts of the cleansing Spirit and the disciplined believer who has separated himself from wickedness.

---

7. See, e.g., my comments on 1 Tim 1:3 in *1 Timothy*.

8. See Fee, *1 and 2 Timothy, Titus*, 262; Marshall, *Pastoral Epistles*, 762.

Second, this "someone" will become "useful for the master" (εὔχρηστον τῷ δεσπότῃ). The reference to "master" recalls 1 Tim 6:1–2 where Christian slaves are called to regard their own "masters" (δεσπότας) as worthy of all honor (6:1), all the more if their "masters" (δεσπότας) are believers (6:2). There may be a subtle reminder here that all are both free in Christ and under his mastery. This notion was suggested already in 2:4 where Paul declared, "None who-is-a-soldier gets entangled in the affairs of life, that he might please the one-who-enlists-soldiers." Similarly, in 2:15 Paul writes, "Strive to present yourself approved to God, a worker without-shame, handling-orthodoxly the word of truth." Salvation in Christ is lordship-salvation; thus the believer focuses on pleasing and becoming "useful"—profitable, serviceable—to the "master." This is impossible unless "someone" is deliberate about "purifying" himself from the negative influence and heresies of the agitators.

Finally, such a person becomes "toward all good work ready" (εἰς πᾶν ἔργον ἀγαθὸν).[9] The phrase echoes Paul's description of the widow that qualifies for help, not just because of her age but also because of her reputation (1 Tim 5:1): she is known for immersing herself "in commendable works (ἔργοις)," for having devoted herself "to all good work" (παντὶ ἔργῳ ἀγαθῷ).[10] Similarly, rich believers are exhorted "to-do-good-work (ἀγαθοεργεῖν), to be rich in commendable works (ἔργοις)" (1 Tim 6:18). In particular, the work of the elder is described as a "commendable work (ἔργου)" (1 Tim 3:1), manifested primarily in the care of one's own household (1:2–7). While the rich use of commendable/good works should not limit our understanding of 2 Tim 2:21 to just the office of overseer, the participle "ready" (ἡτοιμασμένον), which connotes being prepared, seems to suggest a special position. Indeed, the participle recalls Paul's use of soldier and athlete imagery, both of which highlight unique roles relative to the ordinary citizen.

Verse 22—"But youthful desires flee (φεῦγε), but pursue righteousness (δίωκε δὲ δικαιοσύνην), faith (πίστιν), love (ἀγάπην), peace"—is

---

9. Towner, *Letters*, 542: "Third, Paul employs the 'good works' language typical of these letters to coworkers to summarize the visible outworking of being 'holy' to God and 'useful': 'prepared to do any good work.' The phrase parallels 3:7 and Titus 3:1 where the concept depicts authentic faith from the standpoint of the outward service it produces." For further reflection on the ideas of authentic faith and its visible—and inevitable—outworkings, see Jeon, *True Faith*; Jeon, *Christianity Philanthropy*.

10. Paul seems to use the adjectives καλός and ἀγαθός interchangeably, perhaps with the nuance of the former being outwardly obvious, the latter being inherently good.

an obvious echo of 1 Tim 6:11: "But you, O human being of God, these things flee (φεῦγε); but pursue righteousness (δίωκε δὲ δικαιοσύνην), godliness, faith (πίστιν), love (ἀγάπην), steadfastness, gentleness." In the previous context, Paul is describing the "love of money" that plunges many "into a snare, into many senseless and harmful desires (ἐπιθυμίας)" (1 Tim 6:9–10). The occurrence of "desires" (ἐπιθυμίας) in 2 Tim 2:22 suggests that the apostle might have in mind the corrupting power of money and thus exhorts Timothy to flee from an obsession with it. But the immediate context and the qualifier "youthful" (νεωτερικὰς), which can also mean "adolescent" or "juvenile,"[11] suggest otherwise. "Youthful" stands in obvious contrast to the maturity of those that have endured hardship (soldiers, athletes, and farmers). Paul uses these metaphors to describe the discipline of any believer, a discipline marked by a deliberate decision to mature in the word of truth and to avoid irreverent babble (2 Tim 2:14–16).[12] Therefore, 2 Tim 2:22 does not appear to be a summons to "flee" the love of money but the gangrene-words of the false teachers.[13]

Typical of Paul, the charge to "flee" one thing is coupled with a charge to "pursue" (δίωκε) another. Again, there is a clear similarity to the virtues listed in 1 Tim 6:11.[14] There, Paul proclaims, "but pursue justice (δίωκε δὲ δικαιοσύνην), godliness, faith (πίστιν), love (ἀγάπην), steadfastness, gentleness," and calls for near-identical virtues in 2 Tim 2:22: "but pursue righteousness, faith, love (δίωκε δὲ δικαιοσύνην πίστιν ἀγάπην), peace." The differences that do occur in each list suggest that Paul drew somewhat freely from a cache of virtues, although given Paul's special concern for endurance in 2 Timothy, it is striking that he excludes "steadfastness" (ὑπομονὴν). "Faith" and "love" occur together to express

---

11. Friberg and Friberg, *Analytical Greek New Testament*, s.v.

12. Some suggest that "youthful desires" may refer to a lust for innovation; see, e.g., Metzger, "Die *neōterikai epithymiai* in 2 Tim 2.22." Towner adds: "In any case, sexual lust does not seem to be the focus, and the plurality of the whole construction suggests a broad pattern of behavior rather than a particular weakness. Various kinds of behavior characterized by impetuous or rash acts without thought to consequences could easily be in view; the context suggests that those related to argument and abrupt innovation would be uppermost in mind" (*Letters*, 544).

13. See Westfall, "Moral Dilemma," 245. For the verb "flee" (φεύγω), see my comments on 1 Tim 6:11 in *1 Timothy*.

14. See my comments on 1 Tim 6:11 in *1 Timothy*. We should observe that Paul would take virtues familiar to his audience and redefine them in view of Christ's first and second epiphany. For instance, sobriety would be redefined as living deliberately as believers recall Christ's resurrection and his return.

the inseparable relationship between "faith" in God and "love" for his people.[15] The inclusion of "peace" (εἰρήνην) was intentional: Timothy is to reject the argumentative spirit of the agitators with a non-combative disposition. By doing so, not unlike Martin Luther King Jr., he would perhaps win over some of the opponents.

The most notable difference between 1 Tim 6:11 and 2 Tim 2:22 is the prepositional phrase that follows in 2 Tim 2:22: "with those who invoke the Lord from a pure heart" (μετὰ τῶν ἐπικαλουμένων τὸν κύριον ἐκ καθαρᾶς καρδίας). Paul depicts the effort to purify the self not as an individual pursuit but as a shared effort with other true believers.[16] That such individuals "invoke the Lord" recalls Paul's earlier description of genuine believers as those "that-name the name of the Lord" (2:19).[17] The phrase "pure heart" echoes 1 Tim 1:5 where Paul explains that his charge to silence the false teachers is aimed at love that issues from "a pure heart (ἐκ καθαρᾶς καρδίας) and a good conscience and a sincere faith." This triplet describes genuine believers. The occurrence of the single phrase "pure heart" may be shorthand to describe believers who neither engage in heresy nor have been overturned by it.

2 Timothy 2:23

WHAT TO DISREGARD TO BECOME A USEFUL VESSEL

(B ELEMENT)

The B element, which is solely comprised of v. 23, makes clear what is implicit in the previous A element. What are "these" that Timothy should purify himself from? From what "youthful desires" should he flee? In 2 Tim 2:23 of the B element, Paul specifies, "But moronic and

15. This juxtaposition of "faith" and "love" occurs regularly in Paul; see, e.g., Phlm 5 and my comments in *Unreconciled* or 1 Tim 1:5 and my comments in *1 Timothy*. Towner, *Letters*, 544: "Together they sum up the Christian life in terms of the 'vertical' or mystical faith relationship with God and the 'horizontal' or relational outworking of that faith in other-oriented service."

16. Köstenberger, *1–2 Timothy and Titus*, 251: "Yet the quest for holiness needn't be a lonely enterprise, as though believers should retreat to their closets and engage in quiet meditation. Instead, holiness should be pursued in community."

17. See also Rom 10:12, 13; 1 Cor 1:2; 2 Cor 1:23. The descriptor "those who call on the Lord" was a somewhat regular designation of the early church based on the OT; see, e.g., Ps 86:5; Isa 55:6.

without-instruction controversies disregard." The noun "controversy" (ζητήσεις) recalls 1 Tim 6:4, where Paul describes the prototypical agitator as one that has a nauseating interest in "controversies" (ζητήσεις). In both 1 Tim 6:4 and 2 Tim 2:23, Paul summarizes the destructive consequences of such controversies. In the former, he says from "controversies and word-fights (λογομαχίας) come envy, dissension, blasphemy, evil suspicions."[18] In the latter, Paul says that "they birth fights (μάχας)."[19] Here again we have Paul's negative assessment of the irreverent "controversies" of the agitators: they accomplish nothing good.

The apostle does not withhold his assessment of these "controversies"—they are "moronic and without-education" (μωρὰς καὶ ἀπαιδεύτους). The former adjective requires little comment;[20] the second probably means lacking the education of revelation, that is, such controversy is not tutored in the teaching of Christ, which has been uniquely revealed and entrusted to the apostle. Together, the verb "disregard" (παραιτοῦ) and the descriptors "moronic and without-education" echo 1 Tim 4:7 where Paul writes, "But irreverent and old-women myths disregard (παραιτοῦ). But train yourself toward godliness." (Note the use of athletic imagery.) The redundancy of Paul's exhortation to have nothing to do with myths, speculations, and controversies suggests that some believers continued to do otherwise.

The B element concludes with a terse explanation of why Timothy should avoid idiotic controversies: "knowing that (εἰδὼς ὅτι) they birth fights." There may be some echo of 2 Tim 1:15, "You know this (οἶδας τοῦτο) . . ." It is as if Paul is appealing to Timothy to remember the things he already knows from experience.[21] The only "good" that comes from engaging in divisive controversies is "fights" that distract believers from the gospel and their calling to abound in philanthropy. Paul's use of birthing language (γεννῶσιν) accords with his proclivity to use graphic images to make a point. According to 2:23, engagement in controversy is essentially no different from planting seeds of division that will "birth" destruction in a matter of time.

18. See my comments on the verse and term in 1 Timothy.

19. See my comments on the term as it occurs in Titus 3:9 in To Exhort and Reprove.

20. Towner, Letters, 545: "'Foolish' (Titus 3:9) describes the verbal wrangling as frivolous and unskilled because it produces nothing useful." See, again, my comments on Titus 3:9 in To Exhort and Reprove.

21. See also 1 Tim 1:8, 9; 3:15.

2 Timothy 2:24—3:5a

The Gentle and Savvy Vessel

(B' Element)

The B' element begins with an explicit contrast given what Paul just said about the effect of controversies: "But (δέ) it is necessary for the slave of the Lord not to fight." The infinitive "to fight" (μάχεσθαι) parallels "fights" (μάχας) in 2:23 of the corresponding B element. It also makes clear that controversies do not necessarily result in fights but rather fighters themselves; that is, people—not propositions—ultimately engage in quarrels. Fighting, in the sense of quarreling over useless and divisive controversies, is unfitting for the "slave of the Lord."[22] The mention of "slave" (δοῦλον) recalls the opening image of vessels useful for the "master" (2:21). Here, in 2:24 it becomes clear that by "master" Paul means the "Lord" (κυρίου). Useful vessels, then, are to be understood as "slaves" of Christ. The mention of "slaves" also recalls Paul's instructions to believers who are "slaves" (δοῦλοι) under a yoke (1 Tim 6:1). The phrase "slave of the Lord" is another reminder that no believer is truly free. Rather, all live under the lordship of Christ; and as people under a master, there are obligations that force Paul to use "it is necessary" (δεῖ) language.[23] Paul's language is purposefully forceful: Fights must not characterize anyone that aspires to become a vessel useful for the master.

As we would expect of Paul, having stated that "slave of the Lord" must not be belligerent, he proceeds to outline fitting characteristics. In a sense, he echoes his earlier statements in 2:21–22 of what it means to purify the self and pursue righteousness. In stark contrast ("rather"; ἀλλά), the "slave of the Lord" must "be (εἶναι) gentle to all, able-to-teach, forbearing, in respectfulness instructing those who oppose." This description recalls Paul's instructions on what prospective elders "must be" like (δεῖ . . . εἶναι). First, the "slave of the Lord" must be "gentle to all" (ἤπιον . . . πρὸς πάντας). In context, "gentle" means non-belligerent.[24]

---

22. The phrase "slave of the Lord" was a common self-designation for Paul and his co-laborers (e.g., Rom 1:1; Gal 1:10; Phil 1:1; Titus 1:1). It derived from the OT where key figures (e.g., Moses, Joshua) held the authoritative title "servant of the Lord" (e.g., Josh 1:1). For further reflection, see my comments on Titus 1:1 in *To Exhort and Reprove*.

23. See esp. 1 Tim 3:15; also 1 Tim 3:2, 7.

24. Towner, *Letters*, 546: "In addition to its link with paternal care, [ἤπιον] could

Noteworthy is the specification "to all," which in 2 Timothy likely means even to the agitators and apostates. "Able-to-teach" (διδακτικόν) recalls not just Paul's descriptor of aspiring elders who must be "able to teach" (διδακτικόν; 1 Tim 3:2), but also Paul's condemnation of the false teachers who must be charged not "to-teach-heterodoxy" (ἑτεροδιδασκαλεῖν; 1 Tim 1:3). Whereas these troublemakers make ignorant assertions because they do not understand the law correctly, the worker of Christ must make every effort to handle correctly the word of truth (2 Tim 2:15). Third, the "slave of the Lord" must be "forbearing" (ἀνεξίκακον). Danker explains the nuance of this adjective: "practicing restraint in the face of what does not measure up to high standards."[25] The Friberg lexicon adds, "bearing difficulties without resentment." In other words, the adjective means handling κακός with grace. This last attribute captures the essence of gospel-ministry. Paul can personally attest to this as he is writing from prison and experiencing widespread abandonment.

The fourth descriptor breaks from the previous adjectives through the use of a participle phrase: "in gentleness instructing those who oppose." The prepositional phrase "in gentleness" precedes the participle and therefore carries an emphatic force. The nuance of the adjective "gentleness" (πραΰτητι) is "meekness as strength that accommodates to another's weakness."[26] Indeed, this is extraordinary strength—to withhold the force of one's presence and words in order to facilitate communication and even reconciliation with another.[27] This quality is especially necessary in situations marked by conflict and quarrel. The main descriptor "instructing" (παιδεύοντα) parallels the adjective "without-instruction" (ἀπαιδεύτους) in v. 23 of the corresponding B element. This parallelism identifies whom Paul has in mind with the participle "those who oppose" (ἀντιδιατιθεμένους): they are without-instruction and without regard for apostolic teaching and authority. Timothy is to gently instruct such agitators. Paul may have in view here church discipline. In 1 Tim 1:20, Paul indicates that he has handed over Hymenaeus and Alexander to Satan

---

also be a characteristic of authority figures, suggesting that authority in this context would lead to seeking to nurture others."

25. Danker in BDAG, s.v.

26. Friberg and Friberg, *Analytical Greek New Testament*, s.v. See also Titus 3:2 and my related comments in *To Exhort and Reprove*.

27. Towner, *Letters*, 547: "This attitude gathers together the qualities of gentleness and tolerance into a disposition of patient openness that is particularly necessary for the Christian response in confrontational situations."

"that they may be instructed (παιδευθῶσιν) not to blaspheme." This former instance of the verb παιδεύω points in the direction that 2 Tim 2:25 is less about instructing those "without-instruction"; doing so, after all, would be a blatant contradiction to Paul's repeated exhortation to have nothing to do with the teachers and teaching of heresy (2:16–18). Rather, 2 Tim 2:25 seems to be a summons to discipline those who oppose but to do so with tremendous grace and forbearance.

Paul suggests that "perchance to them God may give repentance toward a knowledge of truth." The operative phrase here is "toward a knowledge of truth" (εἰς ἐπίγνωσιν ἀληθείας). This exact phrase occurs in 1 Tim 2:4 where Paul says that "God desires all people to be saved and to come toward a knowledge of truth" (εἰς ἐπίγνωσιν ἀληθείας). The "and" (καί) in 1 Tim 2:4 is likely epexegetical; that is, "to be saved" is to come "toward a knowledge of truth."[28] True "repentance" (μετάνοιαν), as 2 Tim 2:25 indicates, leads to salvation, a comprehension and embrace of the truth of the gospel;[29] and the ordinary means through which "God may give (δώῃ αὐτοῖς ὁ θεός) repentance" is through instruction and exhortation, especially by those in authority. The kind of "repentance" that leads to salvation may or may not happen—the Lord is sovereign; hence, "perchance" (μήποτε). In the case of Hymenaeus, being handed over to Satan did not achieve the outcome Paul had hoped for (1 Tim 1:20). Nevertheless, 2 Tim 2:25 makes clear that the purpose of all church discipline is restoration. To this end, it is necessary for the slave of the Lord "to be gentle to all, able-to-teach, forbearing, in respectfulness instructing those who oppose."

Verse 26 views the possibility of restoration from another angle. The first half of the verse reads, "and they may become-sober-again from the snare of the devil (τῆς τοῦ διαβόλου παγίδος)." The καί suggests a loose relationship between the two verses, something akin to repentance leading to an awakening. Instructive for interpreting this verse is 1 Tim 3:6–7. Here, describing prospective elders, Paul indicates: "He must not be a new convert, in order that he might not—by becoming puffed up—fall into the condemnation of the devil (διαβόλου). But it is necessary to have a commendable witness from outsiders, in order that he might not fall into disgrace and the snare of the devil (παγίδα τοῦ διαβόλου)."[30] These

---

28. For further reflection on this verse, see my comments in 1 Timothy.

29. For further reflection on the theme of repentance in 2 Tim 2:25, see Boda, "Return to Me," 173.

30. See my comments on these verses in 1 Timothy.

verses suggest that "those who oppose" in 2 Tim 2:25–26 are those who have become leaders prematurely among the believers. Their immaturity is evidenced especially by their fascination with false teaching, which throughout the Bible is associated with the devil.[31] Moreover, the reference to becoming "sober-again" (ἀνανήψωσιν)—"to come to one's senses, to no longer think wrong thoughts"[32]—is likely describing the outworking of becoming "puffed up" (1 Tim 3:6) through false teaching.[33]

The mention of "snare" (παγίδος) also recalls 1 Tim 6:9: "But those who desire to be rich fall into temptation and a snare (παγίδα) and many foolish and harmful desires." While there is little mention of money so far in 2 Timothy, the continuity between these two letters does not make it impossible that the loss of sobriety in 2 Tim 2:26 is related to a love of money. To "become-sober-again" could mean freedom from the folly of greed as stated in 1 Tim 6:17: "As for the rich in this present age, charge them not to be haughty, nor to set their hopes on the uncertainty of riches, but on God, who richly provides us with everything to enjoy."

The connection between 2 Tim 2:26 and 1 Tim 6:9 is strengthened by the closing participle phrase: "having-been-captured by him toward that will." The participle "having-been-captured" (ἐζωγρημένοι) evokes imagery similar to that of 1 Tim 6:9–10. In this earlier passage, Paul describes the desire and love for money as a force that has the unusual ability to capture and plunge people into ruin and destruction. The verb ζωγρέω literally means to "capture alive; of fish and animals."[34] This nuance echoes Eph 2:1–2 where Paul talks of unbelievers as "the living dead" who have been captured by the "prince of the power of the air."[35] Under

31. Köstenberger, *1–2 Timothy and Titus*, 252: "Trapping people in a web of lies has been the devil's practice from the beginning (Gen 3:1–7). Those who persist in falsehood show that they're caught in spiritual bondage." Towner, *Letters*, 549: "The phrase 'trap of the devil' has already occurred as a description of the temptations that belong to Satan's domain (see on 1 Tim 3:7). By implication, those teaching or subjected to the heresy are thought to have strayed into the devil's territory . . . The equation of the false teaching with the devil's influence is not unexpected (1 Tim 5:15)."

32. Friberg and Friberg, *Analytical Greek New Testament*, s.v.

33. Towner, *Letters*, 549: "Almost with the idea that false teaching is a potent soporific or narcotic, the effect of corrective teaching (namely, repentance) is described as 'sobering up,' which in moral discussions depicts a 'coming to one's senses.'"

34. Friberg and Friberg, *Analytical Greek New Testament*, s.v.

35. Towner, *Letters*, 550: "While in some context the verb on which it is based can mean 'rescue,' it was also used to depict those taken captive in war (LXX Deut 20:16) and often subjected to cruel torture and slavery by the captors. The perfect tense of the participle is perhaps a more apt description of the state of the capitves (i.e., in Satan's

the devil's grip, they are acting "toward that will" (εἰς τὸ ἐκείνου θέλημα), that is, they are doing his bidding by propagating heterodoxy. This stands in obvious contrast to Paul, who identifies himself as "an apostle of Christ Jesus through the will (θελήματος) of God."[36] As Timothy engages those that have abandoned sound doctrine, he must remember that the struggle is not merely between human beings. As Paul serves as God's appointed apostle and Timothy as "the slave of the Lord" (2 Tim 2:24), so too the agitators labor as slaves of the devil.[37] In his endeavor to become a useful vessel to the master, Timothy is to bear in mind the spiritual nature of the conflict. To see clearly—to see reality—is to see spiritually.

In 2 Tim 3:1 Paul continues to prepare Timothy to endure suffering by equipping him with a mature—prophetic—outlook on the present and near future. Verse 1 begins with the imperative, "But this perceive that . . ." (τοῦτο δὲ γίνωσκε, ὅτι). The command contrasts the parallel statement "knowing that" (εἰδὼς ὅτι) in 2 Tim 2:23 of the corresponding B element: Timothy is aware in the former instance, perhaps less aware in this second instance. Thus, the command likely means, "Accept what I am about to say."[38] The summons to "perceive" echoes Paul's earlier command, "Understand what I am saying; for to you the Lord will give insight in all-things" (2 Tim 2:7). Timothy, along with all believers, must not be naïve about people, life, and ministry. The statement, "You know this, that all that are in Asia turned-from me" (2 Tim 1:15), was meant to reiterate what people are like. Paul is not a misanthrope; yet, he is terribly aware

---

clutches) prior to escape . . . Consequently, 'having been taken captive by him' both explains the situation from which they escape (by coming to their senses) and further defines the nature of the 'devil's trap' as captivity."

36. Towner, *Letters*, 550: "One of the things at stake from at least 2:19 has been the clash of opposing figures—Timothy/false teachers, Moses/Korah, implements for honor/implements for dishonor, God/the devil—which finally issues in the image of a struggle between God and the devil for the souls of people. From the parenetic perspective, Timothy enters this struggle as an agent of Christ ('the Lord's servant') to face the agent of the devil (false teachers under his thrall, in his service)."

37. Köstenberger, *1–2 Timothy and Titus*, 252: "As Paul wrote to the Ephesians, our struggle isn't against flesh and blood but against the devil and his forces (Eph 6:10–18). Christian ministry entails waging spiritual warfare (2 Cor 10:3–5; 11:2–3). Thus Timothy should adopt a ministering stance toward the false teachers; perhaps some of them can be set free from spiritual bondage."

38. Towner, *Letters*, 553: "The phrase used to catch [Timothy's] attention is similar to that used in 1:15, with an important difference; there Paul called to mind knowledge that Timothy already had ('this [what follows] you know'), here he instructs him with the present tense imperative 'know this' (i.e., accept what I am about to tell you)."

that allegiance to the gospel will entail suffering, including imprisonment and abandonment. To be a useful vessel to the master entails having a biblical understanding of the times and especially of people.

"The last days" (ἐσχάταις ἡμέραις) marks the present age that precedes "that day" of Paul's vindication (2 Tim 1:12), "that day" when Onesiphorus will receive mercy from the Lord (2 Tim 1:18). The phrase "the last days" is not referring to some period in the future but to the present age between the first and second manifestation of Christ Jesus.[39] Paul wants Timothy to have a very clear sense that "in the last days there will come difficult times (ἐνστήσονται καιροὶ χαλεποί)." The verb "there will come" connotes impending threat and inevitable hardship. This echoes 1 Tim 4:1: "Now the Spirit expressly says that in later times (καιροῖς) some will depart from the faith by devoting themselves to deceitful spirits and demonic teachings."[40] Apostasy is in the air. With respect to people, the adjective "difficult" (χαλεποί) means "fierce, violent, dangerous."[41] Given this prophetic outlook, Timothy should not be surprised by the present suffering Paul is experiencing nor by the impending apostasy of many. Instead, Timothy must exhibit sobriety and prudence in all his endeavors, being fully cognizant of what "the last days" will entail.[42]

In 2 Tim 3:2, Paul begins to delineate how people will be "difficult" "in these last days" by employing the vice-list technique that was common in Jewish and Greek ethical literature.[43] He asserts by way of in-

---

39. Towner, *Letters*, 553: "And in various other ways it becomes clear that the present age of the Spirit (launched by Jesus' ministry, death, and resurrection) is in fact 'the last days' (1 Cor 10:11; 1 Pet 1:20; 1 John 2:18). Used in this way, the phrase was understood to imply that with Jesus' appearance, the End, marked by divine intervention, had been inaugurated and would culminate in God's final intervention (in the parousia of Christ) complete salvation and execute judgment."

40. Here in 1 Tim 4:1, as well as in 1 Tim 2:6 and 6:15, "time" (καιρός) carries the connotation of an "appointed" or "designated" period. If that is the case, then its occurrence in 2 Tim 3:1 may have a similar sense: it is a period of suffering appointed by God. This is not insignificant because of the general tendency to view seasons of suffering as expressions of God's absence.

41. Friberg and Friberg, *Analytical Greek New Testament*, s.v.

42. Köstenberger, *1–2 Timothy and Titus*, 225: "As Paul has written to the Ephesians, believers should be wise in how they live and make the most of every opportunity 'because the days are evil' (Eph 5:15–16)."

43. Towner, *Letters*, 552–53: "Such lists were often crafted for oral presentation, so that repetition of sounds and other rhythmic devices sharped the impact." Towner observes (553n2): "In vv. 2–4, nine words beginning with *a*; the *oi*- ending occurs fifteen times; the *ph*-sound eight times, five of them in compounds built on the stem *phil*."

troduction, "For human beings will be . . ." (ἔσονται γὰρ οἱ ἄνθρωποι). Paul's description of humanity appears misanthropic.[44] But it is helpful to keep in mind his apostolic labor to bring salvation to all people, which is indicative of his love for humanity. In addition, Paul's apparent misanthropy sheds some perspective on Paul's earlier statements in 1 Timothy: "First of all, then, I urge that supplications . . . be made for all human beings (ἀνθρώπων)" (1 Tim 2:1); "God desires all human beings (ἀνθρώπους) to be saved" (1 Tim 2:4); "For to this end we toil and strive, because we have our hope set on the living God, who is the Savior of all human beings (ἀνθρώπων)" (1 Tim 4:10). The juxtaposition of the vice-list that follows in 2 Tim 3:2–5a and these statements from 1 Timothy deepens our understanding of Paul's gospel: Jesus died for the unlovely, as epitomized in Paul himself (1 Tim 1:12–15). Thus, what follows in the vice-list is not an expression of Paul's misanthropic tendencies but a description of humanity that is meant to sober Timothy to the realities of life and ministry—human beings are fundamentally flawed beings in need of sovereign grace.

As we reflect on the vice-list, we should contrast it with the qualities of aspiring elders and deacons included in 1 Tim 3:1–13. The first two vices are "lovers-of-self, lovers-of-money" (φίλαυτοι, φιλάργυροι). These terms are perhaps mentioned first to reiterate what Paul says in Romans 1, namely that everyone is a worshiper. Every person gives himself to something or someone. The apostle argues that "human beings" are first and foremost devoted to the self instead of loving God above anything else; in short, they are selfish.[45] Second, they are "lovers-of-money." This echoes Paul's description of money in 1 Tim 6:10: "For the love-of-money (φιλαργυρία) is the root of all kinds of evil." Noteworthy is how Paul says in 1 Tim 3:3 that the aspiring elder must not be a "lover-of-money" (ἀφιλάργυρον). Similarly, the aspiring deacon must not [be] "greedy-for-dishonest-gain" (αἰσχροκερδεῖς, 1 Tim 3:8). Given elders and deacons are

---

These observations reiterate our thesis that 2 Timothy was written to be performed as a rhetorical piece before the audience of gathered believers.

44. By "human beings," Paul likely has in view specifically professing believers that had apostatized. Nevertheless, I am not entirely convinced that we should limit the scope of Paul's comments in this vice-list to this group (see, e.g., Towner, *Letters*, 554–55). To be sure, Paul is seeking to equip Timothy with a mature outlook on ministry, but such a perspective is very deficient if it lacks a more general understanding of how all "human beings" behave.

45. Interestingly, Philo connected love-of-self with atheism; see Towner, *Letters*, 555. This is worth further reflection.

supposed to embody the height of spiritual renewal, a "lover-of-money" represents what human beings are by nature.

Verse 2 goes on to include "boasters, arrogant, blasphemous." "Boasters" (ἀλαζόνες) connotes egotism, self-aggrandizement, and disproportionate confidence in the self. It is a natural outworking of loving—of trusting in—money because earthly wealth leads to a delusional sense of self-sufficiency.[46] Similarly, "arrogant" (ὑπερήφανοι) means to put on display one's position or accomplishments. Whatever distinction Paul sought to highlight between "boasters" and "arrogant" is unclear. But both reiterate Paul's initial descriptor, namely that people will be "lovers-of-self." This includes attempting to get others to join in their worship of themselves by showboating their feats. "Blasphemous" (βλάσφημοι) recalls Paul's self-description as a "blasphemer" (βλάσφημον) who once persecuted the church and denied Christ's lordship (1 Tim 1:13). Its inclusion here suggests that "human beings" will deny the reality and consequences of Christ's unique identity as the Son of God.

The next set of adjectives on the whole share a common alpha-prefix: "to their parents without-obedience, without-gratitude, without-holiness, without-feeling, without-reconciliation, devilish, without-self-control, without-tameness, without-loving-good" (3:2b–3).[47] "To their parents without-obedience" (γονεῦσιν ἀπειθεῖς) suggests a disregard for the natural order that God has established.[48] To rebel against authority is a strong theme in 1 Timothy where Paul presents the false teachers as those that rebel against Paul's apostolic authority.[49] "Without-gratitude" (ἀχάριστοι) is to be unthankful. Paul asserts that everything God has created—particularly marriage and food—is to be "received with thanksgiving by those who believe and know the truth" (1 Tim 4:3). Thanksgiving to the Maker and Giver of all good things is one way to express recognition of God's sovereign rule and mercy. This holds true particularly for believers that have received the gift of eternal life through the death and resurrection

---

46. See 1 Tim 6:17. Towner, *Letters*, 556: "This word lends itself well to descriptions of those who in their arrogance take themselves to be gods and in so doing oppose the one true God; human conceit that refuses to acknowledge God."

47. See similarly 1 Tim 1:9.

48. The translation here is deliberate, reflecting the linguistic transition to the vices marked off by the alpha prefix. Towner, *Letters*, 556: "At this point in the list, there is a slight shift in the rhythm as two words are used to construct the vice and a transition is made to negative words beginning with the Greek *a-* prefix."

49. See Titus 1:16 where Paul identifies this quality with the false teachers; see also Titus 3:3 and my comments in *To Exhort and Reprove* on both verses.

of the Son and the outpouring of the Spirit. "Without-holiness" (ἀνόσιοι) also occurs in the vice-list of 1 Tim 1:9, where it is coupled with the qualifier "profane." The basic sense of "without-holiness" is to live without any appreciation and reverence for the sacred.[50]

Verse 3 continues the list. "Without-feeling" (ἄστοργοι) means to lack affection, specifically the natural affection "of children and parents."[51] The suggestion is that human beings will become so increasingly depraved "in the last days" that they will lack even natural affections. "Without-reconciliation" means "implacable"—a stubborn commitment to hold on to resentment and bitterness, an unwillingness to make a treaty.[52] This represents a disposition opposite to that of God who has reconciled himself to humanity through the human Jesus (1 Tim 2:4–6). "Devilish" (διάβολοι), which momentarily breaks the alpha-prefix pattern, likely connotes "slanderous," being untruthful like the devil. It can also have the specific sense of maligning the reputation of those who are innocent.[53] This term occurs somewhat frequently in 1 and 2 Timothy.[54] In several of these instances, Paul associates the devil with a snare or trap. The sense here in 2 Tim 3:2 may be that people will fall increasingly under his influence and become more like him, especially with respect to deceit and rebelliousness.

"Without-self-control" (ἀκρατεῖς) represents the opposite of σωφρονισμός, which connotes moderation, temperance, prudence, discipline. "Self-control" is the trademark of all who profess godliness.[55] Earlier in the letter Paul declared that God has given to him and Timothy a Spirit of "power and love and self-control (σωφρονισμοῦ)" (2 Tim 1:7). To be "without-self-control," then, is to lack a basic Christian quality. "Without-tameness" (ἀνήμεροι) means "savage" or "brutal" like wild animals.[56] Paul underscored a few verses earlier that the slave of the Lord must not be belligerent but gentle to all. Savagery represents the antithesis of the gentleness that should mark God's people. "Without-loving-good"

50. Towner, *Letters*, 557: "The term views these sinners in terms of actions that show disregard for sacred duties or laws, or as people who live in rejection of sacred norms."

51. BDAG, s.v.

52. Friberg and Friberg, *Analytical Greek New Testament*, s.v.

53. Towner, *Letters*, 557.

54. 1 Tim 3:6, 7, 11; 2 Tim 2:26.

55. See, e.g., 1 Tim 2:9, 15 and my comments in *1 Timothy*.

56. See Titus 1:12 where Paul uses more explicit language to describe the agitators.

(ἀφιλάγαθοι) echoes the initial attributes of "lovers-of-self" and "lovers-of-money." Here Paul reiterates that human beings are lovers—just not lovers of that which is "good."[57] The sense here is that they have little, if any, interest in honoring God by abounding in good works toward mankind. In other words, people will become more like anti-philanthropists.[58]

Verse 4 continues the vice list: "treacherous, reckless, puffed-up, lovers-of-pleasure rather-than lovers-of-God." "Treacherous" (προδόται) means disloyal. It is an apt descriptor of those who have turned away from Paul and the gospel (1:15). The term also recalls Judas who betrayed Jesus because he was a lover-of-self and a lover-of-money. "Reckless" (προπετεῖς) literally means "falling headlong" and is figuratively applied here to mean "thoughtless."[59] Paul probably means something akin to living without a sense of the divine. More specifically, it likely means the lack of intentionality in life despite God's revelation in Christ Jesus. "Puffed-up" (τετυφωμένοι) means very proud. This term is used to describe the elder that has been appointed prematurely and has therefore become "puffed-up" (τυφωθείς, 1 Tim 3:6). It is also used to describe the false teachers who reject sound teaching and, as a result, become "puffed-up" (τετύφωται, 1 Tim 6:4). In a sense, it is the defining marker of all who reject the gospel because grace effects the opposite character.

Verse 4 concludes with a forceful contrast: "lovers-of-pleasure rather than lovers-of-God." "Lovers-of-pleasure" (φιλήδονοι) likely has something more specific in view than general hedonism. It could mean lovers-of-sensual-pleasure, which stands in opposition to God and is spiritually destructive.[60] The contrast "rather than" (μᾶλλον ἤ) reminds us that all people are lovers and worshipers. The problem is that some are loving the wrong things and persons. They love themselves, money, and pleasure instead of loving the one true God. There seems to be some echo here of 1 Tim 6:10 and 17 where Paul describes the pitfalls of loving and placing one's ultimate hope in money instead of God.

---

57. Towner, *Letters*, 558: "Within the list, this 'disinterest in good' is the corollary of the first vice, 'an excessive interest in self.' The willful inward turn of the heart and emotions robs the individual of the capacity to love the good."

58. Cf. Jeon, *Christian Philanthropy*, which underscores how God's own love-for-mankind is meant to create a people who are devoted to doing tangible and abundant good to all. See also Titus 1:8 and my comments in *To Exhort and Reprove*.

59. Friberg and Friberg, *Analytical Greek New Testament*, s.v.

60. Friberg and Friberg, *Analytical Greek New Testament*, s.v.

Paul concludes this vice list with the summary condemnation: "having the form of godliness but its power denying." The controlling thought is that in the last days people will appear godly but prove otherwise: their behavior and attitude expose their counterfeit faith. The term "form" (μόρφωσιν) means "outward appearance" or "external shape." Paul's point in the first half of the condemnation is that many will "have" (ἔχοντες) the mold of "godliness" (εὐσεβείας). This is helpful to highlight because the word "heretic" can conjure images of dark and brutal villains. The apostle, however, indicates otherwise. False teachers and troublemakers will very much "look Christian."[61] At the same time, such imposters "deny" (ἠρνημένοι) the transformative and tangible "power" (δύναμιν) of "godliness." The mention of "power" is significant because Paul uses it twice in the letter to indicate a marker of true faith. According to 2 Tim 1:7 God has given believers a "spirit of . . . power (δυνάμεως) and love and self-control." In the very next verse, the apostle exhorts Timothy to "share-together for the gospel according to the power (δύναμιν) of God" (2 Tim 1:8). Paul's point in 2 Tim 3:5a is that people will appear godly, but the sincerity of their faith—or the lack of—will be evidenced in their application of divine power, especially as that power is expressed in the ability to endure suffering.

This point of appearing godly but denying its reality is found also in 1 Timothy. Paul says of the supposed believer: "But if anyone does not provide for his relatives, and especially for the members of his household, he has denied (ἤρνηται) the faith and is worse than an unbeliever" (1 Tim 5:8). Paul argues that believers must "first learn to show godliness (εὐσεβεῖν) to their own household . . . for this is pleasing in the sight of God" (1 Tim 5:4).[62] In this 1 Timothy passage, the professing believers exhibit "the form of godliness" but effectively "deny its power" by their refusal to care for their own. Similarly, the false teachers deny "the teaching that accords with godliness (εὐσέβειαν)" (1 Tim 6:3) and imagine that "godliness (εὐσέβειαν) is a means of gain" (1 Tim 6:5). Here too Paul argues that these false teachers put on a show of "godliness," but their love for money manifests their ungodliness. True "godliness," in contrast to "the form of godliness," makes tangible differences for the believer. Finally, in the second chapter of 2 Timothy, Paul argues that "the power

---

61. The term "godliness" (εὐσέβεια) indicates authentic Christian existence; see its multiple occurrences in 1 Timothy (2:2; 3:16; 4:7, 8; 6:3, 5, 6, 11).

62. For further reflections, see my comments in *1 Timothy*. See also Titus 1:16 and my comments in *To Exhort and Reprove*.

of God"—if it is not denied—will empower the believer not to "deny (ἀρνησόμεθα) him" (2 Tim 2:12); that is, true "godliness" is revealed through the "power" to persevere.

2 Timothy 3:5b–6

Becoming a Useful Vessel by Avoiding Household Breakers

(A' Element)

Verse 5b initiates the closing A' element (3:5b–6). Following his vice-list, Paul inserts the exhortation, "and these (τούτους) turn-from." Paul echoes a similar command in 2:21 of the corresponding A element ("if someone purifies himself from these [τούτων]"). No doubt Paul has teased out through the chiastic progression—particularly in 3:2–5a—whom "these" refer to. Perhaps the best way to understand the negative command "and these turn-from" (ἀποτρέπου) is to view it as a contrast to the positive command in 2:22, also found in the corresponding A element: "pursue righteousness, faith, love, peace with those who invoke the Lord from a pure heart." The present tense of the command "turn-from" suggests that Paul is referencing to a present reality. Moreover, to "turn-from" such persons may have in view church-discipline, which Paul mentions in 2:25–26. To separate from those that profess godliness but deny its power could take the form of excluding them from the fellowship of the saints through church discipline for the sake of their restoration.

Verse 6, which concludes the fourth microchiasm, continues Paul's description of what people will be like "in the last days," though it is clear now that he is referring to the false teachers. He writes, "For from these are those-who-slip into the households and captivate foolish-women who-are-weighed with sins." Paul begins the sentence with the explanatory "for" (γάρ), which suggests that he does not suppose Timothy is beyond the reach of temptation. He too can go astray through the small but regular influence of these troublemakers; hence, the command to "turn-from" such persons.

The phrase "from these" (ἐκ τούτων) suggests that Paul is thinking of a sub-group from "these" (τούτους; 2 Tim 3:5b). Paul describes this sub-set as "those-who-slip into the households and captivate foolish-women." The image is vivid: "those-who-slip" (οἱ ἐνδύνοντες) describes secret in-filtrators who worm their way into homes. The mention of "households" (οἰκίας) is significant for two reasons. First, it recalls the opening illustration of a "great house (οἰκίᾳ)" in the corresponding A element (2:20-22). The occurrence of "household" in the A' element suggests some relationship between the wooden and clay vessels mentioned in 2:20 and these furtive infiltrators. Second, the "household" is the controlling image in 1 Timothy.[63] Just as the false teachers were disrupting God's "household," so too this subgroup is upsetting specific "households" by captivating certain women. The use of the participle "captivate" (αἰχμαλωτίζοντες) is ironic, given Paul himself is currently a prisoner. The sense of the verb in this context is "to gain mastery over."

Paul shifts focus in the remainder of 3:6 from the troublemakers to their targets. It is unclear why women were more susceptible to the false teaching, although it is clear that Paul is referring to a specific subset of women.[64] Paul specifies that he has in mind "foolish-women who-are-weighed with sins, led by many desires." Paul's discussion of younger widows (1 Tim 5:11-15) may be instructive here. Paul says of the "younger widows" that they have sexual desires (5:11) that are so strong that they are drawn from their commitment to Christ (5:12). Also, they are foolish in that they are idlers going about from house to house as gossips and busybodies (5:13). For these reasons, Paul commands younger widows to marry in order to satiate their sexual desires and busy themselves with good works.[65] The term "foolish-women" (γυναικάρια) in 2 Tim 3:6 literally translates "little women" and is used in a derogatory sense to express idleness, frivolity, and immaturity.[66] In this regard, the term is a fitting descriptor of the younger widows in 1 Tim 5:11-15.

---

63. See my comments in related sections of 1 Timothy; see esp. my comments on 1 Tim 3:5 and 3:15.

64. Towner, Letters, 561-62: "Many recent scholars link this tendency to prey on women with Gnosticism. But the practice of singling out women was far more widespread and connected with the belief that they were more easily swayed by novel ideas than were men. In some way or other, the focus on women might have been compensation for the false teachers' commitment to an ascetical regime (i.e., religious activity among women in place of sexual activity; cf. 1 Tim 4:3). Otherwise, the appeal of the teaching for women is not immediately clear. But from other relevant texts it is reasonable to imagine that the false teaching included a new ascetical approach to the traditional female role in the household and community, or endorsed a cultural trend that was influencing Christian women from outside the church (see on 1 Tim 2:9-15)."

65. For further commends on these "younger widows," see my comments on this section in Jeon, 1 Timothy.

66. Friberg and Friberg, Analytical Greek New Testament, s.v.

Paul goes on to state that these women are "weighed with sins." The participle "weighed" (σεσωρευμένα) means to be "overwhelmed by" or "burdened with" something. The image of being overwhelmed seems to echo the way in which younger widows are overcome by the desire for sexual intimacy. Therefore, the "sins" (ἁμαρτίαις) in view may involve sexual relations outside of the covenant of marriage. This would have been an acute problem, given the false teachers were forbidding marriage (1 Tim 4:3). Either way, whatever specific "sins" Paul has in mind, their weight has made these specific women particularly vulnerable to the influence of the false teachers. Such "foolish-women" are also "led by many desires." This condition may represent the outworking of being so "weighed with sins" that they cannot help but sin. The passive voice of the participle "led" (ἀγόμενα) conveys a lack of strength or resolve. The multiplicity of desires ("many") also reiterates how vulnerable and weak such women are. The term "desires" (ἐπιθυμίαις) echoes its earlier occurrence in 2:22 of the corresponding A element: "But youthful desires flee (ἐπιθυμίας) . . ." This parallelism supports the idea that the "foolish-women" in view are likely the "younger widows" who are filled with many "youthful desires." As noted in our analysis of v. 22, it may be that these "foolish-women" are also preoccupied with the "desire" for more money (1 Tim 6:9). That is, "desire" does not have to be restricted to sexual "desire," given Paul underscores that they are "led by many (ποικίλαις) desires."

Paul's focus, however, is not on these "foolish-women" (which are to be understood in contrast to the godly women he describes in 1 Tim 2 and the godly widow of 1 Tim 5), but on the subgroup of false teachers who take advantage of them.[67] Knowing how weak and vulnerable this subgroup of widows is, these imposters of godliness take advantage of them by worming into their homes and using their "many desires" against them. This is especially heinous. Indeed, the downward spiral implicit in the vice list has prepared Paul's audience to hear this final assessment of the false teachers: they take advantage of the most vulnerable. Again, Paul's exhortation is that Timothy is to "turn-from" these, which likely means not just avoidance but also discipline.

---

67. Köstenberger, *1–2 Timothy and Titus*, 258: "The overall picture is that these women lack dignity and self-restraint, are weak mentally and morally, are caught in bondage to their sinful desires, and are trapped in a cycle of futility . . . Nevertheless, primary culpability rests not with the victims of the false teaching but with the false teachers."

7

2 Timothy 3:7–17

Remain in Salvation through Faith in Christ Jesus

(D' UNIT)

THIS CHAPTER EXAMINES THE fifth of eight microchiastic units within the 2 Timothy macrochiasm. Having warned Timothy against the influence of agitators, Paul encourages Timothy to persevere by abiding in Christ. He picks up on his description of the wayward women and exhorts Timothy to anchor himself in the things he has already learned, especially from the apostle.

The Fifth Microchiastic Unit

The fourth of eight microchiasms within 2 Timothy is composed carefully of four elements (A-B-B'-A'). Linguistic parallels are indicated by the Greek text.

A. 7 always learning (μανθάνοντα) and never toward a knowledge of the truth having-power (δυνάμενα) to come. 8a But in the way Jannes and Jambres opposed Moses, thus these also oppose the truth, human beings corrupted in mind,

    B. 8b without-qualification regarding the faith (τὴν πίστιν).
    9 Rather they will not progress upon much (προκόψουσιν

ἐπὶ πλεῖον); for the without-mindedness of theirs will be
plain to all, as was (ἐγένετο) that also of those.

B′. 10 But you yourself have followed the teaching of mine, the
way, the purpose, the faith (τῇ πίστει), the long-suffering,
the love, the endurance, 11 the persecutions, the sufferings that were (ἐγένετο) to me at Antioch, at Iconium,
at Lystra—which persecutions I also bore-up—and from
all the Lord rescued me. 12 But also all who-desire to live
in-a-godly-manner in Christ Jesus will be persecuted,
13 but evil human beings and impostors will progress to
worse (προκόψουσιν ἐπὶ τὸ χεῖρον), deceiving and being
deceived.

A′. 14 But you yourself endure in the things you learned (ἔμαθε) and
were-persuaded-of, knowing from those you learned (ἔμαθες), 15
and that from childhood the sacred writings you have known that
have-power (δυνάμενά) to wisen you for salvation through faith
in Christ Jesus. 16 All Scripture is God-Spirited and useful toward
teaching, toward reproof, toward correction, toward training in
righteousness, 17 that complete may be the human being of God,
toward all good work equipped.

2 Timothy 3:7–8a

THE ROAD TO NOWHERE

(A ELEMENT)

Paul's final descriptor of the vulnerable women focuses on their inability
to repent: "always learning and never toward a knowledge of the truth
having-power to come." Notice the rhythmic quality of the contrast between "always" (πάντοτε) and "never" (μηδέποτε). It is somewhat striking
that the verb "learning" (μανθάνοντα) occurs in 1 and 2 Timothy mainly
in relation to women: "A woman in quietness must learn" (μανθανέτω;
1 Tim 2:11); "Besides that, [younger widows] learn (μανθάνουσιν) to be
idlers" (1 Tim 5:13). In any case, in 2 Tim 3:7 the apostle underscores the
regularity—perhaps the frenetic quality—of their learning. "The picture
drawn depicts them as constantly seeking out every kind of teaching . . . to

grasping at any and all teaching."[1] Despite all their efforts, however, they seem incapable of change. The force of the verb "being-able" (δυνάμενα) is highlighted elsewhere. In 1 Tim 6:7, Paul indicates that human beings "brought nothing into the world and that we are not able (δυνάμεθα) to take anything out." A few verses later, he says that God "dwells in unapproachable light, whom no one has ever seen or is able (δύναται) to see" (1 Tim 6:16). Closer to home, Paul declared that even "if we are-without-faith, he remains faithful—for he is not able (δύναται) to deny himself" (2 Tim 2:13). Thus, in his selection of this verb, the apostle underscores a critical flaw in the spirituality of these erudite women.

As noted already in 2:25 of the corresponding D element, the phrase "toward a knowledge of the truth" (εἰς ἐπίγνωσιν ἀληθείας) refers to repentance.[2] Its occurrence here is significant, filling out the operative term "perhaps" (μήποτε) in 2 Tim 2:25. While Paul hopes that some might repent, that is, "come toward a knowledge of the truth" through church-discipline, he recognizes that there are some—humanly speaking—that may "never" change despite their vast learning.

Returning specifically to the agitators that worm their way into the homes of impressionable women, Paul draws a comparison from Israel's history. He writes: "But in the way Jannes and Jambres opposed Moses, thus these also oppose the truth." Paul associates the false teachers with "Jannes and Jambres" ("in the way . . . thus . . .") by underscoring how both groups oppose God's servants and revelation. We are not given a great deal of information in the exodus narrative of how "Jannes and Jambres" (Ἰάννης καὶ Ἰαμβρῆς) challenged "Moses" (Μωϋσεῖ), other than that they sought to replicate Aaron's miracles.[3] The nature of the opposi-

---

1. Towner, *Letters*, 563.

2. Regarding the different occurrences of the phrase "knowledge of the truth," see 1 Tim 2:4; Titus 1:1; and my respective comments in *1 Timothy* and *To Exhort and Reprove*.

3. Some argue, however, that Jannes and Jambres were Jewish opponents of Moses from among the Israelites; see Köstenberger on the debate around the identity of these men in *1–2 Timothy and Titus*, 258–59. Regardless of the actual sources of their names, this much is clear, namely that both men represented opposition to God and his divine purposes. Towner explains (*Letters*, 564): "What is noticeable, apart from varieities of spelling and variance from single to double mention of the two characters, is the way the tradition elevated their roles to archetypal status. They came to represent Moses' archnemeses, who would counter his displays of divine power with various tricks of their own; and by their association with various stories (such as Balaam's servants or sons, trailing Israel through the wilderness, and instigating the Golden Calf rebellion), they acquired a symbolic status as opponents of the truth. Paul's purpose is to place

tion seems to have been something along the lines of giving a pretense of power. Perhaps most noteworthy here is that Paul compares himself, as he does in 2 Cor 3:4–18, to one of the most important figures in the OT. In doing so, he again reiterates his status as a servant in the line of uniquely appointed prophetic servants of the Lord.[4]

The verb "oppose" (literally "stand-against") occurs twice in 3:8a (ἀντέστησαν, ἀνθίστανται) to reiterate the parallelism between "these" (οὗτοι), that is, the false teachers, and Jannes and Jambres. The comparison, however, is not exact. Whereas in the first instance the opposition was against a person (Moses), in the second instance it is against "the truth" (τῇ ἀληθείᾳ). The "truth," as we have noted, is the "truth" of Paul's gospel.[5] But this distinction is overstated because Paul identified so deeply with "the truth" that to reject his gospel or his apostleship was one and the same.[6] Thus, when he writes, "these also oppose the truth," he is essentially saying, "these also oppose me, a second and greater Moses."

Of such persons, Paul adds two qualifiers. First, they are "human beings corrupted in mind." The use of "human beings" (ἄνθρωποι) recalls its identical occurrence in the nominative plural in 3:2: "For human beings (ἄνθρωποι) will be lovers-of-self . . ."[7] The progression from the D unit (3:8a) to the D' unit (3:2) suggests that "Jannes and Jambres" stand as archetypes of all depraved "human beings." Verse 8a also echoes 1 Tim 6:5 where Paul describes the false teachers as "human beings corrupted in mind" (διεφθαρμένων ἀνθρώπων τὸν νοῦν).[8] The "mind" in Paul's letter's refers to"the faculty of moral perception and insight" or even the "total inner orientation."[9] The corruption of their minds is evident in the way these false teachers suppose that "godliness is a means of gain": their love of money keeps them from understanding and embracing the

---

the false teachers troubling the Ephesian church into the same category as those who oppose God's work and who will consequently never succeed, and more implicitly to establish the connection between Moses's authority as YHWH's specially appointed servant and his own apostolic ministry (just as in 2:18–19)."

4. See previous note.

5. See my comments on 1 Tim 2:4, 7; cf. 3:15; 4:3; 6:5; 2 Tim 2:15, 18, 25.

6. See esp. Gal 1:11–12.

7. This is in distinction to "faithful human beings (ἀνθρώποις)," which occurs in the dative case, who are able to teach others (2 Tim 2:2).

8. See also Titus 1:15 and my comments in *To Exhort and Reprove*. In 1–2 Timothy and Titus, Paul describes his opponents by underscoring the fallen quality of their minds.

9. Friberg and Friberg, *Analytical Greek New Testament*, s.v. See, e.g., Rom 7:25.

gospel.[10] Similarly, in 3:8a such corruption is evident in their willingness to invade the homes of weak and impressionable women. Paul's point is that these false teachers are so depraved "in mind" that they cannot possibly function as models of "truth" for the believers.

2 Timothy 3:8b–9

THE OUTCOME OF THE ROAD TO NOWHERE

(B ELEMENT)

In the B element, Paul continues his condemnation of the false teachers by adding they are "without-qualification regarding the faith" (3:8b).[11] The phrase "regarding the faith" (περὶ τὴν πίστιν) occurs twice in 1 Timothy at the bookends of the letter to describe the agitators: at the beginning of 1 Timothy, "have become a shipwreck regarding the faith (περὶ τὴν πίστιν; 1:19)" and at the end, "have swerved regarding the faith (περὶ τὴν πίστιν; 6:21)." In a sense, 2 Tim 3:8b functions as a climax to these previous statements: given the false teachers have become a shipwreck and have missed the mark, they have proven that they are "disqualified regarding the faith." Paul's statement regarding the prospective deacon elucidates the meaning of the adjective "disqualified" (ἀδόκιμοι): "But these deacons must indeed be tested (δοκιμαζέσθωσαν) first, then they-must-serve-as-deacons, being above-reproach" (3:10). "Disqualified" in context likely means that these professing teachers have been tested and have been found wanting because of their love of money and their attack on the weak and vulnerable. Such behaviors expose the absence of true conversion and communion with God.

Returning to the present situation, the apostle assures Timothy of the fate of these false teachers in 3:9a: "Rather they will not progress (οὐ προκόψουσιν) upon much." This pronouncement recalls 2 Tim 2:16b: "for upon more irreverence they will progress" (ἐπὶ πλεῖον γὰρ προκόψουσιν ἀσεβείας). On the surface it may appear that things are faring well for these troublemakers even as Paul suffers alone in prison. In reality, however, the only "progress" they are making is into deeper

10. For further reflection, see my comments on 1 Tim 6:5 (and following) in *1 Timothy*.

11. Titus 1:16: "God they profess to know, but by their works deny, being detestable and disobedient and disqualified (ἀδόκιμοι) for all good work."

ungodliness. Moreover, as was the case with Moses's opponents, any apparent "progress" they enjoy will soon end. The prepositional phrase "upon much" (ἐπὶ πλεῖον) can mean "at length" or "very far." Thus, v. 9a stresses that their end is imminent; hence the useful translation of the NASB, "But they will not make further progress."

Paul goes on to explain (γάρ) why their progress will be short-lived: "for the without-mindedness of theirs will be plain to all (πᾶσιν), as was that also of those." The noun "without-mindedness" (ἄνοια), which could be translated more basically as "folly," stands in stark contrast to Timothy who will receive insight from the Lord "in all [things]" (πᾶσιν; 2 Tim 2:7). The descriptor "plain" (ἔκδηλος) means that their foolishness will become abundantly obvious. Given, however, that their folly is not evident in the present moment, the question must be raised: When will all this take place? Moreover, to whom will it become "plain"? Does "all" include everyone in general or to all the believers? 1 Tim 4:15, which reflects some conceptual similarity, suggests that Paul may be speaking (in 2 Tim 2:9) about the present: "These things practice . . . that your progress might be evident to all" (πᾶσιν). Perhaps it is the case, then, that the folly of these false teachers will soon become evident to all the believers. However, the overall outlook of 2 Timothy is on the day of final judgement.[12] Moreover, Paul possessed the maturity to know that not all injustice and sorrow will be undone in this life. Thus, it seems more likely that this manifestation of folly will be made plain to all human beings on the day of judgment.

This interpretation gains support from the closing statement "as was that also of those" (ὡς καὶ ἡ ἐκείνων ἐγένετο). Paul is referring to the folly of Jannes and Jambres. Paul could be referring to how the serpent from Aaron's staff quickly defeated the serpents of Pharaoh's wise men and sorcerers (Exod 7:11–12). But there is no indication that after this event, the hearts and minds of all were changed. More than likely, their folly became evident after God's destructive judgment brought Pharaoh to his knees.[13] The point, however, of all this is to remind Timothy and the believers

---

12. See, e.g., my comments on 2 Tim 1:16–18.

13. Towner, *Letters*, 567: "The closing statement compares the folly of the present-day opponents with that of Jannes and Jambres . . . the futility of their opposition to the God of Israel was finally demonstrated when they could no longer produce imitations of the miracles worked by Moses (see Exod 7:12; 8:18; 9:11)." See also the extended comments on the identity of Jannes and Jambres and their rhetorical function in the passage by Köstenberger, *1–2 Timothy and Titus*, 258–61.

with him of God's ultimate victory, even—and perhaps especially—in the face of apparent defeat.

2 Timothy 3:10-13

THE ROAD TO SOMEWHERE

(B' ELEMENT)

Having made clear the final outcome of those opposed to the truth of the gospel, Paul now completes the thought of 3:5. The compliment Paul provides to the command "avoid such people" is that Timothy would remember the path he has followed up to now.[14] In a sense, the B' element echoes the theme of remembrance found in the opening of the letter (1:3-7).

Paul begins this element by reminding Timothy: "But you yourself have followed the teaching of mine, the way, the purpose, the faith, the long-suffering, the love, the endurance."[15] The repetition of the article is intentional, communicating a rhythmic quality to the reminder; one can almost hear a dramatic pause at the end of each noun. The declaration "But you yourself" (Σὺ δέ) is intended to draw a clear line between Timothy and those that oppose Paul. The apostle seems fond of using this phrasing to mark off a strong contrast. For instance, in 1 Tim 6:10, Paul says that the love of money is the root of all evils and that some have wandered from the faith because of their desire for it. Verse 11 begins with the same words: "But you yourself (Σὺ δέ), O human being of God, these things flee." Even as many give themselves over to money and heresy, Timothy is to "follow" (παρηκολούθησάς) Paul's gospel; that is, he is to give his full attention and energy to upholding the truth he has received. This verb recalls 1 Tim 4:6 where Paul exhorts Timothy to transmit the

---

14. Towner, *Letters*, 569–70: "Still within the broader framework of parenesis to Timothy (3:1—4:8), this section renews the call to Timothy to follow Paul and share in the apostolic sufferings. It is presented as the antithesis to the ways of the opponents, a technique that Paul uses in each letter to Timothy to denounce error and accentuate genuine godliness. To sharpen the contrast, Paul matches the vice list above (vv. 2–5) with a commendatory list of nine virtues and experiences that characterized his ministry."

15. The placement of the personal pronoun μου before all the "virtues" that follow indicates that the proper sense of the verse is, "But you yourself have followed my teaching, my way, my purpose, my faith, etc."

sound "words of the faith and of the commendable teaching" that he has "followed" (παρηκολούθηκας) to "the brothers." Now, Paul is summoning Timothy himself to continue in the faith that he has been commending in the face of apostasy.

Second, Timothy 3:10 contains the first occurrence of "teaching" (διδασκαλία). But this term occurs abundantly in 1 Timothy.[16] The "teaching" in 1 Timothy is specifically "healthy teaching that is according to the gospel" (1:10–11). Paul's teaching, then, is his gospel. Noteworthy is the priority "teaching" has in this "list of virtues." "Conduct" (ἀγωγῇ) means more than just behavior. It is the pursuit of a deliberate lifestyle—the "act of conducting one's life in a certain way."[17] As Paul's letters evidence, the apostle viewed his life as a stage for the gospel to play out. Therefore, his partners for the gospel and the beneficiaries of his ministry had a tangible expression of what it means to live in step with the gospel. This held true especially for Timothy. "Purpose" (προθέσει) recalls Paul's earlier declaration of how God saved his people "not according to our works; rather according to his own purpose (πρόθεσιν) and grace" (1:9). Paul has already expressed his purpose in terms of faithfulness to his calling as preacher, apostle, and teacher. Paul's purpose in life is to guard what has been entrusted to him "since his aim is to please the one who enlisted him" (2:4). Paul's purpose aligns with divine purpose because both seek to advance salvation for God's elect, especially among the Gentiles.

"Faith" (πίστει) can refer to the act of having faith in God, expressed concretely in faithfulness, or the content of faith. Given that its occurrence here parallels "the faith" (τὴν πίστιν) in 3:8b of the corresponding B element, the former is more likely. The chiastic movement conveys a basic contrast: the false teachers are found wanting "regarding the faith" whereas Paul has demonstrated—especially through his suffering—that he possesses genuine "faith" in God. "Long-suffering" (μακροθυμίᾳ), commonly translated as "patience," recalls Paul's "testimony": "But I received mercy for this reason, that in me, as the foremost, Jesus Christ might display his perfect long-suffering (μακροθυμίαν) as an example to those who were to believe in him for eternal life" (1 Tim 1:16). Its mention here in v. 10 underscores how Paul's own experience of Christ's long-suffering has enabled him to suffer patiently for the sake of the gospel. "Love" (ἀγάπη) is referring to the supernatural gift that comes

16. See 1 Tim 1:10; 4:1, 6, 13, 16; 5:17; 6:1, 3. See also related terms like ἑτεροδιδασκαλεῖν in 1 Tim 1:3 and νομοδιδάσκαλοι in 1:7.

17. See my further comments in *Living Intentionally*.

from union with Christ. In 2 Tim 1:13 Paul exhorted, "Follow the pattern of the sound words that you have heard from me, in the faith and love (ἀγάπη) that are in Christ Jesus."[18] Such "love" is from God and is expressed in love for the saints.

"Endurance" (ὑπομονῇ) echoes Paul's earlier words: "Therefore I endure (ὑπομένω) everything for the sake of the elect" (2:10). The mention of Paul's own "endurance" is significant because again it is an indirect summons for Timothy to do likewise: "if we endure (ὑπομένομεν), we will also reign with him" (2 :12). "Endurance," in a sense, captures the abiding theme of the letter—that Timothy would endure in the faith he has received (1:3–7); that Timothy would endure even as Paul has endured all suffering (1:8–11); that Timothy should endure, following the example of Onesiphorus (1:13—2:1); that Timothy should consider the endurance exhibited by soldiers, athletes, and farmers (2:4–19); that without endurance it is impossible to become a useful vessel for God (2:20—3:6).

Verse 11 is marked off from 3:10 most likely because it appears that Paul shifts to focus on specific incidents versus specific qualities.[19] This shift may serve to bring special attention to what follows. The apostle makes reference to "the persecutions, the sufferings that were to me at Antioch, at Iconium, at Lystra." "Persecutions" (διωγμοῖς), which literally translates "pursuits, chases," might be referring to how Jews chased Paul down until he was presumed dead (Acts 14:19–20). One can only imagine how unnerving it must have been to have his life under constant impending danger because of the gospel. "Sufferings" (παθήμασιν) include the emotional turmoil Paul must have experienced while trying to attend to the needs of various churches. The term certainly includes the physical sufferings he endured as well. Taken together, "persecutions" and "sufferings" distinguish Paul as an apostle that has identified fully with the Lord in contrast to the antagonists that resemble Jannes and Jambres. Moreover, Paul's mention of these experiences reiterates to Timothy and the audience that all genuine disciples should expect some degree of "persecutions" and "sufferings" if they are following Christ.

Paul guards against abstraction by specifying such suffering "were to me at Antioch, at Iconium, at Lystra" (οἷά μοι ἐγένετο ἐν Ἀντιοχείᾳ, ἐν Ἰκονίῳ, ἐν Λύστροις). The echo of ἐγένετο to its parallel occurrence in 3:9b seems to underscore the historicity of what transpired: as the folly of

---

18. See also my comments on 2 Tim 2:22.

19. Note also the shift from singular to plural nouns.

Moses's opposition actually happened, so too did Paul's persecution and suffering. Acts 13:13—14:23 provides some insight into the sort of persecutions and sufferings Paul endured: jealousy and opposition, including reviling (13:45); persecution—being driven out of Iconium (13:50–51); continuous opposition from the Jews who sought to thwart their efforts (14:2); failed attempts to be stoned (14:5); fleeing for safety (14:6); being worshipped (14:8–18); dragged out, stoned, and left for dead (14:19–20). The force of these references to Antioch, Iconium, and Lystra underscores that Paul was no stranger to suffering: he suffered deeply and regularly in order to bring the gospel especially to the Gentiles. Also, this reference to the past contextualizes Paul's present imprisonment: suffering is the norm for all who aspire to live for Christ.[20]

Paul is careful to bring attention not just to his persecutions and sufferings but, more so, to his endurance: "which persecutions I also bore-up."[21] The verb "bore-up" (ὑπήνεγκα) means that he did not falter under the heavy burden of ministry. That is, he endured by faithfully carrying out his calling as a preacher, apostle, and teacher for the sake of the elect. This is especially extraordinary given that in Lystra Paul not only was stoned and dragged out of the city, but also survived. Anyone that survives such a traumatic experience would have been tempted to cave in to fear and despair. Paul, however, asserts that he did not lose hope but continued to hold up amid all the suffering.

Verse 11, however, does not end with Paul's perseverance but on God's deliverance: "and from all the Lord rescued me." The verb "rescued" (ἐρρύσατο) means "bringing someone out of severe and acute danger."[22] The use here is somewhat ironic, given Paul is in prison. In context, however, Paul is describing how God spared him of death at Antioch, Iconium, and Lystra even in the face of such harrowing circumstances. More so, the declaration is a clear echo of Ps 33:20 LXX: "and out of them

---

20. Towner, *Letters*, 574: "The point of this return to the past is not to introduce new information, for Timothy probably joined Paul not too many months after these episodes (Acts 16:1), and he would have known well the experiences of Paul in Lystra and Iconium (16:2). What Paul does is to remind him of the pattern that is still in effect; therefore, in a sense, Paul's Roman imprisonment is simply a matter of consistency."

21. The relative clause here serves neither as a bridge to recall the first half of 3:11 (e.g., TNIV) nor as an emphasis on the degree of Paul's suffering (NRSV). Instead, it underscores Paul's endurance of the persecutions and sufferings he experienced. Given the letter's burden is to encourage endurance, we should not be surprised that Paul again reiterates his own perseverance as an example for Timothy to remember.

22. Friberg and Friberg, *Analytical Greek New Testament*, s.v.

all the Lord will deliver them."[23] The psalm is speaking of the righteous. By appropriating the promise of deliverance, Paul is aligning himself with the prophets of old, and particularly with Jesus, the final righteous prophet that experienced ultimate deliverance. This self-identification with the saints of the past recalls Paul's opening description of Timothy's faith as that which he inherited from his grandmother Lois and his mother Eunice (1:5). Paul's point is that God will be faithful in delivering Paul and Timothy just as he exhibited such faithfulness to the saints of old. Therefore, Timothy and all that follow in his footsteps need only to continue in the teaching and faith they have received.

The force of the "all" (πάντων) is that such deliverance was not a one-time occurrence. Rather, we witness God's faithfulness and sovereignty over an array of circumstances. Paul's point is not so much a promise that God will always deliver his servants from danger and death. Rather, Paul's point is that his life is ultimately under the sovereign reign of God. In this sense, he is a prisoner of the Lord—both as one who is in prison for the sake of the gospel and as one who is where he is according to the rule of God.

In v. 12, Paul then describes how his own experience provides a type for all believers: "But also all who-desire to live in-a-godly-manner in Christ Jesus will be persecuted." Paul states this almost as a maxim: this is the fate of all believers. This is the force of the future tense "*will* be persecuted" (διωχθήσονται). The maxim-like quality is also reflected in the use of "all" (πάντες): there is no exception. The "all" is specified as "those who-desire to live in-a-godly-manner in Christ Jesus" (οἱ θέλοντες εὐσεβῶς ζῆν ἐν Χριστῷ Ἰησοῦ). The verb "desire" occurs in several other places in 1 Timothy to express an earnest and controlling desire.[24] Paul, then, is distinguishing the "godly" from those who, according to 3:5 of the corresponding D element, have the "appearance of godliness (εὐσεβείας)" but deny its power or those that are "always learning and never toward a knowledge of the truth having-power to come" (3:7).

The sense of "godly" (εὐσεβῶς) here is probably referring to the avoidance of false teaching and the pursuit of sound doctrine versus a general sense of pursuing righteousness.[25] Similarly, it is the pursuit of

23. A comparison of the Greek brings out the force of the parallelism:

Ps 33:20 LXX: καὶ ἐκ πασῶν αὐτῶν ῥύσεται αὐτούς

2 Tim 3:11: καὶ ἐκ πάντων με ἐρρύσατο ὁ κύριος

24. See 1 Tim 1:7; 2:4; 5:11.

25. See esp. 1 Tim 4:7 and 6:3; see also 1 Tim 2:2; 3:16; 4:8; 6:5, 6, 11.

a lifestyle that corresponds to the gospel of grace. Such godliness is only possible by virtue of being "in Christ Jesus" (ἐν Χριστῷ Ἰησοῦ), a phrase that occurs regularly in this letter.[26] Paul's basic verdict is that those who make a sincere effort to work out a lifestyle that accords with being united to Christ will inevitably suffer—albeit to a different degree—the same fate he suffered. They "will be persecuted."

It is important not to miss the force of Paul's words. He is saying to Timothy—and to all believers—that he should not be surprised by suffering. The apostle is not suggesting that Timothy should pursue suffering, as if Christianity were an instrument for masochism. But Paul recognizes that having an appropriate framework for suffering makes all the difference in the actual experience of suffering. He alludes to this in his brief comments on his own calling: "for which I was appointed a preacher and apostle and teacher, which is why I suffer as I do" (1:11–12a). This is also implied in Paul's use of the examples of soldier, athlete, and farmer. No one goes into any of these professions assuming that they will not experience suffering. In his concern to promote faithfulness and endurance on the part of Timothy, Paul reiterates what Jesus himself stated, namely, that persecution, rejection, and imprisonment represent the normal experience of the authentic servant of the Lord. Those who "pursue (δίωκε) righteousness" (2:22) will inevitably "be persecuted" (διωχθήσονται).

In contrast ("but"; δέ) to the godly are "evil human beings and impostors" (πονηροὶ . . . ἄνθρωποι καὶ γόητες). Such "evil human beings" diverge from "faithful human beings (πιστοῖς ἀνθρώποις), who will be able to also teach others" the gospel (2:2). Whether Paul is specifying the identity of "evil human beings" or referring to a different group by "impostors" (γόητες) is unclear.[27] Still, the two share the commonality of duplicity. Of such persons Paul says they will "progress to worse" (προκόψουσιν ἐπὶ τὸ χεῖρον). This is an obvious parallelism to what Paul says of the false teachers in 3:9: "they will not progress upon much" (προκόψουσιν ἐπὶ πλεῖον). Together, the portrait conveys the complementary image of the false teachers' inability to move forward and their "progress" toward nowhere. Although it may appear that they are "winning out," Timothy can be as confident of their destruction as his own persecution.

Paul concludes his condemnation with the final descriptor "deceiving and being deceived" (πλανῶντες καὶ πλανώμενοι). The sense is that

26. See 2 Tim 1:1, 9, 13; 2:1, 10.

27. If the former, the καί is epexegetical and specifies that Paul has in view specifically duplicitous men.

deception feeds off itself, leading deceivers to bring others into deeper darkness as they themselves become increasingly deceived.[28] Already Paul described how the "impostors" deceive: "For among them are those who creep into households and capture weak women . . ." (3:6). The "impostors" accomplish this by promoting false doctrine and perpetuating a lifestyle antithetical to the gospel. Paul, however, does not detail exactly how the "evil human beings" themselves are "deceived." It could be that they are under the control of the devil; or they might suppose that their temporary and present "success" will shield them from final judgment (1:16). That is, their current "progress" may leave the misimpression that they are headed to glory. But, like Jannes and Jambres, they will be proven wrong when God's power is manifested on "that day."

2 Timothy 3:14–17

THE SURE ROAD TO LIFE

(A' ELEMENT)

Paul initiates the final A' element by summoning Timothy to follow a different path ("but"; δέ) from the impostors who seem to be progressing but are in fact deceived. The apostle begins with the command: "But you yourself endure in the things you learned and were-persuaded-of." The personal pronoun is emphatic: "But you yourself" (σύ).[29] As is characteristic of Paul in 1 and 2 Timothy, having spoken of the character and fate of those who oppose the gospel, he calls Timothy to be otherwise. That is, being aware of the realities set forth in 3:12–13, Timothy is to live purposefully, pursuing a different way.

The use of the verb "endure" (μένε) reiterates the main theme of the letter: endurance in the face of widespread apostasy. Repeatedly throughout this letter, both implicitly and explicitly, Paul has summoned Timothy to endure in the faith and in his calling (e.g., 2:13). Now Paul specifies that he is to "endure in the things you learned and were-persuaded-of." Here, "the things" (ἐν οἷς) refers to those things he has received directly from Paul through instruction and example.

---

28. We find something similar at the end of Titus 3:3 where Paul says trouble-makers are "hated by others and hating one another." Indeed, sin is a downward and perpetuating cycle that grace alone can check.

29. See similarly 3:10. The repetition here signals the start of a new section.

The verb "learned" (ἔμαθες) recalls Paul's descriptions of the wayward women who are "always learning" (μανθάνοντα) but never maturing. The implication is obvious: Timothy is to do otherwise. He is to preserve the teaching of the gospel, delving further into the glories of calvary, and pursue a lifestyle that conforms to deeper repentance. The coupling ("and," καί) with the verb "were-persuaded-of" (ἐπιστώθης) underscores that Timothy's learning was more than knowledge acquisition. Rather, it was so compelling because it was modeled by his spiritual father and his grandmother and mother. The force of the latter verb is for Timothy not to become unhinged from the things that Timothy "learned" from his spiritual predecessors. Again, we see an emphasis in this letter on the importance of continuing in the path of previous saints through deep reflection on their teaching and example.

Paul grounds the exhortation with the participle phrase "knowing from those you learned." Paul uses the participle "knowing" (εἰδώς) in a similar fashion in 2:23 of the corresponding D element: "But moronic and without-instruction controversies disregard, knowing (εἰδώς) that they birth fights."[30] Timothy knows from his ministry experience how secondary debates lead to gratuitous and explosive conflicts. Similarly, here in 3:14, Paul exhorts endurance since Timothy "knows" personally and profoundly (experientially) those from whom he "learned" (ἔμαθες) the things of the gospel. The plural pronoun "those" (τίνων) extends the exemplar of fortitude beyond the apostle. Indeed, Timothy has had the unique benefit of multiple examples of faith, including—but not limited to—his grandmother Lois and his mother Eunice (1:5), and his co-laborer Onesiphorus (1:16–18). Perhaps the most relevant "thing" that Timothy "learned" from these models was not just the inevitability of persecution but an endurance rooted in God's faithfulness.

Verse 15 continues to outline the object of "knowing": "and that from childhood the sacred writings you have known." There is a clear echo between the participle "knowing" (εἰδὼς) and the indicative verb "you have known" (οἶδας). The mention of "childhood" (βρέφους), which also translates to infancy, again recalls Timothy's upbringing in a believing household (1:4–5). This reference to an earlier part of the letter suggests to the audience that Paul is beginning to draw the letter to a close. More importantly, it poignantly reminds Timothy of his extensive spiritual lineage—something that he must uphold even in the face of persecution.

---

30. See also 1 Tim 1:9.

"Sacred writings" (ἱερὰ γράμματα) is likely a reference to the OT. The term "writing" carries a didactic nuance: "of education letters, learning."[31] In this sense, the term is polemical: "sacred writings" stand in contrast to the heresies of the false teachers. Paul specifies that these writings are instructional because they "have-power (δυνάμενά) to wisen you for salvation." This quality recalls the deficiency of the wayward women who are never "having-power" (δυνάμενα) to repent and be saved according to 3:7 of the corresponding A element. The parallelism is suggestive, insinuating that the wayward do not change because they hold fast to the teachings of the agitators instead of Paul's gospel.

But how do the "sacred writings" "wisen (σε σοφίσαι) you for salvation"? The answer rests in the conclusion of 3:15: "through faith in Christ Jesus." Paul indicates an idea that he did not believe prior to his conversion. He is proposing a hermeneutical principle here, namely that the OT leads to saving wisdom only when it is interpreted in light of the "salvation" that comes "through faith in Christ Jesus" (διὰ πίστεως τῆς ἐν Χριστῷ Ἰησοῦ).[32] In other words, Paul is proposing what is referred to in some circles as a "Christo-telic" or "Christo-centric" interpretive model for reading all of the Bible.[33] The OT, then, is ultimately a narrative that concerns itself primarily with the question of salvation. In various times and in various ways, the OT as a whole points to how God would accomplish salvation through his Son. In sum, Paul is summoning Timothy to retain the only approach to reading and interpreting the OT that will lead to salvation.

Reflecting further on the unique nature of "the sacred writings," in v. 16 Paul declares, "All Scripture is God-Spirited and useful toward teaching, toward reproof, toward correction, toward training in

31. Friberg and Friberg, *Analytical Greek New Testament*, s.v.

32. Paul uses this almost exact phrase in 2:10 when he writes, "All-things I endure for-the-sake of the elect, that they themselves might also obtain the salvation that [is] in Christ Jesus" (σωτηρίας . . . τῆς ἐν Χριστῷ Ἰησοῦ).

33. Towner, *Letters*, 584: "It does direct attention to the need to interpret and understand the holy writings by means of the Christian lens and from within a genuine relationship with Christ. For Paul, Christ is the climax of the biblical story, and the biblical story interprets Christ; the OT Scriptures and the Christ-event are integrally related." Köstenberger, *1–2 Timothy and Titus*, 266: "With regard to the false teachers, Paul's point here seems to be that the Scriptures . . . are indeed of great value . . . but only if understood as pointing toward faith in Christ. Rather than using the Scriptures with an emphasis on law and the observance of its particular stipulations, a proper appreciation of the value of Scripture entails recognition of its true God-intended salvation-historical purpose."

righteousness." "Scripture" (γραφή) occurs also in 1 Tim 5:18 where Paul provides the basis for the generous remuneration of teaching elders: "For the Scripture (γραφή) says . . ." In this former instance, Paul implies the authority "Scripture" should have in the lives of believers. Significant to our interpretation of 2 Tim 3:16 is that Paul states that "all (πᾶσα) Scripture" is authoritative, not just select parts.[34] We see this authoritative view of Scripture reflected in the way Paul freely uses different—and, sometimes seemingly random—parts of the OT to exhort and reprove.

Of this holy text Paul makes both theological and pragmatic declarations. First, "all Scripture is God-Spirited (θεόπνευστος)," which means that it is God-breathed.[35] Paul is making a statement that is foreign to the minds of a scientific and materialistic modern society. He is asserting that there is something fundamentally unique and extraordinary about Scripture, which sets it apart from any other written text. "All Scripture" has been divinely inspired and therefore has an abiding and pervasive authority over people that no other text can claim. Its functional value, as we will see, rests in its ontology as the uniquely God-breathed-out-text.[36] Paul's exhortation is for Timothy to immerse himself deeply in this divine and therefore trustworthy text versus the duplicitous teachings of "evil human beings and impostors."

According to the apostle, the divine nature of Scripture is also what makes it eminently "profitable" (ὠφέλιμος) for the life and vibrancy of the church.[37] This adjective is significant as it reflects one of the main

34. See Towner's extensive analysis of the phrase "All Scripture" in *Letters*, 585–88. He concludes: "Given the 'functional,' distributive way in which Scripture is envisaged, the logical conclusion is that Paul wished to affirm that divine inspiration applies evenly, text by text, to the entire OT." Köstenberger, however, indicates: "However, since no specific passage is referred to, it's more likely that Paul here views Scripture in its totality ('all Scripture' used as a collective phrase)" (*1-2 Timothy and Titus*, 266n135). In the end, the two interpretations yield little difference because both positions highlight that every part, or all, of the OT is inspired by God. Still Köstenberger argues for "all" because it would then include "the nascent writings of the Christian faith containing the gospel of Christ which Paul preached" (266n136). See esp. Swinson, *What Is Scripture?*, 115–59.

35. Friberg and Friberg, *Analytical Greek New Testament*, s.v. This term does not occur anywhere else in the Old and New Testaments.

36. Warfield, *Inspiration and Authority of the Bible*, 134: "[Scripture] is the product of the creative breath of God, and, because of this its Divine origination, is of supreme value for all holy purposes."

37. Paul also uses this adjective twice in 1 Tim 4:8 to distinguish between the value of bodily training and of spiritual training. See my comments in Jeon, *1 Timothy*.

themes in the letter. Earlier Paul spoke of soldiers, athletes, and farmers who must live disciplined lives in order to please their enlisting officer, to win the prize, or to enjoy the harvest (2:4–6). People of such vocations tend to be selective and deliberate about their lifestyles, pursuing things that are only "profitable" with respect to their goal. Also, Paul warned Timothy against getting involved with any irreverent babble that leads people into more ungodliness (2:16). Finally, Paul compared honorable vessels to dishonorable vessels, indicating that if Timothy aspires to be the former, he must set himself apart as holy in order to become useful to the master of the house (2:20–23). In this regard, Paul has been priming Timothy to think in terms of "cost-benefit" analysis: he is to consider on a regular basis what is "profitable," useful, and beneficial versus what is not. In other words, Paul summons Timothy to be very purposeful by attending to the "Scripture."

Paul outlines four ways "toward" (πρός) which God's inspired word can be used. The fourfold repetition of the preposition "toward" is rhetorical, underscoring the usefulness of Scripture. First, it is profitable toward the activity of "teaching" (διδασκαλίαν). This term occurs regularly in 1 Timothy.[38] It is not any "teaching" but the "teaching" reflective of and consistent with Paul's "teaching" of the gospel (2 Tim 3:10), which itself stems from God's revelation. In this sense, it sets the standard of orthodoxy from which Timothy must "teach" all believers. Second, it is profitable toward "reproof" (ἐλεγμόν). Because the Scripture is God's inspired text, it becomes the basis for making judgments between right and wrong: all relativism dissipates in light of revelation. Believers can—and should—reprove others because of a divine text that transcends any personal whims or culture.[39]

Third, it is profitable toward "correction" (ἐπανόρθωσιν). Paul likely has in view restoration. If "reproof" refers to bringing to light behavior and belief that contradict sound doctrine, "correction" focuses on what form restoration and reconciliation take. Finally, Scripture is profitable toward "training in righteousness" (παιδείαν τὴν ἐν δικαιοσύνῃ). Twice in these two letters Paul's uses the exact phrase, "But pursue righteousness

38. See 1 Tim 1:10; 4:1, 6, 13, 16; 5:17; 6:1, 3.

39. Towner, *Letters*, 590–91: "The term covers a range of activities all related to the process of making someone aware of sin, which begins with the educative act designed to produce self-awareness of sin and proceeds to the more immediately disciplinary stage of calling one up short for some specific misbehavior, and finally reaches the point at which 'rebuke' is so harsh that it becomes punitive."

(δικαιοσύνην)" (1 Tim 6:11; 2 Tim 2:22). The term "training" (παιδείαν) often refers to a father's discipline or any sort of general instruction that results in improved behavior.[40] It involves pruning vices and adding virtues. It echoes earlier images in the letter, particularly that of an athlete. Coupled with 1 Tim 6:11 and 2 Tim 2:22, the term "training" focuses on growing in "righteousness" by pursuing a lifestyle that accords with God's gift of "righteousness." Such a pursuit contrasts the life of those that are ever learning but never changing according to 3:7 in the corresponding A element. Such a pursuit also contrasts the preoccupations of the false teachers who fixate on "moronic and without-instruction (ἀπαιδεύτους) controversies." They are untrained because they fail to abide in the divinely inspired Scripture and instead chase silly myths and genealogies. Paul's desire is for his spiritual son to be otherwise. Then, and only then, can he lead others to life eternal.

Verse 17, which concludes both the A′ element and the D′ microchiasm, ends with the declaration, "that complete may be the human being of God, toward all good work completed."[41] There is a clear echo here between "the human being of God" (ὁ τοῦ θεοῦ ἄνθρωπος) and "O human being of God" (ὦ ἄνθρωπε θεοῦ) in Paul's summons in 1 Tim 6:11. The "human being" in v. 11 stands in stark contrast to "human beings (ἀνθρώπων) depraved in mind and deprived of truth" (1 Tim 6:5) and to "human beings" (ἀνθρώπων) who are slaves to money (1 Tim 6:9).[42] The "human being of God" is characterized by the pursuit of righteousness, godliness, and faith (1 Tim 6:11) as manifested concretely in his commitment to Scripture. The context here makes clear that Paul is referring primarily to Timothy.

Paul asserts that the "human being" that looks to Scripture as the basis of all ministry will be "complete" (ἄρτιος); this is the purpose (ἵνα) of Scripture. He then explains what he means through the phrase "toward all good work completed" (πρὸς πᾶν ἔργον ἀγαθὸν ἐξηρτισμένος). The meaning of the participle "completed" is "finished, ready, equipped" as with an athlete that is about to compete, a soldier that is about to battle, a

---

40. Friberg and Friberg, *Analytical Greek New Testament*, s.v. For further reflection on the term—especially on how it relates to household imagery, see Krumbiegel, *Erziehung in den Pastoralbriefen*, 39–53, 105.

41. There is an obvious word-play between the adjective "complete" (ἄρτιος) and the verb "to complete" (ἐξαρτίζω).

42. See my comments on "O human being of God" and the related section in Jeon, *1 Timothy*.

laborer that is about to harvest. The phrase echoes Paul's earlier statement in 2:21: "Therefore, if someone purifies himself from these (τούτων), he will be a vessel toward honor, sanctified, useful for the master, toward all good work ready (εἰς πᾶν ἔργον ἀγαθὸν ἡτοιμασμένον)." Paul thus answers the somewhat lingering question of how a person can cleanse himself from what is dishonorable from 2:20–21: namely, by enduring in the divine Scripture that outlines the way toward salvation and the way of ministry, turning away from heresy.

8

2 Timothy 4:1–8

*I Have Fought the Good Fight
and Kept the Faith for That Day*

(C' UNIT)

THIS CHAPTER EXAMINES THE sixth of eight microchiastic units within the 2 Timothy macrochiasm.

Having exhorted Timothy to turn from the false teachers and to endure in the example and teaching he has received, the apostle now presents himself again as an example of faithfulness.

The Sixth Microchiastic Unit

The sixth of eight microchiasms within 2 Timothy is composed carefully of four elements (A-B-B'-A'). Linguistic parallels are indicated by the Greek text.

A. 4:1 I charge you in-the-presence-of God and Christ Jesus, who is about to judge (κρίνειν) the living and the dead, and [by] the manifestation of his (τὴν ἐπιφάνειαν αὐτοῦ) and the kingdom of his:

    B. 2 preach the word, stand-ready (ἐπίστηθι) in-season (εὐκαίρως), out-of-season (ἀκαίρως), reprove, rebuke,

2 TIMOTHY 4:1-8 147

exhort, in all long-suffering and doctrine. 3 For there will be a season (γὰρ καιρός) when sound teaching they will not tolerate, rather according to their own desires for-themselves they—itching [regarding] the hearing (τὴν ἀκοήν)—will accumulate teachers,

B'. 4 and on-the-one-hand the hearing (τὴν ἀκοήν) of the truth they will-turn-away, on-the-other-hand upon the myths they will-turn-aside. 5 But you yourself be sober in all [things], bear-hardship, the work of an evangelist do, the service of yours fulfill. 6 For (γάρ) I myself am al-ready being-poured-out-as-a-drink-offering, and the time (καιρός) of my departure has stood-over (ἐφέστηκεν). 7 The commendable agony I have agonized, the race I have-finished, the faith I have kept. 8a Henceforth is-laid-up for me the crown of righteousness,

A'. 8b which the Lord will recompense to me on that day, the just judge (κριτής), but not only to me; rather and to all who have loved his manifestation (τὴν ἐπιφάνειαν αὐτοῦ).

2 Timothy 4:1

THE "INDICATIVE"

(A ELEMENT)

Paul begins the A element of the sixth microchiasm (4:1–8) with the for-mulaic words: "I charge you in-the-presence-of God and Christ Jesus" (Διαμαρτύρομαι ἐνώπιον τοῦ θεοῦ καὶ Χριστοῦ Ἰησοῦ). This exact word-ing is found in 1 Tim 5:21.[1] The context of 1 Tim 5:21 is instructions and exhortations concerning elders of the church, which includes their public discipline if any persist in sin.[2] Similar language is found in 2 Tim 2:14 of the corresponding C microchiasm: "These things remind, charging them in-the-presence-of God (διαμαρτυρόμενος ἐνώπιον τοῦ θεοῦ) not to word-fight." Thus we have a movement from Timothy giving a solemn charge to Timothy receiving one. By calling "God and Christ Jesus" as

---

1. 1 Tim 5:21 includes elect angels: "Διαμαρτύρομαι ἐνώπιον τοῦ θεοῦ καὶ Χριστοῦ Ἰησοῦ καὶ τῶν ἐκλεκτῶν ἀγγέλων."

2. See my comments in 1 Timothy.

witnesses, Paul is stressing the weighty obligation Timothy has to fulfill his ministry.

The apostle expands on his charge in two ways. First, Paul describes "Christ Jesus" as the one "who is about to judge the living and the dead." The participle "who-is-about-to" (μέλλοντος) occurs several times in 1 Timothy to indicate a sure, future reality.[3] The idea of Christ's final judgment (κρίνειν) echoes Paul's earlier statements of the Lord granting mercy to Onesiphorus on "that day" (1:16–17). The contrasting participles "the living and the dead" (ζῶντας καὶ νεκρούς) could—and probably should—be taken literally; namely, that when Christ returns he will judge those who are still alive as well as those that have died and are raised on the day of final judgment.[4] Thus the juxtaposition of "the living and the dead" conveys a sense of the comprehensive quality of Christ's judgment: none shall be excluded from his judgment. As Timothy and the audience hear this solemn charge, they are to endure in light of the inevitable judgment that will fall upon all mankind. The clear sense that Paul wishes to reiterate is that someday all, "the living and dead," will stand before Christ to receive his judgment. Timothy's decision to "endure in the things you learned" should depend on this inevitable and future reality versus the apparent "victory" of the protagonists.[5]

The second expansion reads "and [by] the manifestation of his and the kingdom of his." Earlier in the letter Paul uses the term "manifestation" (ἐπιφάνειαν) to refer to Christ's first "manifestation": the grace of God "was manifested (φανερωθεῖσαν) through the manifestation (ἐπιφανείας) of our Savior Christ Jesus" (1:10). If we look even further back, the term occurs in 1 Tim 6:14 to refer to Christ's second appearing: "to keep the commandment unstained and free from reproach until the manifestation (ἐπιφανείας) of our Lord Jesus Christ." Paul toggles easily between these two manifestations because they set the "bookends" for the Christian life. Paul's addition of "the kingdom of his" (τὴν βασιλείαν αὐτου) is somewhat striking, given the noticeable absence of "kingdom" language in Paul's letters.[6] Nevertheless, in 1 Timothy the related term

3. See 1 Tim 1:16; 4:8; 6:19.

4. See 1 Thess 4:13–16.

5. Köstenberger, *1–2 Timothy and Titus*, 271: "As Timothy discharges his duties as Paul's apostolic delegate and in keeping with Paul's own practice (2 Cor 5:9–11), the apostle wants Timothy to be ever conscious of the reality of God and the certainty of Christ's return."

6. Although "'appearing' and 'kingdom' may relate to one another closely in the

"king" (βασιλεύς) occurs both in the beginning (1:17) and end (6:15) of the letter. In both instances, Jesus is exalted as "the king" who is exalted forever and who will be exalted by all people at the second manifestation of Christ. In a sense, "kingdom" and "king" refer to the same reality, the exalted rule of Christ when he returns to judge all human beings. Timothy is to live with deep hope in view of this coming "kingdom" of which he is already a "soldier."[7]

2 Timothy 4:2–4

The Imperative Given Inevitable Eschatological Apostasy

(B Element)

Having established the proper perspective—the "indicative"—Paul now proceeds to provide Timothy with a list of imperatives: "preach the word, stand-ready in-season, out-of-season, reprove, rebuke, exhort, in all long-suffering and doctrine." The first imperative "preach the word" (κήρυξον τὸν λόγον) is a summons for Timothy, the child, to continue the work of Paul, his father, who is unabashed in reiterating his unique appointment as "preacher (κῆρυξ) and apostle and teacher" (2 Tim 1:11).[8] The "word" refers mainly to the "word of the gospel," namely that Christ came to save sinners (1 Tim 1:15). This is the central content and aim of all preaching. The second imperative is to "stand-ready in-season, out-of-season." The verb "stand- ready" (ἐπίστηθι) conveys the sense of alertness and preparedness. The juxtaposing adverbs "in-season, out-of-season" (εὐκαίρως ἀκαίρως) eloquently convey the simple idea "always."[9] Taken

form of a hendiadys, giving something like the meaning, 'his appearing through (or in) his kingdom'" (Towner, *Letters*, 598–99).

7. Towner, *Letters*, 598: "In Pauline thought, 'kingdom' could be viewed from the perspective of the present experience of salvation; but frequently for the believer it is the symbol of the consummation of salvation and of Christ's final victory, when he takes up his place as universal ruler, savior, and judge . . . And it is the positive note of triump that is uppermost in mind here (4:8)."

8. See also 1 Tim 2:7 and my related comments in *1 Timothy*.

9. Towner, *Letters*, 600–601: "Modifying the command verb is the opposing pair of adverbs . . . which means 'when the time is convenient [and] when the time is inconvenient . . . a more likely background for the contrasting adverbial phrase has been shown to be the secular philosophical debates of that time . . . where the need to

together, these words depict a soldier who is always prepared to stand fast against attack. The use of this verb is intentional, echoing again Paul's earlier depiction of the Christian life in terms of a soldier of Christ (2:3–4).

The next two imperatives "reprove, rebuke" (ἔλεγξον, ἐπιτίμησον) flow somewhat naturally, given what Paul has said of the inspired Scripture. Given all Scripture is profitable toward "reproof" (ἐλεγμόν) and "correction" (ἐπανόρθωσιν), Timothy should be engaged in reproving and rebuking the saints for their edification and salvation. Perhaps the nuance between these two imperatives is that the former involves private correct, the latter public discipline. In the case of this letter, the former would apply more to believers under the care of Timothy who have been influenced by the troublemakers; the latter to the troublemakers themselves. The last imperative is to "exhort" (παρακάλεσον). This verb occurs four times in 1 Timothy to describe both the activity of Paul (1:3; 2:1) and Timothy (5:1; 6:2) who alone stand as God's authoritative representatives among the believers. Verse 6:2 probably illuminates best the force of the verb, given its juxtaposition with the command to "teach": to "exhort" is to command a certain lifestyle that corresponds to the teaching of the gospel. As Paul is so concerned to express in all his letters, the gospel is consequential truth, that is, it has deep and wide implications for the way believers must live.

All this—preaching, being ready, reproving, rebuking, and exhorting—is to be done "in all long-suffering and doctrine."[10] "Long-suffering" (μακροθυμία) recalls not just Paul's own "long-suffering" (μακροθυμία; 3:10) but, more so, the "long-suffering" of Christ as exhibited paradigmatically in Paul's conversion (1 Tim 1:16). The kind of "long-suffering" Paul has in view stems from maintaining the eschatological perspective

---

discern the appropriate time to speak so as to be most persuasive to a particular audience was stressed . . . As applied in the present context, the force of the phrase would be to command Timothy to disregard this convention of rhetoricians. Explanations for this advice suggest either that Paul (the author) regarded the audience (chiefly the opponents) as too evil for this fine point of rhetorical strategy to make any difference, or that his concern is rather that the need is so extremely urgent that truth must be addressed to the church immediately and persistently."

10. Concerning the last three duties, Köstenberger, 1–2 Timothy and Titus, 273: "The fact that the words rendered 'rebuke, correct, and encourage' are all partially overlapping in meaning suggests that Paul is concerned here to convey the spectrum of functions a person such as Timothy will be called to exercise in the local congregation, ranging from encouragement and affirmation to mild correction or even strong rebuke. To know what is needed in a particular situation calls for considerable wisdom and discernment."

expressed in the prior verse, which describes Christ's return, his judgment, and the manifestation of his kingdom. As one lexical explanation states, "patience [is] a state of emotional quietness in the face of unfavorable circumstances . . . long-suffering."[11] Such "patience" is possible only in light of the hope of Christ's return and final vindication. The qualifier "in all" (ἐν πάσῃ) could relate to both "long-suffering and teaching," but it is more likely that it qualifies just "long-suffering"; hence, "great patience" (NASB).[12]

The precise meaning of "doctrine" (διδαχῇ) is unclear. Although many translations use "teaching," doing so obscures the use of a different term here from the more typical Greek term διδασκαλία, which is also commonly translated as "teaching." It has both an active and passive sense, the former referring to the activity of instruction, the latter to what is taught, i.e., doctrine.[13] The latter seems to fit the context, namely that Timothy should preach, remain alert, reprove, rebuke, and exhort according to the "doctrine" he has received from Paul.

Verse 3 begins an explanation ("for"; γάρ) for Paul's command to preach, rebuke, and exhort: "For there will be a season when sound teaching they will not endure." The future tense of "there will be" (ἔσται) may be referring to a particular season in the future.[14] Yet, not unlike the allusion to Christ's future judgment, the sense might be that "there will definitely come a time . . ." More so, this general rejection of sound teaching seems to describe the present situation. Given Paul's elliptical eschatology which encompasses the period between Christ's first and second coming, his "future final age" could easily refer to the present.[15] Apostasy, then, is an inevitable eschatological reality. The term "season" follows on the heels of the juxtaposed adverbs "in-season" (εὐκαίρως) and "out-of-season" (ἀκαίρως). Paul's message is clear: even in the "season" of heresy, Timothy must endure in every good endeavor.

At this time "sound teaching they will not endure." The verb "tolerate" (ἀνέξονται) means "to accept as valid."[16] The object of rejection is "sound teaching" (ὑγιαινούσης διδασκαλίας). This exact phrase occurs

11. Friberg and Friberg, *Analytical Greek New Testament*, s.v.

12. If the qualifier "in all" applies also to "doctrine," it means "careful instruction" or "via the application of all truth/doctrine."

13. Friberg and Friberg, *Analytical Greek New Testament*, s.v.

14. See the occurrences of the verb in 2:21 and 3:9.

15. For a treatment on Paul's elliptical eschatology, see Gaffin, *By Faith*, 30–32.

16. Friberg and Friberg, *Analytical Greek New Testament*, s.v.

in 1 Tim 1:10 as the standard that accords with the gospel. It serves as the basis for all godly conduct, which the false teachers discard. Similarly, in 1 Tim 6:3, Paul asserts that those who reject the "sound (ὑγιαίνουσιν) words of our Lord Jesus Christ and the teaching (διδασκαλίᾳ) that accords with godliness" are puffed up and ignorant. Finally, earlier in 2 Tim 1 :13, Paul exhorts Timothy to hold fast to the "sound (ὑγιαινόντων) words that you have heard from me." Thus, the first half of v. 4 declares that there will undoubtedly come a time when many will reject the gospel. Ironically, Paul's remedy to this inevitable reality is to summon Timothy to continually proclaim the truth of the gospel: it is exactly because people will cease to listen that Timothy must continue to preach the word. It is as if Paul is suggesting that silence during apostasy will slowly lead even those who remain faithful to forget what they have followed and come to believe.

The second half of v. 3 completes Paul's explanation. On the one hand, as Paul has indicated already, they will reject words of life and truth. On the other hand ("rather"; ἀλλά), they will not just accept false teaching but will in fact pursue it: "according to their own desires for-themselves they—itching [regarding] the hearing (τὴν ἀκοήν)—will accumulate teachers." "Desires" already occurred twice in the letter to describe "youthful desires" (ἐπιθυμίας; 2:22) and captivating "desires" (ἐπιθυμίαις; 3:6). It also occurred in 1 Tim 6:9 to describe those who display an inordinate longing to become rich and therefore fall "into many senseless and harmful desires (ἐπιθυμίας)." We can assume its occurrence here is also negative. The emphasis seems to fall on the adjective "own (ἰδίας) desires," thus recalling Paul's earlier diagnosis that in the final days people will be "lovers-of-self, lovers-of-money, and lovers-of-pleasure rather than lovers-of-God" (3:2–4). That is, people will live "according to" (κατά) the desires of their own hearts rather than the dictates of the gospel.

The verb "accumulate" (ἐπισωρεύσουσιν) paints the picture of piling up, heaping together, or growing a large sum. Such "teachers" (διδασκάλους) stand in obvious contrast to Paul, who has been uniquely appointed as "preacher and apostle and teacher (διδάσκαλος)" of the gospel (2 Tim 1:11).[17] Whereas Paul speaks according to the revelation of

17. See also 1 Tim 2:7. Towner, *Letters*, 604: "The irony is created by the use of the term 'teachers' . . . It comes just after (and in strong contrast to, *all*) the reference to 'sound teaching' (*didaskalias*), which produces the cognitive dissonance that in effect means 'false teachers.' The mockery is heightened by means of the striking verb 'to

God in Christ Jesus, these supposed "teachers" are hired hands who say only what their audience wants to hear. Paul aptly describes this audience as those "itching regarding the hearing" (κνηθόμενοι τὴν ἀκοήν), that is, as those who hear only what they want to hear.[18] Paul's point is that Timothy must preach and teach in a context where individuals do not want to listen. To buy into the contemporary pervasive belief in objectivity is to commit the sin of incredible naiveté.

2 Timothy 4:4–5

Enduring Even in Apostasy

(B' Element)

Verse 4 offers a parallel contrast to v. 3. First, Paul begins by asserting, "and on-the-one-hand (μέν) the hearing of the truth they will turn-away."[19] This echoes his statement that "sound teaching they will not tolerate" (3:3a). "The truth" (τῆς ἀληθείας) has already been mentioned five times in the letter.[20] It is best understood as "the truth" of the gospel through which one comes to salvation (1 Tim 2:4). In 2 Timothy "the truth" is strongly correlated with repentance (2 Tim 2:25; 3:7). The verb "turn-away" (ἀποστρέψουσιν) echoes its earlier occurrence in 1:15, where Paul indicated that "All that are in Asia turned-away (ἀπεστράφησάν) from me." Once again, Paul identifies himself so closely with his gospel that a rejection of the gospel is synonymous with a rejection of the apostle himself. There also appears to be an echo of 2 Tim 2:18 where Paul described Hymenaeus and Philetus as "the-someones-who regarding the truth (ἀλήθειαν) have swerved." These reverberations of earlier terms and themes of the letter suggest to the audience that Paul is beginning to bring his letter to a close. Finally, the noun "the hearing" (τὴν ἀκοήν)

accumulate or pile up,' which almost gives the impression of stockpiling teachers. At the same time, this verb (*episōreuō*) sets up an echo that, when followed back to its source in 3:6 (*sōreuō*), provides the perfect example in foolish, susceptible women burdened by their sins."

18. Note the phrase κνηθόμενοι τὴν ἀκοήν is idiomatic: "literally *itch with respect to hearing*, i.e., crave to hear what one wants to hear (2T 4.3)" (Friberg and Friberg, *Analytical Greek New Testament*, s.v.).

19. In other words, they will turn the listening of their ears—what they hear—away from the truth.

20. See 2 Tim 2:15, 18, 25; 3:7, 8.

echoes its parallel occurrence in the corresponding B element. The persons in view are so biased in what they want to hear (3:3b) that they turn away from an honest "hearing" of the gospel. In sum, the first half of v. 4 calls attention to a refusal to consider the gospel and respond with contrition.

Paul goes on to describe ("on the other hand"; δέ) that "upon the myths they will-turn-aside." The use of this term is purposeful: Paul is characterizing the false teaching as mere fictions and legends that no sensible person should take seriously. "Myths" (μύθους) stand in contrast to the gospel. In 1 Tim 1:4, Paul describes the troublemakers as those who give themselves over to "myths" (μύθοις) rather than the progress of the gospel. Similarly, in 1 Tim 4:7, "myths" (μύθους) stand in contrast to "commendable doctrine." The verb "turn-off" (ἐκτραπήσονται) occurrs twice in 1 Timothy to describe the false teachers and heretics: they have "turned-off (ἐξετράπησαν) into empty-words" (1:6); they have "turned-off (ἐξετράπησαν) after Satan" (5:15). Thus, what Timothy has already observed among the false teachers will hold true for many as he continues to minister. In sum, v. 4 portrays humanity as moving deeper into darkness, particularly through the false teachers who will say what people want to hear instead of what they need to hear, namely, Christ, his judgment, and his kingdom (4:1).

Verse 5, which contains four imperatives, conveys that Paul does not suppose that Timothy is above temptation and apostasy. He warns, "But you yourself be-sober in all [things]." The inclusion of the pronoun "you" (σύ) is certainly emphatic: This, in contrast, is how *you* are to be. The imperative "be sober" (νῆφε) echoes what Paul says is absolutely necessary for aspiring elders and deacons—"sobriety" (νηφάλιος; 3:2, 11). The sense of the verb is "to be clear-headed, be self-possessed," the opposite state of holding any wine.[21] This contrasts the condition of those who have become ever more self-deluded because of their itching ears. Timothy, however, given his position among the believers, must remain clear-headed "in all" (ἐν πᾶσιν) matters. At bedrock for such sobriety involves upholding the reality of Christ's judgment and the appearing of the kingdom.

The second imperative is to "bear-hardship" (κακοπάθησον). In a sense, this imperative can be viewed as a summary exhortation for the entire letter. Early in the letter Paul exhorted Timothy not to be ashamed

21. Friberg and Friberg, *Analytical Greek New Testament*, s.v.

of the apostle but to share in suffering for the gospel (1:8). He then underscored his own suffering as a preacher, apostle, and teacher: "I am suffering-as-an-evildoer (κακοπαθῶ) until bonds" (2:9). Nevertheless, Paul, Timothy's spiritual father, continues to persevere in hope of eternal life. The summons, then, to "bear-hardship" is a call for Timothy to imitate Paul by persisting in all good despite the inevitable reality of suffering for the gospel.

The last two imperatives "the work of an evangelist do, the service of yours fulfill" give shape to what bearing hardship looks like. "Evangelist" (εὐαγγελιστοῦ) refers to "one who brings or announces good news"; in other words, a preacher or teacher of the gospel, a divinely appointed position.[22] "The work" (ἔργον) in view includes the activities delineated in 4:2—preaching, always being alert, reproving, rebuking, and exhorting. The term also brings to mind its earlier occurrences in 2:21 and 3:17: Timothy is prepared to carry out "all good work (ἔργον)" on behalf of his Master because the Scriptures have equipped him for "all good work (ἔργον)." All that is needed now is a renewed resolve to "do" (ποίησον) the work that God has already equipped him to do.

In other words, Timothy must "fulfill" (πληροφόρησον) his "service" (διακονίαν). The noun "service" echoes Paul's conversion and calling: "I thank him who has given me strength, Christ Jesus our Lord, because he judged me faithful, appointing me to his service (διακονίαν)" (1 Tim 1:12). "Service" in 2 Tim 4:5 probably means something similar—gospel-ministry, an entrustment from the risen Lord that must be satisfied. The exhortation to "fulfill" this calling echoes Paul's earlier exhortation "to rekindle the gift of God, which is in you through the laying on of my hands" (1:6). Instead of turning away because of shame or suffering, Timothy is to remember the promise of Christ's return, endure hardship, and continue the work of an evangelist. In this way, he will bring his "service" to full completion and thus please the One that has enlisted him.

Verse 6 begins with an explanatory statement (γάρ) for the preceding commands. The precise relationship between v. 6 and what precedes it in the previous elements is not entirely clear. Verse 6a, which reads, "For I myself am already being-poured-out-as-a-drink-offering," suggests that

---

22. Köstenberger suggest this nuance: "Apparently, Timothy's calling wasn't primarily that of pastor but that of an apostolic delegate who consolidated the fruit of Paul's preaching before moving on to other fields" (*1–2 Timothy and Titus*, 274–75). See also Combs, "Biblical Role of the Evangelist," 44.

Paul doubts he has much time left to live. This being the case, he seeks to encourage his spiritual son to continue the work of his spiritual father.[23]

The first half of v. 6 provides a vivid image: "I myself am already being-poured-out-as-a-drink-offering."[24] The adverb "already" (ἤδη) and the present tense of the verb suggest that Paul's immediate imprisonment and suffering reflect the present reality depicted by the verb. The passive voice suggests that this is according to the sovereign will of God and not primarily through the machinations of man. Moreover, the image of sacrifice reiterates that the gospel cannot go forth without the suffering of the saints. This suffering, in turn, recalls Christ's own blood by which sinners are saved. Thus, Paul views his impending death as a divine necessity by which the gospel goes forth.[25]

The second half of v. 6 confirms that Paul believes he is nearing death: "and the time of my departure has stood-near."[26] The term "time" (καιρός), which echoes its occurrence in 4:3a, means a divinely appointed time, a particular season.[27] Again, the apostle maintains that all of his life is according to the sovereign rule of God. Paul specifies that it is the "time" of his "departure" (ἀναλύσεώς), which literally means "breaking up, dissolution." The term is a euphemism for death. The verb "stood-near" (ἐφέστηκεν) echoes Paul's exhortation to "stand-ready" in 4:2 of the corresponding B element. "Time" here is personified, standing near-and-ready to perform its duty of dissolution. Paul's exhortations— particularly in the corresponding B element—should thus be heard as a father's final words to his beloved son and partner in the gospel.

23. Towner, *Letters*, 610: "Verse 6 opens with the emphatic personal pronoun 'I.' This personal reference corresponds to the dramatic summary begun with 'but you' in the previous verse. With this shift, Paul grounds Timothy's commission in the urgency of the experience about to overtake him."

24. The verb means to "offer a libation, pour out a drink offering; metaphorically and passive in the NT, of martyrdom *be poured out as a libation*, i.e., *be put to death, have one's life blood poured out*" (Friberg and Friberg, *Analytical Greek New Testament*, s.v.)

25. Towner, *Letters*, 609: "There are indeed grounds for thinking that Paul may be echoing the Philippians letter at this point [2:12–18; 3:12] . . . What is presented as a distant possibility in the earlier setting has now become an imminent certainty in Paul's mind. For Timothy, who knew the letter to the Philippians (Phil 1:1), the echo of a passage containing Paul's theological evaluation of his crisis would have been all the more poignant a device to enact the handing over of ministry responsibilities."

26. Contra Prior, *Paul, the Letter-Writer*, 98–103 who argues that Paul expects to be released soon.

27. See also 1 Tim 2:6; 4:1; 6:15.

Seeking to rouse Timothy to faithfulness in light of the impending vacuum in leadership, Paul adds his famous threefold declaration: "The commendable agony I have agonized, the race I have finished, the faith I have kept." "The commendable agony I have agonized" (τὸν καλὸν ἀγῶνα ἠγώνισμαι) echoes Paul's closing exhortation in 1 Tim 6:12: "Agonize the commendable agony of faith."[28] The almost precise echo makes clear that Paul is again presenting himself as a model of endurance. The term "agony" literally refers to an athletic contest but applies metaphorically here to costly struggle. The athletic terminology recalls Paul's comparison of serving as a solder of Christ to an athlete in training. Paul qualifies this "agony" as "commendable" because the pain and even death of its participants will lead to salvation for many. But the repetition of "agony" and its verbal cognate reiterate what Paul has underscored throughout this letter, namely that the pursuit of Christ entails deep and regular suffering.

Paul continues the athletic imagery in the second declaration: "The race I have- completed." The verb "have-finished" (τετέλεκα) conveys the sense of completion. The verb echoes what Paul demands of Timothy—to "fulfill" the service that has been entrusted to him (4:5). The image of the "race" (δρόμον) reiterates the athletic motif. It also vividly conveys how Timothy and all believers are to view life. Christ the Lord has set each person on a "race" that is fraught with challenge and opposition. But they must finish the race, just as Christ did, in order to win the prize to which they have been called to.

The third declaration is, "the faith I have kept" (τὴν πίστιν τετήρηκα). The sense here is not merely that Paul continues to believe in the Lord Jesus Christ for salvation. The context of the letter suggests something more specific. Paul has "kept the faith" in the sense that, as a soldier of Christ, he has preserved sound doctrine and promoted godliness even in the face of much opposition. This final declaration indicates that faithfulness is possible despite widespread apostasy and persistent opposition. By presenting himself as the victorious athlete and devoted soldier, Paul seeks to inspire Timothy and all believers to "go and do likewise."[29]

28. See my comments in 1 Timothy.

29. Towner, however, contends that Paul maintains the athletic imagery in all three declarations (Letters, 613): "The third metaphor at its most basic level depicts Paul as having kept a pledge: 'I have kept the faith.' It may be best to see its reference, if not its point of origin, as keeping the rules of the race. This maintains the athletic theme throughout the series of metaphors."

The B' element concludes on a note of hope: "Henceforth is-laid-up for me the crown of righteousness." The adverb "henceforth" (λοιπόν) indicates that, for believers, there will definitely be a real and tangible consequence for fighting the good fight, finishing the race, and keeping the faith. Paul specifies first that this prize will come from the Lord. We know this from what Paul said earlier regarding Onesiphorus (1:16–18), and from the divine passive of the verb "is laid-up" (ἀπόκειταί). The verb means "to store up" or "reserve." The promise is that the Master is preparing to reward his servants for completing the service entrusted to them. Second, the reward is immensely personal versus transactional. The inclusion of the personal pronoun "for me" (μοι) expresses this.

"Crown" (στέφανος) literally refers to "an adornment worn around the head, given as an award in athletic contests."[30] Its occurrence here is fitting, given the wide use of athletic imagery. Paul's point is that the athlete's "life" portrays well the Christian's life: endurance in the face of challenge will climax in the receipt of glory. Paul specifies this "crown" as "the crown of righteousness" (δικαιοσύνης). This is the fourth and final time this term occurs in these two letters.[31] "Righteousness" in these letters contrasts with a love of money (1 Tim 6:11), youthful passions (2 Tim 2:22), and heresy (2 Tim 3:16). The receipt of the "crown of righteousness," then, means that each person will ultimately get what he or she has desired most.[32] This prize stands in contrast to those who, because of their itching ears, have sought the "prize" of hearing whatever agrees with their own passions.[33] Indeed, the promise of eschatological rewards

---

30. Friberg and Friberg, *Analytical Greek New Testament*, s.v.

31. See also 1 Tim 6:11; 2 Tim 2:22; 3:16.

32. Towner makes a helpful nuance; *Letters*, 615: "The imagery [of a crown of righteousness] would seem to demand that a sense of 'reward' be maintained, and this is strengthened by the context (vv. 7, 8b). We need to allow Paul to combine several thoughts: (a) righteousness as a gift from God that has yet to be fully received; (b) the need for the believer to 'cooperate' in this process by means of his/her faithful response to God in godly living; (c) the concept of 'righteousness,' including the note of 'vindication' . . . With the symbolism of the crown and athletics, Paul especially combines again the indicative and imperative of Christian living—what God has done and will do is woven together mysteriously with the possibility and necessity of appropriate response."

33. Lewis aptly summarizes the point that, in the end, each person gets what (s)he ultimately wants: "There are only two kinds of people in the end: those who say to God, 'Thy will be done,' and those to whom God says, in the end, 'Thy will be done.' All that are in Hell, choose it. Without that self-choice there could be no Hell" (*Great Divorce*, 69).

recalls the imagery of Christ's coming judgment (4:1). Again, this perspective should renew Timothy and all the believers in their resolution to uphold sound doctrine and promote godliness. The righteous Judge will not forget every good deed done in faith.

2 Timothy 4:8b

The Promise to All Who Have Longed for Christ's Return

(A' ELEMENT)

This sixth microchiasm concludes with 2 Tim 4:8b, which forms the A' element. Paul declares that his hope for future vindication is true for all believers.

Verse 8b begins by identifying the passive agent of the verb "is laid-up": "which the Lord will recompense to me on that day." Again, Paul reiterates what he has said throughout this letter, namely that there will come a day of accounting, and that standing on the throne of judgment will be "the Lord" (ὁ κύριος), none other than Christ Jesus.[34] Somewhat striking is the verb "will recompense" (ἀποδώσει)—as if God were a debtor to any. The verb carries the nuance of paying back an obligation.[35] Probably the best way to understand this is not so much in terms of the Creator owing anything to the creature, but God working according to his justice. Indeed, this is why Paul identifies "the Lord" here as "the just judge" (ὁ δίκαιος κριτής). The one "who is about to judge (κρίνειν) the living and the dead" according to 4:1 of the corresponding A element is the "just judge." Apart from this reality, why would anyone compete in the race? If there is no assurance of a "just judge," its participants would have little incentive to persevere. Christian hope is founded on the reality that Christ Jesus "will recompense" his servants according to his perfect justice.[36]

The phrase "on that day" (ἐν ἐκείνῃ τῇ ἡμέρᾳ) is significant, echoing the day of judgment outlined in 4:1 of the corresponding A element. This phrase also echoes its earlier occurrence in 1:18 where Paul prayed that

---

34. See 2 Tim 1:16, 18; 2:7, 19, 22, 24; 3:11.

35. See esp. the occurrence of this verb in 1 Tim 5:4 and my comments in Jeon, *1 Timothy*.

36. Towner, *Letters*, 616: "A possible polemical challenge to the imperial judgment handed down against Paul should not be discounted."

the Lord would give mercy to Onesiphorus "on that day" (ἐν ἐκείνῃ τῇ ἡμέρᾳ). An eschatological mindset is critical to endurance in suffering for the gospel. Paul himself declared earlier, "I am not ashamed, for I know to-the-one I have faith and I am convinced that he is powerful to guard my entrustment toward that day (ἐκείνην τὴν ἡμέραν)" (1:12). All soldiers, athletes, and farmers live with a similar mindset. They sacrifice, practice, and labor with the hope of future reward (2:4–6). The warnings in 2:11–13 were also given with a view toward Christ's return and the manifestation of his kingdom. The folly of men whose predecessors are Jannes and Jambres will be revealed when Christ judges the world (3:7–9). Thus, here again in 4:8b Paul reminds Timothy and all the believers with him to live each day with a sense of "that day." As Lewis put so well, "If you read history you will find that the Christians who did most for the present world were just those who though most of the next."[37]

Verse 8b ends with the assurance that Paul's hope is available to all believers: "but not only to me; rather and to all who have loved the manifestation of his." Paul contends that the hope of future glory and vindication is "but not only to me" (οὐ μόνον δὲ ἐμοι). Like a good father, he is seeking to assure Timothy that his son and all believers can share in this hope of divine recompense. The contrast is highlighted through the use of the emphatic disjunction "rather" (ἀλλά): this hope is for "all who have loved (ἠγαπηκόσιν) the manifestation of his," not just for the apostle. The "all" (πᾶσιν) that is specified differs from those who are "lovers-of-self, lovers-of-money (φίλαυτοι φιλάργυροι) . . . without-loving-good (ἀφιλάγαθοι) . . . lovers-of-pleasure (φιλήδονοι)" (3:1–5). This "all" align themselves with Paul by sharing in his longing for "the manifestation of his" (τὴν ἐπιφάνειαν αὐτοῦ), a phrase which echoes 4:1. In other words, believers are those who endure in preaching the word, reproving, rebuking, and exhorting because they live in anticipation of "the manifestation of his and the kingdom of his." In this way, they demonstrate that they are truly children of Paul, following his model of faithfulness.

---

37. Lewis, *Mere Christianity*, in *Complete C. S. Lewis Signature Classics*, 111.

9

2 Timothy 4:9–21

The Lord Will Save Me from All Evil—
But You Must Come

(B' UNIT)

THIS CHAPTER EXAMINES THE seventh of eight microchiastic units within the 2 Timothy macrochiasm. Having exhorted Timothy and the believers with him to live in hope of Christ's return and eschatological judgment, Paul begins to conclude this letter with a series of personal remarks. Notable is the interplay between Paul's hope in Timothy's arrival and his persistent confidence in the Lord's deliverance.

The Seventh Microchiastic Unit

The seventh of eight microchiasms within 2 Timothy is composed carefully of four elements (A-B-B'-A'). Linguistic parallels are indicated by the Greek text.

A. 9 Do-your-best to come (Σπούδασον ἐλθεῖν) to me quickly. 10 For Demas deserted me, loving the present age, and journeyed toward Thessalonica, Crescens toward Galatia, Titus toward Dalmatia. 11 Luke alone is with me. Taking-up Mark, bring [him] with you, for to me he is useful toward service. 12 But Tychicus I sent toward Ephesus. 13 The cloak that I left (ἀπέλιπον) in Troas with Carpus—when-you-come bring, and the books, especially the parchments. ¹⁴ᵃ Alexander the coppersmith displayed many evils to me;

> B. ¹⁴ᵇ to him the Lord (κύριος) will recompense him according to his works (ἔργα). ¹⁵ Him you yourself guard [against], for strongly he opposed our words. ¹⁶ In my first defense none was present with me; rather all left me; may it not be charged to them! ¹⁷ But the Lord (κύριός) was present with me and strengthened me, so that through me the proclamation might be fulfilled and all the Gentiles might hear it; and I was rescued (ἐρρύσθην) from the lion's mouth.
>
> B'. ¹⁸ Rescue (ῥύσεταί) me the Lord (κύριος) will from all evil work (ἔργου) and will save [me] into his heavenly kingdom; to him be the glory for the eternities of eternities; amen. ¹⁹ Greet Prisca and Aquila and the household of Onesiphorus. ²⁰ᵃ Erastus remained at Corinth,

A'. ²⁰ᵇ but Trophimus, being ill, I left (ἀπέλιπον) at Miletus. ²¹ Do your best to come (Σπούδασον . . . ἐλθεῖν) before winter. Eubulus and Pudens and Linus and Claudia and all the brothers greets *you*.

2 Timothy 4:9–14a

Personal Remarks and Requests

(A Element)

Paul begins the A element of the seventh microchiasm (4:1–8) with the directive, "Do-your-best to come to me quickly." Some interpret this to mean that Paul does not suppose he is really going to die.[1] While this is possible, the request itself may signal that Paul does in fact believe his demise is close at hand. Given this, it makes sense for him to command his spiritual son to "do-your-best" (σπούδασον), which, like its earlier occurrence in 2:15, means to make every effort. The force of this verb is reiterated to the point of redundancy through the adverb "quickly" (ταχέως). Perhaps what is a bit difficult to reconcile is whether Paul wants

---

1. But see 4:6–7 and my earlier comments.

Timothy to stay among the believers in Ephesus to preserve and promote Paul's gospel. If he is asking Timothy to make haste "to come to me" (ἐλθεῖν πρός με), it would seem that Timothy would have to prematurely conclude his ministry. More likely, especially given all the emphasis on endurance, Paul is commanding Timothy to come as soon as he has completed his work in Ephesus. Either way, what is clear is that Paul longs to see Timothy (1:4).

Verse 10 states explicitly the reason (γάρ) for this urgent request: Paul is basically alone. "For Demas deserted me, loving the present age, and journeyed toward Thessalonica, Crescens toward Galatia, Titus toward Dalmatia." In a sense, Paul is not giving new information. Already in 1:15 he stated that all in Asia had turned away from him. The reiteration of earlier themes likely signals to the audience that Paul is wrapping up the letter.

Little is known about Demas aside from references in Colossians 4:14 and Phlm 24. He was likely an intimate co-laborer for the gospel at some point. Significant, however, is the participle phrase Paul uses to describe Demas—"loving this present age" (ἀγαπήσας τὸν νῦν αἰῶνα). The verb recalls what Paul just declared in 4:8, namely that the crown of righteousness is reserved not just for Paul but also to "all who have loved (ἠγαπηκόσιν) the manifestation of his." In other words, believers are those who are not in love with the "present age" but long for Christ's return and their own future vindication. Indeed, the phrase "the present age" recalls 1 Tim 6:17 where Paul specifies those who are "rich in this present age (νῦν αἰῶνι)." Such affluent believers are exhorted to use their wealth to abound in good (6:18) so that they might store up for themselves treasures in the age to come. The mark of genuine faith is living in the "present age" in view of the "future age." In a glaring way, what is lacking for Demas is such Christian hope. Rather, he serves as a paradigm of all that love self, money, and pleasure above God (3:2–4) and that turn away from sound teaching (4:3–4).[2] This worldly love has been expressed tangibly in vivid language: "For Demas deserted me . . . and journeyed toward Thessalonica" (με ἐγκατέλιπεν . . . καὶ ἐπορεύθη εἰς

---

2. Quinn and Wacker (*First and Second Letters to Timothy*, 808) suggest Demas despised the poverty of apostolic ministry and longed for more material comfort; Marshall (*Pastoral Epistles*, 815) proposes that Demas was ashamed of identifying with the imprisoned apostle.

Θεσσαλονίκην).[3] It is not lost on Timothy and the believers with him that Demas stands as a foil to Onesiphorus (1:16–18).

Whether we are to continue to apply Paul's negative assessment to Crescens and Titus is unlikely. All that is said is that "Crescens [journeyed] toward Galatia, Titus toward Dalmatia" (Κρήσκης εἰς Γαλατίαν, Τίτος εἰς Δαλματίαν). These two were probably commissioned by the apostle to serve in his place in these respective areas.[4] The Letter to Titus itself leans us more toward concluding that Paul does not assess Crescens, whom we know very little about, or Titus in the same way as Demas. The more relevant point is that Paul feels alone because—quite literally—he is alone.

Paul continues his personal remarks by providing updates on Luke and Mark. He first states, "Luke alone is with me" (Λουκᾶς ἐστιν μόνος μετ' ἐμοῦ). This clarifies that Paul is not technically alone. Nevertheless, the inclusion of the adjective "only," which Paul uses twice in 1 Tim 6:15–16 to describe God as the "only" true God, reiterates Paul's sense of aloneness.[5] It is possible that Luke is serving as Paul's amanuensis.

Paul then mentions Mark: "Taking-up Mark, bring [him] with you, for to me he is useful toward service." This is a somewhat startling comment, given Paul and Barnabas parted ways because Paul did not want to take Mark on their second missionary journey.[6] What Paul makes abundantly clear is Mark's usefulness—"for to me he is useful for service" (ἔστιν γάρ μοι εὔχρηστος εἰς διακονίαν). The term "useful" recalls Paul's earlier description of anyone that cleanses himself and thereby becomes "useful (εὔχρηστον) to the master" (2:21). Mark is thus presented as an exemplar

3. Paul, however, may not have in view complete apostasy. Towner, *Letters*, 622–23: "What became of him is not known, but it is noteworthy that the language used to describe his desertion, which stops short of associating him with the opponents, seems closer in tone to that used by Luke to describe John Mark's lapse (Acts 15:38). There is thus no reason to think that his desertion from the Pauline team, as serious as that was in Paul's eyes, indicates his rejection of the faith or even necessarily his retirement from Christian service. In other words, apostasy as such does not seem to be in view." See similarly Kelly, *Pastoral Epistles*, 212–13; Köstenberger, *1–2 Timothy and Titus*, 280.

4. Though there is some ambiguity about "Galatia" because the term can refer to either the Roman province in Asia or Gaul; see Towner, *Letters*, 623: "'Galatia' is probably a reference to Asiatic Galatia."

5. This situation and its impact on Paul can perhaps best be appreciated if we recall Paul's understanding of the corporate quality of the Christian life versus more modern and Western individualistic and pietistic forms of Christianity.

6. See Phlm 24 and my comments in *Unreconciled*.

of a useful vessel for gospel-ministry. The phrase "toward service" recalls not just Paul's command for Timothy to fulfill his "service" (διακονίαν, 2 Tim 4:5), but also Paul's own appointment by Christ "toward service" (εἰς διακονίαν, 1 Tim 1:12). Paul could not be clearer about his esteem for Mark. Thus, the forceful command "Taking-up Mark, bring [him] with you" (Μᾶρκον ἀναλαβὼν ἄγε μετὰ σεαυτου). It sounds almost as if Paul is as eager to see Mark as he is Timothy.

The last personal reference to Paul's compatriots is to Tychicus: "But Tychicus I sent toward Ephesus" (Τύχικον δὲ ἀπέστειλα εἰς Ἔφεσον). It is noteworthy that Paul offers little comment on any of these persons. He assumes Timothy and the audience would have been familiar with all these individuals. Here too little can be said about "Tychicus." He is mentioned in Acts 20:4, Eph 6:21–22, and Col 4:7 as a trusted emissary for Paul. Perhaps significant is the explicit language "sent toward Ephesus": Tychicus may be delivering the letter to Timothy and serving as his substitute; but we cannot be sure of this.[7] What is clear is that he is acting on the apostle's orders.

Paul now proceeds to make some personal requests: "The cloak that I left (ἀπέλιπον) in Troas with Carpus—when you come bring, and the books, especially the parchments" (4:13). Some brief comments. First, it is clear that Paul expects Timothy will "come" (ἐρχόμενος), that is, the two will be reunited. Second, the items Timothy is to bring include a "cloak" (φαιλόνην) that Paul "left" (ἀπέλιπον) with Carpus—specifically "books" (βιβλία)—and "parchments" (μεμβράνας) presumably for writing. The mention of a specific piece of clothing brings to mind Paul's closing words in 1 Timothy: "For we brought nothing into the world, and we cannot take anything out of the world. But if we have food and clothing, with these we will be content" (6:7–8). Paul seems to be modeling here a modest and content life even in the face of imprisonment. The mention of "books" and "parchments" is suggestive of Paul's own commitment to "endure in the things you learned . . . and . . . the sacred writings" (3:14–15). Paul does not suppose that he has "arrived." Rather, we see an ongoing zeal to learn in order to better fulfill his work as teacher, preacher, and apostle.[8] The adverb "especially" (μάλιστα) may be indicative of Paul's

---

7. Köstenberger, *1–2 Timothy and Titus*, 282: "Moreover, Paul anticipates sending Tychicus to Ephesus, presumably in order to deliver the present letter and perhaps also to relieve Timothy upon his arrival so that Timothy can depart for Rome to be with Paul." See also Towner, *Letters*, 626–27.

8. Towner, *Letters*, 630: "What further can we learn from this reference? From the

desire to write more letters to various persons and churches, especially if his death is looming.

The A element concludes with v. 14a: "Alexander the coppersmith displayed many evils to me." It is quite possible that the "Alexander" (Ἀλέξανδρος) in view is the same "Alexander" (Ἀλέξανδρος) whom Paul handed over to Satan in order to be disciplined (1 Tim 1:20). The mention here at the end of 2 Timothy in contrast to the beginning of 1 Timothy suggests the persisting challenge this individual posed. In addition to the mention of his craft as a "coppersmith" (χαλκεὺς), Paul underscores that "Alexander" did him great harm.[9] The verb "displayed" (ἐνεδείξατο) echoes Paul's conversion account where Paul declares that his call to ministry was so that Christ might "display" (ἐνδείξηται) his perfect patience to all who would come to believe (1 Tim 1:16). "Alexander" serves almost as an anti-type to Christ who showed favor, mercy, and grace—all good things—to Paul. The specification of "many" (πολλά) highlights the unrelenting quality of Alexander's opposition to Paul.

2 Timothy 4:14b-17

The Lord's Faithfulness to Paul in the Face of Persecution

(B ELEMENT)

The B element begins with a declarative assurance: "to him the Lord (κύριος) will recompense according to his works." Paul uses the same verb here ("recompense"; ἀποδώσει) as in 4:8 where he asserted, "The Lord will recompense (ἀποδώσει) to me on that day." The Lord, then, is again reiterated as the equal dispenser of both prize and punishment: to the one that endures in righteousness and fulfills his calling, he will award life; to the one committed to doing evil, he will "recompense" accordingly. In other words, "the Lord" is the righteous judge

---

perspective of the historical Pauline mission, Paul's request reveals that he was a man of letters devoted to the study of the Scriptures, who, if at all possible, wanted to have his writings and writing materials (from notebooks containing personal correspondence to early Christian and biblical texts) close at hand."

9. Towner, *Letters*, 631: "Paul's reference would be to false charges made by Alexander (in Troas) that led to his arrest by the Roman authorities. Naturally this narrower interpretation, which is plausible and should not be ruled out, would tie up some loose ends very nicely. In either case the reference may be to Alexander's part in Paul's arrest and subsequent trial; and apparently it is Alexander's location as Paul writes that makes him a threat to Timothy."

that makes pronouncements "according to [a person's] works" (κατὰ τὰ ἔργα αὐτοῦ).[10] Anyone that has ever experienced injustice knows well that comfort is not found in a god that is nothing but all-loving. Such a "god" cannot bring comfort to the one that has lost loved ones to the many seemingly random acts of violence.[11] Comfort *and* conviction from raising the sword of vindication come from belief in a God that is equally committed to grace and justice.[12]

No doubt the concluding prepositional phrase of v. 4:14b would have been jarring to Paul's audience. After all, in the opening chapter he declared that God "saved us and called to a holy calling not according to our works (κατὰ τὰ ἔργα ἡμῶν); rather according to his own purpose and grace" (1:9). So which is it? Does God repay a person, as he will for Alexander, "according to his works"? Or is grace the decisive factor? The answering is a vexing "yes." The Lord "recompenses" everyone the same way he will repay Alexander, according to his works. The Christian, however, is a new creation in Christ. Specifically, by virtue of his faith-union with the risen Lord, he becomes one with him such that all that is true for Christ is now true for him. This is why the apostle is careful to underscore that God's grace has been given to us "*in* Christ Jesus" (1:9). And because the believer is in him, Christ's righteousness is imputed to the believer as well. Eternal life and glory are "recompensed" truly because God now

10. See also LXX Ps 27:4 (κατὰ τὰ ἔργα αὐτῶν); Ps 61:13 (κατὰ τὰ ἔργα αὐτοῦ). For further reflection on the phrase, see Yinger, *Paul, Judaism, and Judgment according to Deeds*.

11. See Miroslav Volf's comments on the relationship between non-violence and belief in divine vengeance: "My thesis that the practice of nonviolence requires a belief in divine vengeance will be unpopular with many Christians, especially theologians in the West. To the person who is inclined to dismiss it, I suggest imagining that you are delivering a lecture in a war zone (which is where a paper that underlies this chapter was originally delivered). Among your listeners are people whose cities and villages have been first plundered, then burned and leveled to the ground, whose daughters and sisters have been raped, whose fathers and brothers have had their throats slit. The topic of the lecture: a Christian attitude toward violence. The thesis: we should not retaliate since God is perfect noncoercive love. Soon you would discover that it takes the quiet of a suburban home for the birth of the thesis that human nonviolence corresponds to God's refusal to judge. In a scorched land, soaked in the blood of the innocent, it will invariably die. And as one watches it die, one will do well to reflect about many other pleasant captivities of the liberal mind" (*Exclusion and Embrace*, 234).

12. Köstenberger, *1-2 Timothy and Titus*, 284: "Paul knows his struggle is not against flesh and blood, resting content that the Lord (i.e., Christ; cf. vv. 8, 18) will repay this man for what he has done . . . This coheres with Paul's earlier teaching not to take revenge but to leave room for God's wrath (Rom 12:17-21)."

views the believer as if he had perfectly obeyed him. Thus, the believer is judged "according to his works."

Returning to Paul's discussion on Alexander, Timothy is warned, "him you yourself guard [against], for strongly he opposed our words." The operative verb "guard" (φυλάσσου) creates an echo chamber. In 1 Tim 5:21, Paul exhorts, "guard (φυλάξῃς) these things" [concerning the treatment of elders]; and in 1 Tim 6:20, "guard (φύλαξον) the entrustment." In 2 Tim 1:12, "[God] is powerful to guard (φυλάξαι) my entrustment toward that day"; and in 2 Tim 1:14, "The commendable entrustment guard (φύλαξον) through the Holy Spirit." The somewhat frequent repetition of this verb in these letters reiterates one of the controlling images of 2 Timothy—that of a soldier who has been summoned to preserve and promote the gospel. The specification ("you yourself"; σύ) underscores that Alexander poses a continuing threat to Paul and his associates. Again, the apostle does not shy from warning Timothy of people's capacity for evil: he does not want any believer to suppose that human beings are innately good. Timothy must therefore be on "guard" like a soldier readying for the enemy's attack.

Alexander, who first made his appearance in 1 Tim 1:20, however, is not an ordinary foe. Paul makes this clear through the inclusion of the adverb "strongly" (λίαν). Some people will be nuisances in ministry, but that is all. Alexander, however, was a force to be reckoned with.[13] Paul does not include any details beyond the general description "he opposed our words" (ἀντέστη τοῖς ἡμετέροις λόγοις). The verb "opposed" (ἀντέστη) occurred earlier when the apostle described Jannes and James who "opposed" (ἀντέστησαν) Moses (3:8). Verse 15 suggests that Alexander represents the archetype of those who seek to turn many from "our words." He may also typify the sycophant who comes to scratch the ears of those who are inclined to reject the truth of the gospel (4:3–4). Either way, if Timothy is to "fulfill" his ministry (4:5), he cannot be ignorant of Alexander.

As Paul brings his letter to a close, he reflects yet again on the theme of abandonment and aloneness that he noted in 1:15. He recalls—without any bitterness: "In my first defense none was present with me; rather

13. Towner, *Letters*, 634: "What Paul feared and warns of in the case of Alexander was not simply the opposition to the teaching but rather that he might go to the same lengths as he did in the drastic action he took in opposition to Paul (false, incriminating charges against him to the Roman authorities being high on the list of probable explanations)."

all left me; may it not be charged to them." This is a vivid scene, though it is unclear exactly what Paul is referring to.[14] "Defense" (ἀπολογία) is a technical term referring to a speech given to defend oneself.[15] The verb "appeared" (παρεγένετο) means "showing up publicly at a place."[16] The audience can feel the poignant quality of this recollection. As Paul stood to defend himself, he must have looked around. Despite all the years of pouring his life into the lives of many churches and individuals, his defense resembled Jesus's own abandonment on the cross—"*none* (οὐδείς) was present." Moreover, the inclusion of the statement "rather all left me" (ἀλλὰ πάντες με ἐγκατέλιπον) conveys that some had been with him—and could have stood in his defense—but chose to desert him. The previous occurrence of the verb "left" (ἐγκατέλιπον) in 4:10 to describe Demas suggests Paul is referring also to his former colleague—which makes these words all the more painful. As Jesus's disciples deserted him in the Garden of Gethsemane, so now Paul's "disciples" have abandoned him.[17]

The second half of v. 16 is striking because of the obvious contrast with the second half of 4:14b. Whereas with Alexander Paul finds comfort in knowing "the Lord will recompense him," with his deserters he prays "may it not be charged to them!" The verb "charged" (λογισθείη) could translate as "reckon" or "credit." Here too it appears that Paul is echoing Jesus's prayer on the cross: "Father, forgive them, for they know not what they do" (Luke 23:24). Paul pleads for his deserters, asking the righteous judge to treat them with the same mercy that Paul received in his call to ministry (1 Tim 1:12–15).

It is worth pausing here to reflect on the significance of v. 16b. By asking God to show kindness to his deserters, Paul is not only modeling grace but also showing that it is possible to remain as light in the deluge of darkness. To be robbed by a stranger is vexing; to be robbed by a friend is disturbing. In this sense, Paul's former colleagues have hurt him more than even Alexander. Many in Paul's experience of aloneness might have been tempted toward despair and bitterness. Yet, he responds

---

14. Köstenberger, *1-2 Timothy and Titus*, 284: "'First defense' probably relates to Paul's courtroom defense at the initial hearing of his trial in Rome, the *prima actio* or preliminary investigation of the proceedings." For a more detailed analysis, see Towner, *Letters*, 636–38.

15. Friberg and Friberg, *Analytical Greek New Testament*, s.v.

16. Friberg and Friberg, *Analytical Greek New Testament*, s.v.

17. Compare the language of 2 Tim 4:16 and Mark 15:34; see also Ps 21:2.

to his deserters in essentially the same way as he responds to his searcher, Onesimus: for both he asks for God's mercy. The secret to this apparent supernatural ability is given in 1:12—confidence in God's vindication, which frees us from hatred so that we might pray for and bless our enemies.

Lest any suppose that Paul was cut from a unique cloth of superb patience and grace, the apostle is careful and quick to give credit where credit is due: "But the Lord (κύριος) was present with me and strengthened me, so that through me the proclamation might be fulfilled and all the Gentiles might hear it."[18] Here again we see a similar pattern of qualification that we encountered in 1:15–17. In the earlier instance, Paul indicated that all in Asia turned from him, but then he immediately points out how Onesiphorus sought him out earnestly. Here in 4:17 Paul does the same by stating how "the Lord was present with me and strengthened me" even though none remained present with him in his "first defense." The two recollections are so similar that one wonders whether Paul is referring to the same instance. If so, the Lord's presence was materialized through Onesiphorus. If this is the case, the lesson is that the extraordinary (in this case, God's empowering presence) took place through the ordinary (in this case, Onesiphorus).

Noteworthy is the apostle's emphasis in this seventh microchiasm on the theme of presence. The microchiasm flows from Paul's request for Timothy's presence (4:9) to his mention of his absent colleagues (4:10, 15) to his thanksgiving for God's presence. God's presence (παρέστη) should be understood as an empowering presence, as the proceeding verb "strengthened" (ἐνεδυνάμωσέν) suggests. The verb "strengthened" is especially significant for two reasons. First, it is the same verb Paul uses to describe his conversion account: "I give thanks to him who strengthened (ἐνεδυνάμωσέν) me, Christ Jesus our Lord" (1 Tim 1:12). God's empowering presence in this later stage of Paul's ministry underscores God's faithfulness: he will bring to completion every good work he has started through the same power that he first poured into Paul. Second, the verb also occurred in 2 Tim 2:1: "be-strengthened (ἐνδυναμοῦ) in the grace that is in Christ Jesus." Paul has already stated the "universal" quality of God's faithfulness in 4:8: "the Lord will recompense to me on that day, the just judge, but not only to me; rather and to all who have loved the manifestation of his." As Timothy's spiritual father, Paul wants

---

18. See also Acts 18:9–10; 22:17–21; 23:11.

his son to know that the same "Christ Jesus" that has "strengthened" Paul now offers grace for Timothy to "be-strengthened."[19]

Verse 17b makes clear the purpose (ἵνα) of God's empowering presence: "so that through me the proclamation might be fulfilled and all the Gentiles might hear it." The verb "fulfilled" (πληροφορηθῇ) would have caught Timothy's attention. Just a few verses earlier Paul exhorted *him* to "fulfill (πληροφόρησον) his service" (4:5). Now the apostle is insinuating that *God* will enable Timothy to "fulfill" his service even as he has enabled Paul. Specifically, Paul has in mind his gospel "proclamation" (κήρυγμα). The statement "that through me the proclamation might be fulfilled" is profound in light of everything that has happened so far in Paul's life. Paul's "proclamation"—both the act and content of his preaching—has been hampered by imprisonment, abandonment, false teachers, people's waywardness, people's preference for false teachers, and committed agitators. In short, from a human perspective there has been no shortage of obstacles standing in the way of Paul's "proclamation." Yet, Paul asserts that the Lord's presence and strength were sufficient to ensure that "the proclamation might be fulfilled and all the Gentiles might hear it." In short, v. 17b asserts that God's sovereign power will ensure that his divine purpose to bring the gospel to all nations will be accomplished no matter what. The specific reference to the "Gentiles" (ἔθνη) is significant as it recalls Paul's self-identification as "preacher and apostle . . . and teacher of the Gentiles (ἐθνῶν)" (1 Tim 2:7). Proclamation to this group was Paul's unique task relative to Peter; hence the specification "so that *through me* (δι᾽ ἐμοῦ)."

Verse 17 concludes the B element with the summary statement, "and I was rescued from the lion's mouth." The graphic descriptor "lion's mouth" (στόματος λέοντος) literally expresses that on more than one

---

19. Towner, *Letters*, 642: "The second verb phrase explains that in Paul's situation divine presence/help was experienced as 'empowerment.' This is the same verb used in the command to Timothy, in preparation for ministry, in 2:1, creating a link that makes the parenetic dimension of this portrait immediately evident: what Paul commanded earlier in the letter for Timothy is substantiated here on the basis of personal experience."

occasion Paul faced death;[20] but he was "rescued" (ἐρρύσθην).[21] The divine passive underscores God's sovereign rule in all situations. The verb echoes its earlier occurrence in 3:11 where Paul wrote similarly: "the persecutions, the sufferings that were to me at Antioch, at Iconium, at Lystra—which persecutions I also bore-up—and from all the Lord rescued (ἐρρύσατο) me." Here again we see the reminder to Timothy and all the believers with him that each person's life is in God's hands. On the surface, it may seem that a person's life depends on the graces of those in power and with authority. But Paul—in light of what has taken place in his ministry—asserts that this is untrue. The assurance Paul gives is that the Lord will preserve each person's life according to the divine purpose he has received.

2 Timothy 4:18–20a

PAUL'S CONFIDENCE AND FINAL REMARKS

(B' ELEMENT)

20. Compare to Ps 21:22 LXX: "Save me from the lion's mouth (ἐκ στόματος λέοντος)." The precise echo of the phrase in 2 Tim 4:17 suggests that Psalm 21 LXX, which includes the themes of abandonment and rescue, form the background to 2 Tim 4:16–17. For a detailed analysis of this intertextuality, see Smith, 2 Timothy, 163–64; This is not merely a pedantic observation. Instead, the intertextuality reflects Paul's rich theology of union with Christ: "Just as the passion of Christ was viewed through Psalm 22, Paul sees his life through the psalmist's experience and he wants Timothy to do the same" (Smith, 2 Timothy, 164). "In various ways, not least in the contact established with Psalm 21 (LXX), Paul interpreted his final episode of suffering for the gospel in terms of the model left behind by Jesus Christ . . . Nevertheless, Paul's suffering in no way supersedes that of Jesus; it is rather the complementary outworking of one who has taken to himself the cruciform character and behavior of the Lord." See also Towner, Letters, 640–48.

21. Riesner ("Paul's Trial and End," 407) proposes that Paul may be alluding to the Roman Emperor; see similarly Hutson, Timothy and Titus, 205. This, however, is unlikely: "The most likely meaning for the phrase ['from the lion's mouth'] is 'death.' Funerary inscriptions with a lion clutching the head of a man are used to symbolize the power of death. David experienced deliverance from real lions (1 Sam. 17.37) and could therefore be seen as being comfortable, as the notional psalmist, in using the lion as a symbol to portray death (Pss. 7.3; 35.17). Again, the most likely background is Psalm 22. There the psalmist describes the threat of death in terms of 'roaring lions . . . opening their mouths wide against me' . . . Therefore most likely Paul is avowing that he has been delivered from having his case go to a subsequent trial and a verdict of death" (Smith, 2 Timothy, 173).

Having experienced God's faithfulness, Paul looks to his future and expresses in the B' element, "The Lord will rescue me from all evil work and will save [me] into his heavenly kingdom" (4:18).[22] Perhaps worth noting is the multiple instances that the title "the Lord" (κύριος) occurs in the letter.[23] Implicitly, Paul makes the point that Christ Jesus reigns as the sovereign "Lord" irrespective of what the immediate circumstances might suggest. The repetition of the title in 4:17 and 4:18 of the corresponding B and B' elements in addition to the recurrence of the verb rescue ("will rescue"; ῥύσεταί) communicate God's unchanging faithfulness: as the Lord "rescued" Paul then, so now "he will rescue" Paul—not just "from the lion's mouth" but also "from *all* evil work" (ἀπὸ παντὸς ἔργου πονηροῦ). The term "work" recalls Alexander's evil "works" (ἔργα) as noted in 4:14b of the corresponding B element. Paul's great confidence in life—and the reason why he does not need to take up the sword of vengeance—is because "the *Lord*" will rescue him from "all evil work" as typified in Alexander's evil deeds.[24]

The mention of Paul's salvation ("will save"; σώσει) reminds us of the breadth of Paul's "doctrine of salvation." There is the past sense as expressed in 1:9: God "saved (σώσαντος) us and called us to a holy calling." There is also a present sense as expressed in Paul's experience of rescue throughout his ministry and in the related sanctification that took place. Finally, there is the sense of future salvation: "he will save [me] into his heavenly kingdom." Again, the emphasis falls on God's agency, sovereignty, and faithfulness: the salvation God predestined will go forth until Paul has been brought "into the heavenly kingdom" (εἰς τὴν βασιλείαν αὐτοῦ τὴν ἐπουράνιον).[25] The mention of the kingdom recalls 4:1 where Paul charged Timothy "in-the-presence-of God and Christ Jesus . . . and

22. Smith, *2 Timothy*, 173: "So far Paul has declared what God has delivered him *from*. Now he will proclaim what God is saving him *to*. The other side of the story is that regardless of what happens or how many days he lives he knows that through all this, God will save him into his heavenly kingdom."

23. The title occurs sixteen times in total, five of which are clustered between 4:8–22.

24. Towner, *Letters*, 646: "'Every evil attack [deed]' certainly envisages the sort of evil and injustice done to him by the Roman authorities, but the particular configuration also contrasts obviously with the term 'good deeds' that characterizes authentic Christian behavior in these letters."

25. Towner, *Letters*, 647: "The two-part affirmation of the Lord's salvation promise is in Paul's historical context a thorough rejection of the dominion of evil (rulers or opponents) in view of the reality and supremacy of the Lord's dominion/kingdom."

[by] the manifestation of his and the kingdom of his (τὴν βασιλείαν αὐτου)." That Paul is saved "into" his heavenly kingdom means that we will be a part of the "kingdom" Jesus will bring at his second appearing. Elsewhere Paul notes that believers are coheirs of Christ, suggesting that we are not just citizens of the "kingdom" but royal members who will reign with Christ in glory; hence, Paul's earlier declaration, "if we endure, also we will-reign-together" (2:12). The kingdom—not imprisonment, not shame, not alienation—is the final and sure destination of Paul and all who have longed for Christ's return. The mention of the "*heavenly* kingdom" here at the conclusion of the letter reiterates that all endurance comes from the "promise of the life that is in Christ Jesus" (1:1): we can endure every evil deed when we fix our eyes on our final destination.

Fittingly, in view of Paul's emphasis on God's faithfulness expressed climactically in salvation, Paul concludes v. 18 with the doxology: "to him be the glory for the eternities of eternities, amen" (ᾧ ἡ δόξα εἰς τοὺς αἰῶνας τῶν αἰώνων, ἀμήν). There is a faint echo here of 2:10 where Paul indicated, "all-things I endure for-the-sake of the elect, that they themselves might also obtain the salvation that [is] in Christ Jesus with glory eternal (δόξης αἰωνίου)." In this earlier verse, the emphasis falls on Paul—his endurance in the face of persecution and suffering. Yet, as he has underscored, his own faithfulness is the result of God's faithfulness. If any enter into "eternal glory" through Paul, the ultimate reason is the Lord's mercy; thus, Paul rightly declares "to *him* be glory for the eternities of eternities, amen."[26]

A similar doxological statement is found in 1 Tim 1:17: "To the king of the eternities, without-mortality, without-visibility, to the only God, honor and glory for the eternities of eternities, amen (δόξα εἰς τοὺς αἰῶνας τῶν αἰώνων, ἀμήν)." This doxology follows Paul's reflection over his conversion and call to ministry. Paul sees that God's favor toward him began even before his conversion. The similarity of the two doxologies may suggest that Paul is using a well-known hymn,[27] but the repetition may be more purposeful. It seems to highlight how the entire Christian life is about grace from beginning to end: God's grace that first brought

26. Towner, *Letters*, 648: "The concluding 'Amen' . . . punctuates the affirmation as an undeniable fact to which he is completely committed. As a conclusion to the body of the letter, the doxology invites readers to add their voice to Paul's worship."

27. Smith, *2 Timothy*, 173: "This doxology is identical to Gal 1.5 and Heb. 13.21 and very close to other doxologies in terms of content and structure (Rom. 16.27; Phil. 4:20; 1 Pet. 4.11)."

Paul into Christ's service is the same grace that will bring him into his kingdom. How else can Timothy and the believers with him respond other than with a resounding "amen"!

Paul now shifts to giving concluding greetings and final updates on persons of common interest. Verse 20 reads, "Greet Prisca and Aquila and the household of Onesiphorus." Paul is sending greetings to his beloved fellow workers. Prisca and Aquila served as Paul's partners in ministry from the very moment he arrived in Corinth. Paul mentions them in other letters, which suggests they were significant and intimate coworkers.[28] Perhaps more noteworthy is "the household of Onesiphorus" (τὸν Ὀνησιφόρου οἶκον). This phrase recalls Paul's earlier prayer-wish in 1:16: "May the Lord give mercy to the household of Onesiphorus" (τῷ Ὀνησιφόρου οἴκῳ). The mention here again to this "household" signifies how dearly Paul holds them, given especially Onesiphorus sought him out even when all had abandoned him (1:15).[29] Again, we cannot help but wonder if the Lord's presence and strength came through the very ordinary means of a faithful friend. In the overarching concern for endurance, Onesiphorus's kindness to Paul serves as a powerful reminder of what a difference we can make in the lives of even the "super" saints simply by remembering them, another significant theme in the letter.

The B' element concludes with a reference to another of Paul's colleagues: "Erastus remained in Corinth"[30] There may be a double-meaning to the verb "remained" (ἔμεινεν). On the one hand, this may be a simple update to Timothy that Erastus is continuing ministry in Corinth. On the other hand, the use of the verb recalls its earlier explicit occurrences in 2:13—"if we are without-faith, he remains (μένει) faithful"—and

28. See Rom 16:3; 1 Cor 16:19; also Acts 18:26. Almost all commentators note the surprising sequence of mentioning Priscilla first. For example, Smith, *2 Timothy*, 174: "It is doubtful that this is a gesture of courtesy to a woman since when another couple is mentioned together, Adronicus and Junia in Rom 16.7, it is the husband's name that is listed first which is just four verses after Paul refers to Priscilla and Aquila (Rom. 16.3). The reversal of order may [be] because she held a higher social rank than Aquila or she held the primary ministry role of the couple."

29. It is possible that Paul mentions "the household of Onesiphororus" instead of "Onesiphorus" because this dear friend of Paul has passed. But we cannot be sure of this.

30. See Acts 19:22; Rom 16:23. Scholars disagree whether these three references (including 2 Tim 4:20) refer to a single or three different persons; see Brookins, "(In) frequency of the Name 'Erastus' in Antiquity," 496–513; Cadbury, "Erastus of Corinth," 44–45; Marshall, *Pastoral Epistles*, 828; Winter, *Seek the Welfare of the City*, 192–97; Towner, *Letters*, 652.

3:14—"But your yourself remain (μένε) in the things you learned . . ." The selection of this verb to describe Erastus is unlikely arbitrary. In a subtle way, the verb recalls the letter's primary goal, namely to encourage and facilitate endurance on the part of Timothy and all with him. It is quite possible that Timothy heard v. 20a as another exemplar of endurance in ministry.[31] But more relevant to Paul's concern in this microchiasm is that Erastus's remaining in Corinth brings attention again to the fact that Paul is alone.

2 Timothy 4:20b–21

Closing Remarks

(A' Element)

The concluding A' element begins with the final update: "but Trophimus being ill, I left (ἀπέλιπον) at Miletus." The verb "left" (ἀπέλιπον) recalls its corresponding occurrence in 4:13 of the A element. As with the cloak, which Paul left but wishes to have, Trophimus has been "left at Miletus" not because of Paul's preference but because of Trophimus's illness (ἀσθενοῦντα). The broader point Paul is reiterating is that whether for one reason or another, Paul ultimately has been "left" to himself.

Having summarized his personal situation, Paul now reiterates his previous request "Do-your-best to come" (Σπούδασον . . . ἐλθεῖν) with the added detail "before winter" (πρὸ χειμῶνος). The mention of "winter" elucidates Paul's specific request for his cloak.[32] The corresponding request "Do your best to come (Σπούδασον ἐλθεῖν) to me quickly" in 4:9 of the A element is both deepened in its urgency and specificity through the movement from the A element to the A' element. Also, Timothy and the audience realize that Paul's seemingly extravagant words in 1:3–5 are said with utmost sincerity: he truly longs to see Timothy, "so-that I might become-full of joy" (1:4).

---

31. Contra Towner, *Letters*, 652: "Paul's reason for mentioning Erastus at this point is unknown, unless it is simply to explain why he was absent, or to indicate that Timothy might find him en route to Rome."

32. Also, "traveling from Ephesus to Rome mostly by ship, he would need to leave early enough to avoid seaports being closed due to inclement weather (the Mediterranean was impassable from November to March)" (Köstenberger, *1–2 Timothy and Titus*, 288).

Verse 21 concludes with a series of greetings: "Eubulus and Pudens and Linus and Claudia and all the brothers greets you." Nothing is known of these persons for us to make any substantial comments here.[33] Here too Paul may intend to accomplish more than following a customary way to close his letter. The mention of these colleagues is meant to spur Timothy on to endurance as he is reminded of his fellow saints.

---

33. But see Hutson, *First and Second Timothy and Titus*, 206–7.

10

2 Timothy 4:22

The Lord Be with Your Spirit and Grace Be with You

(A' Unit)

THIS CHAPTER EXAMINES THE final of eight microchiastic units within the 2 Timothy macrochiasm.

As is fitting, given Paul's goal to spur Timothy and all the believers with him toward endurance, the apostle concludes the letter with a prayer of blessing.

The Eighth Microchiastic Unit

The final of eight microchiasms within 2 Timothy is composed carefully of several elements (A-B-A'). Linguistic parallels are indicated by the Greek text.

A. 22a The Lord be with (μετά) your spirit.

    B. 22b Grace

A'. 22c be with (μεθ᾽) you all.

Given the brevity of this last unit, we will treat it in a single section.

Second Timothy ends with a prayer of blessing that follows the chiastic movement reflected above. It begins with the wish, "The Lord be with your spirit." The mention of "the Lord" (ὁ κύριος) echoes its many occurrences in the letter.[1] Paul prays that the same "Lord" that will someday return to judge all the earth would strengthen Timothy in the present toward endurance. The Lord's presence and empowerment is not confined to the future, as suggested in 2:7. He is Lord of the past (3:11), present, and future.

The specification of "your *spirit*" (πνεύματός) versus simply "you" seems significant. The term brings us back to the letter's opening, where Paul exhorted Timothy not to be afraid because God has given to him "a spirit (πνεῦμα) . . . of power and love and self-control" (1:7). Thus the "spirit" Timothy now possesses is that which was given to him by the Lord himself. Already, then, Timothy has been graced to perform supernatural work. Moreover, this new "spirit" shares a unique union with the "Holy Spirit" (πνεύματος ἁγίου): "The commendable entrustment guard through the Holy Spirit (πνεύματος) who is housed in us" (1:14).

What, then, is this initial prayer seeking to achieve if both the source and fellowship of the "spirit" Timothy has is already supernatural? More than likely Paul has in view an extra outpouring of God's empowerment—presumably through the Spirit—so that Timothy may perform the task set forth in the letter. Something similar is found in Ephesians where Paul prays for the blessing of enlightenment upon the believers of Ephesus who are already blessed in Christ (Eph 1:16–21). It is not so much that Paul is hoping that these believers would come to a saving knowledge of the gospel. Rather, the prayer that "the eyes of your hearts would be enlightened" (1:18) reflects Paul's hope that they would come to a deeper conviction of the things they already know. In like fashion, Paul's prayer in 2 Tim 4:22 is for God to pour afresh grace upon Timothy so that the "spirit" he has would experience more power for endurance.

The A and A' elements pivot around the single term "grace" (χάρις) in the B element. Its occurrence here in the nominative singular form is intentional, serving as a bookend to its other only nominative form in 1:2: "Grace (χάρις), mercy, peace from God the Father." As noted earlier, the sort of "grace" in view is likely the "exceptional effects produced by God's favor," namely his empowering presence.[2] Though the meaning is similar to its first occurrence, Timothy and the audience are better able to appreciate the need for grace now that Paul has concluded his letter. In receiving the summons to guard the entrustment and endure

---

1. See 1:16, 18; 2:7, 19; 3:11; 4:8, 14, 17, 18.

2. Friberg and Friberg, *Analytical Greek New Testament*, s.v.

in faithfulness, Timothy and the believers are now better positioned to embrace the "grace" that comes through the prayers of others.

The A' element concludes with a repetition of the preposition "with" (μεθ') and the second person plural noun "you all" (ὑμῶν). This imagery of "with-ness" certainly recalls Paul's poignant experience recorded in 4:16–17: on the one hand, in his time of greatest need none stood by him but all deserted him. On the other hand, Paul declares that the Lord remained with him. Not only so, he also delivered him from all evil so that he would be able to complete his task of bringing the gospel to the Gentiles. So now his closing prayer is effectively, "As the Lord was with my spirit, so now may he be with yours, granting you much grace to endure and complete the race set before you." In passing, it should be noted that by praying for grace, Paul is implicitly indicating that any final faithfulness on the part of any believer is the result of God's own faithfulness. In the end, if Timothy endures, it is because the Lord remained with him and gave him grace in answer to Paul's prayer.

As much as the A and A' elements share a common preposition, they differ noticeably in the pronoun. In the first instance, Paul uses the second person *singular* pronoun "you" (σου); in the second, he uses the second person *plural* "you all" (ὑμῶν).[3] This observation simply reiterates that 2 Timothy, like all the NT epistles, was meant to be read aloud (or performed) before the congregation of believers. Given this, while Paul's words were directed primarily to Timothy, they were directed secondarily to the believers with him.[4] Paul, then, concludes his letter of endurance in remembrance not just of Timothy but also all who align themselves with the apostle and the one true gospel.

---

3. See also 1 Tim 6:21; Titus 3:15.

4. Köstenberger, *1–2 Timothy and Titus*, 288: "'Your' (v. 22) is singular, referring to Timothy, who certainly could use encouragement (e.g., 1:5–8). 'With you,' on the other hand, is in the plural (cf. 1 Tim 6:21), indicating that the entire letter, while addressed to Timothy, is to be read in public (cf. Titus 3.15)." Towner, *Letters*, 655: "The benediction . . . is given in two parts, the first of which . . . is directed to Timothy, the second to a wider group."

Bibliography

Bailey, Kenneth E. *Paul through Mediterranean Eyes: Cultural Studies in 1 Corinthians.* Downers Grove: InterVarsity, 2011.

Bassler, Jouette M. *1 and 2 Timothy and Titus.* ANTC. Nashville: Abingdon, 1996.

Bauckham, Richard. "Pseudo-Apostolic Letters." *Journal of Biblical Literature* 107 (1988) 469–94.

Blomberg, Craig L. "The Structure of 2 Corinthians 1–7." *CTR* 4 (1989) 3–20.

Boda, Mark J. *"Return to Me": A Biblical Theology of Repentance.* Nottingham, UK: Apollos, 2015.

Boice, James Montgomery, and Philip Graham Ryken. *The Doctrines of Grace: Rediscovering the Evangelical Gospel.* Wheaton, IL: Crossway, 2009.

Botha, Pieter J. J. "The Verbal Art of the Pauline Letters: Rhetoric, Performance, and Presence." In *Rhetoric and the New Testament: Essays from the 1992 Heidelberg Conference,* edited by Stanley E. Porter and Thomas H. Olbricht, 409–28. JSNTSup 90. Sheffield: Sheffield Academic, 1993.

Brookins, A. Timothy. "The (In)frequency of the Name 'Erastus' in Antiquity: A Literary, Papyrological, and Epigraphical Catalog." *New Testament Studies* 59 (2013) 496–516.

Brouwer, Wayne. *The Literary Development of John 13–17: A Chiastic Reading.* Atlanta: SBL, 2000.

Cadbury, Henry J. "Erastus of Corinth." *Journal of Biblical Literature* 50 (1931) 42–58.

Carson, D. A. *Showing the Spirit: A Theological Exposition of 1 Corinthians 12–14.* Grand Rapids: Baker, 2019.

Clarke, Andrew D. "'Be Imitators of Me': Paul's Model of Leadership." *Tyndale Bulletin* 49 (1998) 329–60.

Combs, William W. "The Biblical Role of the Evangelist." *DBSJ* 7 (2002) 23–48.

Cranfield, C. E. B. "Changes of Person and Number in Paul's Epistles." In *Honouring the Past and Shaping the Future: Religious and Biblical Studies in Wales; Essays in Honour of Gareth Lloyd Jones,* edited by Robert Pope, 112–32. Herefordshire, UK: Gracewing, 2003.

Deppe, Dean B. *The Theological Intentions of Mark's Literary Devices: Markan Intercalculations, Frames, Allusionary Repetitions, Narrative Surprises, and Three Types of Mirroring.* Eugene, OR: Wipf & Stock, 2015.

DeSilva, D. A. "Honor and Shame." In *Dictionary of New Testament Background,* edited by Craig A. Evans and Stanley E. Porter. Downers Grove:: InterVarsity, 2005.

Dewey, Joanna. "Mark as Aural Narrative: Structures as Clues to Understanding." *STR* 36 (1992) 45–56.

———. *The Oral Ethos of the Early Church: Speaking, Writing, and the Gospel of Mark.* BPC 8. Eugene, OR: Cascade, 2013.

Duff, J. "A Reconsideration of Pseudepigraphy in Early Christianity." PhD diss., Oxford University, 1998.

Edwards, Jonathan. *Jonathan Edwards Resolutions; and, Advice to Young Converts.* Edited by Stephen J. Nichols. Phillipsburg, NJ: P & R, 2001.

Fee, Gordon D. *1 and 2 Timothy, Titus.* NIBC 13. Peabody: Hendrickson, 1988.

Frame, John M. *Salvation Belongs to the Lord: An Introduction to Systematic Theology.* Phillipsburg, NJ: P & R, 2006.

Friberg, B., and T. Friberg. *Analytical Greek New Testament.* Grand Rapids: Baker, 1981.

Fuchs, Rüdiger. *Unerwartete Unterschiede: Müssen wir unsere Ansichten über die Pastoralbriefe Revidieren?* BM 12. Wuppertal, Germany: Brockhaus, 2003.

Gaffin, Richard B., Jr. *By Faith, Not by Sight: Paul and the Order of Salvation.* 2nd ed. Phillipsburg, NJ: P & R, 2013.

Gray, Patrick. *Opening Paul's Letters: A Reader's Guide to Genre and Interpretation.* Grand Rapids: Baker, 2012.

Guthrie, Donald. *The Pastoral Epistles: An Introduction and Commentary.* TynNTC 14. Grand Rapids: Eerdmans, 1990.

Hagner, Donald. *The New Testament: A Historical and Theological Introduction.* Grand Rapids: Baker Academic, 2012.

Harvey, John D. *Listening to the Text: Oral Patterning in Paul's Letters.* Grand Rapids: Baker, 1998.

Hearon, Holly E. "The Implications of Orality for Studies of the Biblical Text." In *Performing the Gospel: Orality, Memory, and Mark; Essays Dedicated to Werner Kelber,* edited by Richard A. Horsley et al., 3–20. Minneapolis: Fortress, 2006.

Heil, John Paul. *1–3 John: Worship by Loving God and One Another to Live Eternally.* Cambridge: James Clarke, 2015.

———. *The Book of Revelation: Worship for Life in the Spirit of Prophecy.* Eugene, OR: Cascade, 2014.

———. "The Chiastic Structure and Meaning of Paul's Letter to Philemon." *Bib* 82 (2001) 178–206.

———. *Colossians: Encouragement to Walk in All Wisdom as Holy Ones in Christ.* ECL 4. Atlanta: SBL, 2010.

———. *Ephesians: Empowerment to Walk in Love for the Unity of All in Christ.* SBL 13. Atlanta: SBL, 2007.

———. *The Gospel of John: Worship for Divine Life Eternal.* Eugene, OR: Cascade, 2015.

———. *The Letter of James: Worship to Live By.* Eugene, OR: Cascade, 2012.

———. *Philippians: Let Us Rejoice in Being Conformed to Christ.* ECL 3. Atlanta: SBL, 2010.

———. *Worship in the Letter to the Hebrews.* Eugene, OR: Cascade, 2013.

Herrick, James A. *The History and Theory of Rhetoric: An Introduction.* 5th ed. New York: Routledge, 2013.

Holland, Glenn S. "'Delivery, Delivery, Delivery': Accounting for Performance in the Rhetoric of Paul's Letters." In *Paul and Ancient Rhetoric: Theory and Practice in the Hellenistic Context,* edited by Stanley E. Porter and Bryan R. Dryer, 119–40. New York: Cambridge University Press, 2016.

Horsley, Richard A. *Text and Tradition in Performance and Writing*. BPC 9. Eugene, OR: Cascade, 2013.

Horton, Michael Scott. *Christ the Lord: The Reformation and Lordship Salvation*. Eugene, OR: Wipf & Stock, 2008.

Hutson, Christopher R. *First and Second Timothy and Titus*. Grand Rapids: Baker Academic, 2019.

———. "Was Timothy Timid? On the Rhetoric of Fearlessness (1 Cor. 16:10–11) and Cowardice (2 Tim 1:7)." *Biblical Research* 42 (1997) 58–73.

James, J. D. *The Genuineness and Authorship of the Pastoral Epistles*. London: Longmans, Green, 1906.

Jeon, Paul S. *1 Timothy: A Charge to God's Missional Household*. Vols. 1–3. Eugene, OR: Pickwick, 2017.

———. *Christian Philanthropy: Daily Devotions in Titus 2–3*. Eugene, OR: Resource, 2019.

———. *God's Wisdom for Making Peace: Daily Devotions in the Letter to Philemon*. Eugene, OR: Resource, 2018.

———. *Introducing Romans*. Eugene, OR: Pickwick, 2011.

———. *Living Intentionally before God: Reflections on 1 Thessalonians*. Eugene, OR: Wipf & Stock, 2013.

———. *A New King: Encountering the Risen Son*. Eugene, OR: Wipf & Stock, 2018.

———. *To Exhort and Reprove: Audience Response to the Chiastic Structures of Paul's Letter to Titus*. Eugene, OR: Pickwick, 2012.

———. *True Faith: Reflections on Paul's Letter to Titus*. Eugene, OR: Wipf & Stock, 2012.

———. *Unreconciled: The New Norm*. Eugene, OR: Wipf & Stock, 2018.

Jeremias, Joachim. "Chiasms in den Paulusbriefen." *ZNW* 49 (1958) 145–56.

Johnson, Luke Timothy. *The First and Second Letters to Timothy*. New Haven: Yale University Press, 2008.

———. *Letters to Paul's Delegates: Timothy 1, Timothy 2, Titus*. London: Bloomsbury Academic, 1996.

Keller, Timothy. *Walking with God through Pain and Suffering*. New York: Dutton, 2013.

Kelly, J. N. D. *A Commentary on the Pastoral Epistles*. HNTC. Peabody: Hendrickson, 1987.

Kierspel, Lars. *Charts on the Life, Letters, and Theology of Paul*. Grand Rapids: Kregel, 2012.

Knight, George W., III. *The Pastoral Epistles: A Commentary on the Greek Text*. NIGTC. Grand Rapids: Eerdmans, 1992.

Knight, Philip H. *Shoe Dog: A Memoir by the Creator of Nike*. New York: Scribner, 2018.

Köstenberger, Andreas J. *Commentary on 1–2 Timothy and Titus*. Nashville: Holman Reference, 2017.

Krumbiegel, Friedemann. *Erziehung in Den Pastoralbriefen: Ein Konzept Zur Konsolidierung Der Gemeinden*. Leipzig: Evangelische Verlagsanstalt, 2013.

Kuruvilla, Abraham. *Mark: A Theological Commentary for Preachers*. Eugene, OR: Cascade, 2012.

———. *Text to Praxis: Hermeneutics and Homiletics in Dialogue*. New York: T. & T. Clark, 2009.

Lea, Thomas. "The Early Christian View of Pseudepigraphic Writings." *Journal of the Evangelical Theological Society* 27 (1984) 65–75.

Lewis, C. S. *The Complete C. S. Lewis Signature Classics*. New York: HarperCollins, 2002.

———. *The Four Loves*. New York: Harcourt, Brace & World, 1960.

———. *The Great Divorce*. New York: Macmillan, 1945.

Lips, Hermann von. *Glaube—Gemeinde—Amt: Zum Verständnis der Ordination in den Pastoralbriefen*. FLANT 122. Göttingen: Vandenhoeck & Ruprecht, 1979.

Malherbe, Abraham Johannes. *Light from the Gentiles: Hellenistic Philosophy and Early Christianity: Collected Essays, 1959–2012*. Edited by Carl R. Holladay et al. Leiden: Brill, 2014.

Malherbe, Abraham J. "Medical Imagery in the Pastorals." In *Texts and Testaments: Critical Essays on the Bible and Early Church Fathers; A Volume in Honor of Stuart Dickson Currie*, edited by W. E. March, 19–35. San Antonio: Trinity University Press, 1980.

Malina, Bruce J. *The New Testament World Insights from Cultural Anthropology*. Louisville: Westminster John Knox, 2002.

Marshall, I. Howard. *A Critical and Exegetical Commentary on the Pastoral Epistles*. London: T. & T. Clark, 2007.

———. "The Holy Spirit in the Pastoral Epistles and the Apostolic Fathers." In *The Holy Spirit and Christian Origins: Essays in Honor of James D. G. Gunn*, edited by Stephen C. Barton et al., 257–69. Grand Rapids: Eerdmans, 2004.

———. *The Pastoral Epistles*. ICC. Edinburgh: T. & T. Clark, 1999.

Metzger, Bruce M. *A Textual Commentary on the Greek New Testament (TCGNT)*. 2nd ed. Stuttgart: Deutsche Bibelgesellschaft, 1994.

Metzger, W. "*Die neōterikai epithymiai* in 2 Tim 2.22." *Theologische Zeitschrift* 33 (1977) 129–36.

Molina, Carlos, and Ernest van Eck. "Σφραγίς (*sfragis*) and Its Metaphorical Testimonial Presence in 2 Timothy 2:19." *HTS Teologiese Studies/Theological Studies* 67 (2011) 1–4.

Mounce, William D. *Pastoral Epistles*. WBC 46. Nashville: Nelson, 2000.

Moxness, Halvor. "Honor and Shame." In *The Social Sciences and New Testament Interpretation*, edited by Richard L. Rohrbaugh, 19–40. Peabody: Hendrickson, 1996.

Nässelqvist, Dan. *Public Reading in Early Christianity: Lectors, Manuscripts, and Sound in the Oral Delivery of John 1–4*. Boston: Brill, 2016.

O'Connor, J. Murphy. "2 Timothy Contrasted with 1 Timothy and Titus." *Revue Biblique* 98 (1991) 403–18.

Oberlinner, Lorenz. *Kommentar zum Zweiten Timotheusbrief*. HTKNT. Freiburg: Herder, 1995.

Packer, J. I. *Evangelism and the Sovereignty of God*. Downers Grove: InterVarsity, 2008.

Pitts, Andrew W. "Style and Pseudonymity in Pauline Scholarship: A Register Based Configuration." In *Paul and Pseudepigraphy*, edited by Stanley E. Porter and Gregory P. Fewster, 113–52. Boston: Brill, 2013.

Porter, Stanley E., and Sean A. Adams. "Pauline Epistolography: An Introduction." In *Paul and the Ancient Letter Form*, edited by Stanley E. Porter and Sean A. Adams, 1–8. PS 6. Boston: Brill, 2010.

Poythress, Vern S. "The Church as Family: Why Male Leadership in the Family Requires Male Leadership in the Church." In *Recovering Biblical Manhood and Womanhood*, edited by John Piper and Wayne Grudem, 233–47. Wheaton, IL: Crossway, 1991.

Prior, Michael. *Paul the Letter-Writer and the Second Letter to Timothy.* LNTS. JSNTSup 23. Sheffield: Sheffield Academic, 1989.

Quinn, Jerome D., and William C. Wacker. *The First and Second Letters to Timothy: A New Translation with Notes and Commentary.* Grand Rapids: Eerdmans, 2000.

Rapske, Brian. *The Book of Acts and Paul in Roman Custody.* Grand Rapids: Eerdmans, 1994.

Rhoads, David. "The Art of Translating for Oral Performance." In *Translating Scripture for Sound and Performance: New Direction in Biblical Studies,* edited by James A. Maxey and Ernst R. Wendland, 22–48. BPC 6. Eugene, OR: Cascade, 2012.

———. "Performance Events in Early Christianity: New Testament Writings in an Oral Context." In *The Interface of Orality and Writing: Speaking, Seeing, Writing in the Shaping of New Genres,* edited by Annette Weissenrieder and Robert B. Coote, 166–93. BPC 11. Eugene, OR: Cascade, 2015.

Rhoads, David, and Joanna Dewey. "Performance Criticism: A Paradigm Shift in New Testament Studies." In *From Text to Performance: Narrative and Performance Criticisms in Dialogue and Debate,* edited by Kelly R. Iverson, 10–21. BPC 10. Eugene, OR: Cascade, 2014.

Ridderbos, Herman. *Paul: An Outline of His Theology.* Translated by John Richard De Witt. Grand Rapids: Eerdmans, 1975.

Riesner, Rainer. "Paul's Trial and End according to Second Timothy, *1 Clement,* the Canon Muratori, and the Apocryphal Acts." In *The Last Years of Paul: Essays from the Tarragona Conference,* by Orrey McFarland et al., 391–410. Tübingen: Mohr Siebeck, 2015.

Sampley, J. Paul. "Ruminations Occasioned by the Publication of These Essays and the End of the Seminar." In *Paul and Rhetoric,* edited by J. Paul Sampley and Peter Lampe, ix–xvii. New York: T. & T. Clark, 2010.

Schnabel, Eckhard J. "Paul, Timothy, and Titus: The assumption of a Pseudonymous Author and of Pseudonymous Recipients in the Light of Literary, Theological, and Historical Evidence." In *Do Historical Matters Matter to Faith: A Critical Appraisal of Modern and Postmodern Approaches to Scripture,* edited by James K. Hoffmeier and Dennis R. Magary, 383–404. Wheaton, IL: Crossway, 2012.

Shively, Elizabeth E. *Apocalyptic Imagination in the Gospel of Mark: The Literary and Theological Role of Mark 3:22–30.* Boston: de Gruyter, 2012.

Smit, Peter-Ben. *Paradigms of Being in Christ: A Study of the Epistle to the Philippians.* LNTS. New York: Bloomsbury, 2013.

Smith, Craig A. *2 Timothy.* Sheffield: Sheffield Phoenix, 2016.

Smith, Randall. *Living Hope: Lessons from 2 Timothy.* N.d: GCBI, 2014.

Spicq, C. *Saint Paul: Les Épîtres Pastorales.* 2 vols. EBib. Paris: Gabalda, 1969.

Steele, David N., et al. *The Five Points of Calvinism: Defined, Defended, Documented.* Phillipsburg, NJ: P & R, 2004.

Strange, William A. "'His Letters Are Weighty': Test and Authority in Early Christianity." In *Honouring the Past and Shaping the Future: Religious and Biblical Studies in Wales: Essays in Honour of Gareth Lloyd Jones,* edited by Robert Pope, 112–32. Herefordshire: Gracewing, 2003.

Swinson, L. Timothy. *What Is Scripture? Paul's Use of* Graphe *in the Letters to Timothy.* Eugene, OR: Wipf & Stock, 2014.

Thate, Michael J., et al., eds. *In Christ in Paul: Explorations in Paul's Theology of Union and Participation.* Grand Rapids: Eerdmans, 2018.

Thomas, W. D. "New Testament Characters: IXX. Onesiphorus." *Expository Times* 96 (1985) 116–17.

Thompson, James W. *Preaching Like Paul: Homiletical Wisdom for Today*. Louisville: Westminster John Knox, 2001.

Thomson, Ian H. *Chiasmus in the Pauline Letters*. JSNTSup 111. Sheffield: Sheffield, 1995.

Thornton, Dillon. *Hostility in the House of God: An Investigation of the Opponents in 1 and 2 Timothy*. Bulletin for Biblical Research Supplement 15. Winona Lake: Eisenbrauns, 2016.

Towner, Philip H. *1–2 Timothy and Titus*. IVPNTC. Downers Grove: InterVarsity, 1994.

———. *The Goal of Our Instruction: The Structure of Theology and Ethics in the Pastoral Epistles*. JSNTSup 34. Sheffield: JSOT, 1989.

———. *The Letters to Timothy and Titus*. NIGTC. Grand Rapids: Eerdmans, 2006.

———. "The Use of the Old Testament in the Letters to Timothy and Titus." In *Commentary on the Use of the Old Testament in the New Testament*, edited by G. K. Beale and D. A. Carson. Grand Rapids: Baker Academic, 2007.

Trebilco, Paul. "The Significance and Relevance of the Spirit in the Pastoral Epistles." In *The Holy Spirit and Christian Origins: Essays in Honor of James D. G. Gunn*, edited by Stephen C. Barton et al., 241–56. Grand Rapids: Eerdmans, 2004.

Van Iersel, Bas M. F. *Mark: A Reader-Response Commentary*. Translated by W. H. Bisscheroux. JSNTSup 164. Sheffield: Sheffield Academic, 1998.

Van Nes, Jermo. "On the Origin of the Pastorals' Authenticity Criticism: A 'New' Perspective." *New Testament Studies* 62 (2016) 315–20.

Van Neste, Ray. "Cohesion and Structure in the Pastoral Epistles." In *Entrusted with the Gospel: Paul's Theology in the Pastoral Epistles*, edited by Andreas J. Köstenberger and Terry L. Wilder, 84–104. Nashville: B&H, 2010.

Vena, Osvaldo D. *Jesus, Disciple of the Kingdom: Mark's Christology for a Community in Crisis*. Eugene, OR: Pickwick, 2014.

Volf, Miroslav. *Exclusion and Embrace: A Theological Exploration of Identity, Otherness, and Reconciliation*. Nashville: Abingdon, 2008.

Vos, Geerhardus. *The Pauline Eschatology*. Phillipsburg, NJ: Presbyterian and Reformed, 1991.

Ward, Richard F. "Pauline Voice and Presence as Strategic Communication." *Semeia* 65 (1994) 95–107.

Warfield, B. B. *The Inspiration and Authority of the Bible*. Oxford: Benediction Classics, 2017.

Welch, John W. "Chiasmus in the New Testament." In *Chiasmus in Antiquity: Structures, Analyses, Exegesis*, edited by John W. Welch, 211–49. Hildesheim, Germany: Gerstenberg, 1981.

———. "Criteria for Identifying and Evaluating the Presence of Chiasmus." In *Chiasmus Bibliography*, edited by John W. Welch and Daniel B. McKinlay, 157–74. Provo, UT: Research, 1999.

Westfall, Cynthia Long. "A Moral Dilemma? The Epistolary Body of 2 Timothy." In *Paul and the Ancient Letter Form*, edited by Stanley E. Porter and Sean A. Adams, 213–52. Pauline Studies 6. Leiden: Brill, 2010.

White, John L. "Apostolic Mission and Apostolic Message: Congruence in Paul's Epistolary Rhetoric, Structure and Imagery." In *Origins and Method: Towards a*

New Understanding of Judaism and Christianity; Essays in Honour of John Hurd, edited by Bradley H. McLean, 145–61. JSNTSup 86. Sheffield: Sheffield, 1993.

Winter, Bruce W. *Seek the Welfare of the City: Christians as Benefactors and Citizens.* Grand Rapids: Eerdmans, 1994.

Witherington, Ben, III. *Paul's Letter to the Romans: A Socio-Rhetorical Commentary.* With Darlene Hyatt. Grand Rapids: Eerdmans, 2004.

Yarbrough, Mark M. *Paul's Utilization of Performed Traditions: An Evaluation of the Apostle's Literary, Rhetorical, and Theological Tactics.* New York: T. & T. Clark, 2009.

Yarbrough, Robert W. *The Letters to Timothy and Titus.* Grand Rapids: Eerdmans, 2018.

Yinger, Kent L. *Paul, Judaism, and Judgement according to Deeds.* Cambridge: Cambridge University Press, 2007.